THE ECLIPSE AND RECOVERY OF BEAUTY

A Lonergan Approach

JOHN D. DADOSKY

The Eclipse and Recovery of Beauty

A Lonergan Approach

UNIVERSITY OF TORONTO PRESS
Toronto Buffalo London

© University of Toronto Press 2014
Toronto Buffalo London
www.utppublishing.com
Printed in Canada

ISBN 978-1-4426-4711-4

Printed on acid-free, 100% post-consumer recycled paper with
vegetable-based inks.

Library and Archives Canada Cataloguing in Publication

Dadosky, John Daniel, 1966–, author
The eclipse and recovery of beauty : a Lonergan approach /
John D. Dadosky.

(Longergan studies)
Includes bibliographical references and index.
ISBN 978-1-4426-4711-4 (bound)

1. Aesthetics.   2. Lonergan, Bernard J. F. (Bernard Joseph
Francis), 1904–1984.   I. Title.   II. Series: Lonergan studies

B995.L654D33 2014   191   C2013-906472-9

This book has been published with the help of a grant from the Canadian
Federation for the Humanities and Social Sciences, through the Awards
to Scholarly Publications Program, using funds provided by the Social
Sciences and Humanities Research Council of Canada.

University of Toronto Press acknowledges the financial assistance to its
publishing program of the Canada Council for the Arts and the Ontario
Arts Council.

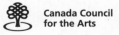

University of Toronto Press acknowledges the financial support of the
Government of Canada through the Canada Book Fund for its publishing
activities.

For my parents Bill and Doris,
in gratitude for the most beautiful gift

Contents

Preface

In August 1994 I stepped out of a traditional Diné (Navajo) *hooghan* into the fresh dry air of the Southwestern desert. I was in Arizona about fifty miles east of the Grand Canyon. I turned clockwise several times to symbolize my return to what the Diné describe as the "corn pollen path" of beauty. This abbreviated version of the Blessingway ceremony soon came to a close, but it raised a question for me that would inevitably lead to the basis for this book – the recovery of beauty.

As I returned to my life off the reservation and began my doctoral studies in theology and philosophy in Toronto, the question about the recovery of beauty persisted. It arose for me again when I encountered the Swiss theologian Hans Urs von Balthasar (1904–1986), who decried the loss of beauty in the West, a topic I will elaborate upon in the coming chapters. I had been encouraged by my encounter with the Navajo because they not only had an entire philosophy that revered beauty, but also had a ritual system for promoting it, protecting it, and restoring it.

The recovery of beauty in the West, however, would be another matter. It would have to be worked out intellectually and philosophically in order to be further appropriated by the broader culture and society. That is the purpose of this book, to propose an intellectual framework for recovering beauty in the West.

The twentieth-century German philosopher Theodor Adorno once criticized the towering figures Hegel and Kant for writing "major aesthetics without understanding anything about art."[1] While any contribution I make to the discussion will pale in comparison to theirs, I must confess that there is a sense in which Adorno's criticism applies also to my work. This book is not about aesthetics and art per se, but it is about beauty. And if Adorno's criticism has any validity, then equally true is that many philosophers of art and aesthetic theorists have little understanding of or interest in beauty – the gaping loss of beauty not only occurs under their watch but is further perpetuated by many of them. Still, one cannot write about beauty without engaging and addressing topics that are generally associated with aesthetics and art, and so I will be addressing those in due course where pertinent.

My original intention for this book was to establish a contemporary Thomistic basis for a philosophy of beauty based on the philosophy of Bernard Lonergan (1904–1984) and then to incorporate some non-Western approaches to beauty in order to get a fuller account. I specifically had in mind the Diné notion of beauty (*hózhó*) and the Japanese notion of *wabi-sabi* because of the unique contributions that each make to the discussion. However, this project soon proved to be too ambitious in scope, and so in this book I have focused on what I know best, Lonergan's thought, and have left aside for now the non-Western approaches for perhaps a subsequent work.

There have been many attempts by Thomists to establish a philosophy of beauty based on the thought of Aquinas, but they often refuse to engage the crucial philosophical movements following the "turn to the subject" (Descartes, Kant, Hume, Hegel, etc.) and the persisting legacy of doubt stemming from these epistemologies. I realized that the eclipse of beauty in the West requires something akin to a philosophical medical procedure in order to establish a philosophy that is capable of affirming the existence of beauty and ameliorating the belief that it is merely in the eye of the beholder. I have tried in the following pages, as a meta-*physician*, to clarify and articulate a philosophy of beauty within Lonergan's philosophy of intentional consciousness. I hope that it gives rise to the further appropriation of other approaches and that it contributes to a theology of beauty. Still, if I am attempting the task of healing in this work, I also keep in mind the adage "Physician, heal thyself!" I have come to realize that the loss of beauty is such a pervasive problem that grappling with it is akin to writing about clean fresh air when one has grown accustomed to breathing smog. I am a product of a culture and intellectual tradition where beauty has been eclipsed by practicality, where form follows function, where beauty is only skin deep, and where violence is increasingly glorified, especially in the various media, new technologies, and digital culture. Therefore, I realize that my attempt in this book may be incomplete and in need of further revisions. I am reminded of the opening lines from Lonergan's preface in *Insight*: "But so prolonged has been my search, so much of it has been a dark struggle with my own flight from understanding, so many have been the half-lights and detours in my slow development."[2]

There are many who helped to bring this project to fruition. I am grateful to the administration, faculty, and students of Regis College at the University of Toronto for their various levels of support over the several years of writing. I am particularly grateful for those students who participated in my seminar *Philosophy and Theology of Beauty* during the past five years. I thank colleagues who gave me support, especially Mark Morelli, Michael Stoeber, James Marsh, and Paul St. Amour. Many friends lent moral support, especially William Hart McNichols, Anne Cahill, Carolyn Green, Robert Turcott, Margo Brousseau, and Wing Chan. I particularly thank Dorothy Cummings, H. Daniel Monsour, and the referees and editors at the University of Toronto Press for their invaluable editorial work and feedback. I am grateful to Robert Doran for his support of the project and for his permission on behalf of the Lonergan Trustees to cite some of Bernard Lonergan's unpublished material.

This book has been published with the help of a grant from the Federation for the Humanities and Social Sciences, through the Awards to Scholarly Publications Program, using funds provided by the Social Sciences and Humanities Research Council of Canada.

Finally, I am grateful to the Association of Theological Schools and the Lilly Foundation for their support for a summer research grant in 2005, to the University of New Mexico and the Catholic Diocese of Santa Fe for a visiting appointment during the 2010–11 academic year, and to the late Joseph Flanagan, SJ (d. 2010) for granting me a post-doctoral fellowship at Boston College in winter 2010.

In his famous and intimate prayer in *Confessions*, St Augustine laments: "Too late have I loved you, oh Beauty so ancient and so new." With the perpetuation of violence and ugliness in societies and with the imminent environmental crises confronting our world today, we cannot afford to be too late. And it will not be enough simply to put policies into place. Such policies need to be grounded within a larger, more integrated worldview, one where beauty, unity, truth, and goodness coincide in harmony. Hence, I invite you to join me on this inquiry to begin to recover beauty in the West so that one day we may be able to say with the Diné:

From the East beauty has been restored
From the South beauty has been restored

From the West beauty has been restored
From the North beauty has been restored
From the zenith in the sky beauty has been restored
From the nadir of the earth beauty has been restored
From all around me beauty has been restored.[3]

Abbreviations

AB Armand Maurer, *About Beauty: A Thomistic Interpretation*
CW Bernard Lonergan, *Collected Works of Bernard Lonergan*
GL Hans Urs von Balthasar, *The Glory of the Lord* (volumes 1, 2, 4, 5)
IN Bernard Lonergan, *Insight: A Study of Human Understanding*
MT Bernard Lonergan, *Method in Theology*
TE Bernard Lonergan, *Topics in Education*
PB Francis J. Kovach, *Philosophy of Beauty*
PL Christopher Alexander, *Nature of Order*, volume 1: *Phenomenon of Life*
ST Thomas Aquinas, *Summa Theologica*

THE ECLIPSE AND RECOVERY OF BEAUTY

A Lonergan Approach

Introduction

"Beauty saves the world." This phrase from Dostoevsky's *The Idiot* contains an extremely important albeit neglected diagnosis and prescription for our contemporary world – the loss of beauty and its recovery. Taking the Swiss theologian Hans Urs von Balthasar as a lead, one can conclude that such a loss leads to a world riddled with scepticism, moral and aesthetic relativism, a fragmentation of knowledge splintered into specialized disciplines, conflicting religious worldviews and, one could also include, escalating ecological crises. These consequences are what make Bathasar's diagnosis of the eclipse of beauty prophetic and extremely relevant to our current theological and philosophical context. He refers to beauty not just as an aesthetic principle but as a fundamental property of being that expresses the pleasure of being in harmony with unity, goodness, and truth.

If it is true that beauty saves the world, then according to Balthasar the loss of beauty threatens or, one might even say, condemns the world. He decries the loss of transcendental beauty in Western philosophy and theology, and his diagnosis has far-reaching implications beyond what even he could have imagined. As such, his passionate plea has secured him a place in the history of Western thought.

Balthasar recognizes, perhaps more than any other Western thinker, that the eclipse of transcendental beauty eventually leads to the relativity of truth and morality, and to a divisiveness that is related to the

Portions of this section, having undergone editorial revisions, appeared in John D. Dadosky, "Philosophy for a Theology of Beauty," *Philosophy & Theology* 19, nos. 1–2 (2007): 7–34.

fragmentation of knowledge. However, I am not using the term *tran-scendental* in the sense that Kant does. For Balthasar, Kant is part of the problem; but I will return to that issue. Rather, I am talking about the transcendental properties of being, such as unity, goodness, truth, and beauty.[1]

A division between or neglect of one of the transcendentals has rami-fications for us as individuals and collectively. For example, one of the effects of the bifurcation between beauty and truth is doubt and relativ-ism, the inability to make aesthetic judgments. Among other things, it becomes difficult to distinguish art from play; the asking price from art dealers and auctions becomes the benchmark for aesthetic value.[2] The following quote from Hume is representative of the relativism and doubt of aesthetic judgments and the loss of beauty:

> Beauty is no quality in things themselves: It exists merely in the mind which contemplates them; and each mind perceives a different beauty. One person may even perceive deformity, where another is sensible of beauty; and every individual ought to acquiesce in his own sentiment, without pretending to regulate those of others. To seek the real beauty, or real deformity, is as fruitless an inquiry, as to pretend to ascertain the real sweet or real bitter.[3]

Likewise, the bifurcation between *beauty* and *goodness* can lead to a sort of split personality within the moral subject. One recalls, for ex-ample, the Nazi officers who had refined and developed aesthetic sen-sibilities and yet committed depraved acts.[4]

Moreover, Balthasar declares of the eclipse of beauty: "if this is how the transcendentals fare because one of them [beauty] has been ban-ished, what will happen to Being itself? … The witness borne by Being becomes untrustworthy for the person who can no longer read the lan-guage of beauty."[5] In other words, the eclipse of *beauty* ultimately leads to the diminishment of meaning, and with this, our very existence is inevitably threatened.

If Balthasar is correct in claiming that one of the chief ailments of modern theology and philosophy has been the eclipse of transcendental beauty, then the restoration of beauty to its proper place in theological and philosophical reflection has ramifications beyond what Balthasar could have imagined. He does not address ecological concerns, pre-sumably because they were not an exigency of his time. However, as-suming he is correct in his analysis of the condition of beauty, then his comments would certainly apply to the current ecological crisis in that the loss of the transcendental beauty threatens the very *being* of our planet. Pollution, global warming, and diminishing natural resources threaten to bring our planet to what Balthasar might have described as "a mere lump of existence" (*GL*, 1, 19).

Second, Balthasar was very concerned that fellow theologians had ceased speaking about the beauty of God. They still speak of the existence, the oneness, the goodness, and the truth of God, but they ignore the beauty of God or have failed to realize its significance. The beauty of God is inextricably related to philosophical reflection on transcendental beauty because God would be the ground on which all being and existence depends. Balthasar wrote a comprehensive theological aesthetics in order to restore transcendental *beauty* to theological reflection. In many respects, it was written in direct response to Kant, to whose legacy much of the modern eclipse of beauty can be traced.

Rather than delve into Balthasar's monumental trilogy, in this work I would like to take his diagnosis of beauty as both a context and a point of departure. Robert Doran addressed this context succinctly when he stated:

> But it may be asked whether von Balthasar's theology does not stand in need of a transcendental grounding in the realm of the beautiful analogous to that which Lonergan's work has received in the realms of the intelligible, the true and the good. Von Balthasar is distrustful of the turn to the subject, largely because of the failures of that turn. But if the turn to the subject has been brought to resolution [by Lonergan] in the areas that concerned Kant in his first two *Critiques*, might it not also be brought to conclusion in the domain that occupied his attention in the third *Critique*?[6]

There are two major limitations to Balthasar's work that have prevented the broader reception of his thought on beauty. I will only mention them here and will go into more detail in chapter 1. The first limitation concerns his Thomism. Because he was suspicious of modern philosophy, he was not willing to engage the more contemporary Thomists who sought to correct the errors in the philosophical turn to the subject in their reappropriation of Thomistic thought. This limits his grounding of beauty (*pulchrum*) to medieval philosophy, and while Aquinas's achievement is extremely important, it alone is not sufficient for the contemporary exigencies of our day. That is, unless it is a Thomism that is able to seriously engage and respond to the movements in modern and contemporary philosophy. As acutely observed by Richard Viladesau,[7] this leaves Balthasar's approach open to the potential danger of fideism.[8]

The second limitation concerns Balthasar's own admission at the beginning of his trilogy that his own thought is "far too Mediterranean." There is a need for an engagement with other cultural and religious as well as non-Western approaches. The Diné (Navajo) notion of beauty is unique for its holistic and comprehensive perspective. It is integral to their culture and traditional religion. They have not lost their notion of beauty although they experience the ongoing challenges of many aboriginal peoples. The Japanese aesthetics of *wabi-sabi* is unique for its ability to recognize the beauty of emptiness and loneliness.

While initially I was hoping to address both of these limitations in Balthasar's approach, in this book I will be dealing only with the first limitation of his thinking on beauty. I will attempt to establish a philosophy of beauty from a transposed Thomistic perspective that has critically engaged the philosophical turn to the subject and can respond to the legacy of doubt and scepticism left in its wake. As said above, I will be engaging the more contemporary Thomistic philosophy of Bernard Lonergan. But Lonergan had little to say explicitly on beauty, so the major portion of this book is dedicated to constructing a philosophy of beauty based upon his epistemology. This is an approach that will be as conducive to transcendental beauty as Balthasar claims for Aquinas's philosophy.

The aim of this book, therefore, is to establish a philosophy for a theology of beauty. The preparation of this philosophy is by way of Lonergan's philosophy of consciousness, which offers a basis for appropriating beauty and judgments of beauty. I proceed as follows:

Chapter 1 summarizes the loss of beauty intellectually in the West as argued by Balthasar. It further outlines some of the conditions and issues surrounding a philosophical recovery of beauty. In addition, I briefly summarize Lonergan's philosophy of consciousness in order to lay the groundwork for subsequent chapters on Nietzsche, Kierkegaard, and Kant and on other topics, such as aesthetic experience, judgments, and the philosophy of art.

Chapter 2 summarizes the transcendentals and Aquinas's treatment of beauty, and some of the controversies and limitations surrounding that treatment. This chapter prepares us to read aspects of Aquinas's philosophy of beauty through a more contemporary Thomistic approach in Lonergan's philosophy of consciousness.

Chapter 3 addresses the relationship between the loss of beauty and the perpetuation of violence. I will focus on Nietzsche's binary aesthetics of the Dionysian and Apollonian as critiqued by René Girard in order to delineate more clearly the link between the loss of beauty and the rise of violence, and a suggestive alternative interpretation of that binary aesthetics.

Chapter 4 takes Balthasar's critique of Kierkegaard's aesthetics as a context for recovering the notion of beauty within the subject. Balthasar believed that Kierkegaard contributed to the loss of beauty by separating the aesthetic from the ethical and religious spheres. However, by viewing the spheres in terms of differentiations and transformations of consciousness, Lonergan's philosophy offers an interpretation of Kierkegaard's stages in such a way that it addresses Balthasar's concern and simultaneously retains the Danish thinker's significant achievements.

Chapter 5 addresses the question of beauty from the first level in Lonergan's theory of consciousness, *experience* or *presentations*. Taking the work of philosopher Robert Schusterman regarding the "end of aesthetic experience" as a context, I approach the question by articulating the powerful, transformative dimensions of aesthetic experience. Further, I take up the question of the sublime as an experience, as articulated by Arthur Schopenhauer, and interpret it in terms of Lonergan's philosophy of consciousness in order to clarify the difference between beauty and the sublime as experienced.

Chapter 6 attempts to interpret how beauty is apprehended at the second level of Lonergan's level of operations – *understanding*. I examine the question from the perspective of the intelligibility of beauty based on Aquinas's three conditions of beauty: clarity, integrity, and harmony/proportion. I argue that Christopher Alexander's principles of beautiful architecture embody these three principles in different ways. In turn, I argue that, for Lonergan at the second level, beauty is to be understood in terms of the grasp of intelligibility, and that the content of the grasp as such reflects Aquinas's three conditions of beauty.

Chapter 7 addresses the issue of judgments of beauty in terms of Lonergan's theory of consciousness. It occurs in the context of responding to Kant's aesthetic judgments and so addresses the issue of judgments of fact and judgments of value together.

Chapter 8 addresses the issue surrounding the fourth level of operations for Lonergan – *decision* (a further expansion upon judgments of value). It likewise speaks to the role of beauty in dramatic living and the creation of beauty in art. It also touches upon what Lonergan speaks of as "fifth level," or *loving*. With this, the question of an ultimate ground of beauty arises, the beauty of God. From there we have come to the threshold of a theology of beauty.

Chapter 9 offers a summary and prospectus towards a theology of beauty based on Lonergan's philosophy. It offers some avenues of development if one is to revisit Balthasar's theological aesthetics from a renewed, transposed, and more contemporary Thomistic approach.

As we noted above, Hume dismisses the search for real beauty as a fruitless inquiry. If beauty is to save the world, we must begin by constructing a more adequate philosophical foundation that does not, as Balthasar does, ignore modern philosophy as a resource, but in engaging its insights does not succumb to the subjectivization of beauty. I believe that Lonergan's philosophical approach is up to the challenge in this project of recovering beauty.[9]

1 The Eclipse of Beauty and Its Recovery

If we are going to take Balthasar's diagnosis of the loss of beauty as a context, several questions arise that need to be addressed in this chapter: (1) Has there been a time when the philosophical foundations for a pleasing synthesis of the transcendentals (including beauty) existed? (2) Where, more precisely, at least in modern times, did we "lose" beauty? (3) What are some of the conditions for the philosophical recovery of beauty in our current situation? (4) How will such a philosophical recovery be attempted in this work?

In regard to the first question, we note that Balthasar devotes a significant portion of his *Herrlichkeit* to various thinkers who have at least implicitly upheld the beauty of God and beauty as a transcendental property of being. However, he suggests that a pleasing synthesis of the transcendentals occurs with the achievement of Thomistic metaphysics, which might surprise some given that Thomas has no systematic treatise on beauty.[1] In regard to the second question, we observe that for Balthasar this historical climax in Thomistic philosophy was short lived and was eclipsed by a subsequent two-pronged demise of metaphysics through Duns Scotus on the one hand and Meister Eckhart on the other. More positively, as I will argue in this chapter, the climax and demise of Thomas's philosophical achievement can be situated within the transition from what Lonergan terms the second and third stages of meaning. In terms of the third question, we will turn again to the work of Lonergan. I will argue for a transposition of Thomistic philosophy

A significant portion of this chapter, with the exception of editorial revisions, appeared in John D. Dadosky, "Philosophy for a Theology of Beauty," *Philosophy & Theology* 19, nos. 1–2 (2007): 7–34.

for what Lonergan calls a third stage of meaning that can reckon with the legacy of Kant and the eclipse of beauty, not by avoiding Kant, but by addressing his concerns, and moving beyond him.

The Achievement of Thomistic Metaphysics and Its Demise

Balthasar laboured to recover a theological aesthetics within contemporary theology. As stated before, his suspicion of modern philosophy with its *turn to the subject* left him unable to articulate the proper philosophical foundations for a modern recovery of beauty. He praised the achievement of Aquinas but did not move beyond him. Therefore, in this book we will be arguing for a transposed philosophy of Aquinas through the thought of Lonergan that can move beyond the distortions in the turn to the subject, but also preserve its necessary insights. I believe that Lonergan's philosophy can properly ground a theological aesthetics because it reckons with the philosophers of doubt, and allows for the incorporation of other cultural notions of beauty that Balthasar admits are lacking in his own aesthetics.

Balthasar devotes several volumes of his *Herrlichkeit* to the loss of beauty as an explicit transcendental property of being. So let us delve right into the heart of the matter and ask: When historically has there been a pleasing metaphysics that could ground each of the transcendentals – truth, goodness, beauty, and unity – and with this, a balanced view of the relationship between nature and grace, all of which could favour a theological aesthetics?

Balthasar is clear: it is the metaphysics of Aquinas. This may seem odd given that beauty is not a central concern for Aquinas. However, it is his "general ontology" rather than his aesthetics, according to Balthasar, that provides the "kairos" moment for articulating the glory of God (*GL*, 4.395): "The metaphysics of Aquinas is thus the philosophical reflection of the free glory of the living God of the Bible and in this way the interior completion of ancient (and thus human) philosophy" (*GL*, 4.406–7). As Aidan Nichols states in his commentary on Balthasar's aesthetics, "St. Thomas's general ontology – as the precious setting for an aesthetics at once metaphysically adequate and biblically controlled – is, in Balthasar's view, the door on which the division of the ages (ancient from modern) itself turns."[2] Indeed, for Balthasar, Aquinas's metaphysics is not only the door, but an unparalleled philosophical achievement. Thomas's "transcendental philosophy of being forms the (higher) centre and mediation between classical and modern metaphysics and in this context is the most valid representative of distinctively Western thought" (*GL*, 4.375). Accordingly, Aquinas represents a historical climax from which there follows a steep decline:

> In Thomas's ontology, the transcendental aesthetics of the classical period (which Dionysus sums up and passes onto Christian theology) achieves a state of balance: Being (*esse*) with which he is concerned and to which he attributes the modalities of the One, the True, the Good and the Beautiful, is the unlimited abundance of reality which is beyond all comprehension, as it, in its emergence from God, attains subsistence and self-possession within the finite entities. Where the balance is not maintained, then there are only two possible ways forward: either to formalize Being to the extent that it becomes the comprehensive concept of reason (which is in the case with Scotus) ... The other way in which Being can be interpreted after Thomas is simply to identify it (once again with God, as Meister Eckhart does). (*GL*, 5.12–13).

For Balthasar it is clear, then, that the metaphysics of Aquinas provides an important historical development and foundation for a theological aesthetics. There one finds a "balanced" view retaining each of the transcendentals and an explicit acknowledgment of the transcendentals (one at least conducive to beauty) as properties of being. ("[W]ith Thomas the true balance is found through his metaphysics of *esse* and *essentia* and his emphasis on secondary causality which that made possible"; *GL*, 4.386.) This achievement is one that "remained without imitators" and effectively "disappears" after the Angelic Doctor (*GL*, 5.9). To extend Nichols's analogy, if Aquinas provides the door between the ancient and modern ages, then it is just as true for Balthasar that subsequent philosophical positions, specifically Duns Scotus (and with him, Ockham) and the mystical theology of Meister Eckhart, close the door to the philosophical foundations of beauty and a subsequent theological aesthetics. Both of these legacies lead in "two false directions," but then they actually "turn into each other," manifesting later as an idealism and rationalism, both of which exclude God.[3]

With Scotus, "being" is a neutral category prevalent throughout intellectual distinctions and relegated to the task of philosophy. The emphasis of the theologian is no longer a reflection upon the being of God but rather on the practical dimension of faith. In contrast, Balthasar does not doubt the authenticity of Eckhart's mystical experiences, but rather the way it is expressed and subsequently misappropriated: being becomes identical with God. In each case, Scotus and Eckhart leave legacies leading to two degenerating views. For Scotus, being becomes strictly an idea (albeit an ultimate one) void of meaning. His legacy extends through Ockham to a period of scholasticism that Lonergan would later call "decadent," to Suárez, to Descartes, and eventually towards the development of a static scientific worldview.

There is a further consequence of the Scotus ontology. Philosophy and theology become separate spheres wherein being is entrusted strictly to the former, while the latter emphasizes practical faith at the expense of contemplation (of the beautiful).[4] The philosophers and theologians can no longer metaphysically ground beauty. To paraphrase Nichols, "Christian thought cannot keep up with Christian inspiration." The reverence for beauty passes to the poets (Dante) and in some cases even to scientists (Teilhard). As for being: "with Suarez, the disastrous shift in the philosophical representation of the 'external' world whereby Being gives way to mental concepts has already taken place. Things are not so much in themselves as for me, and the road to the Königsberg of Kant lies open."[5]

Kant is a particular part of the problem for the loss of beauty, so much so that Balthasar's entire trilogy is a testimony against and response to him. Specifically, each part of this trilogy (*Herrlichkeit*, *Theodramtik*, and *Theologik*) was written in reverse manner as a direct response to Kant's three critiques (*Critique of Pure Reason*, *Critique of Practical Reason*, and *Critique of Judgment* – aesthetics).[6] Likewise, Balthasar's *Herrlichkeit* correlates with transcendental beauty, the *Theodramatik* with goodness, and the *Theologik* with truth.[7] The goal of Balthasar's enterprise is to stitch these transcendentals back together, sealing them inextricably with beauty. By treating beauty first in his trilogy, Balhasar sets out to emphasize transcendental beauty, not only as a property of being, but as the glue that holds the other transcendentals together: "The beautiful guards the other [transcendentals] and sets the seal on them: there is nothing true or good, in the long term, without the light of grace … when the saints interpreted their existence in the light of God's greater glory, they were always the guardians of the beautiful" (*GL*, 2.38–9).

In the legacy of Eckhart, the line between proportionate being and transcendent being is blurred, and therefore incapable of expressing the glory of God. The effects of his legacy extend to Luther, then to Hegel and then, one could add, to Marx. The problem pertains to the "lethal" gap between experience and expression. This gap produces a lack of clarity between the finite and the infinite.[8] For Balthasar this leads to a pantheism: "all this converges, against Eckhart's intention ... towards, in fact, an Indian kind of doctrine that everything is God" (*GL*, 5.45) and its distortion into to the "self-glorifying absolute" of Hegel and Fichte.[9]

Luther reacts to such attempts to confuse the created world with the Creator (revelation) by rejecting any "harmonious" relation between the created world and revelation and with it any *analogia entis*. "Luther's attack on the 'whore' Reason, which aesthetically attempts to achieve a harmony between divinity and humanity," results in what Balthasar describes as an "aesthetic emasculation" of the "Word of God" (*GL*, 1.45). In other words, there is no way to speak of the beauty of God since God is so absolutely different from us and because we are fallen. Therefore, any attempt to express "God's incorruptible splendor" is idolatrous (*GL*, 1.46).

Accordingly, Luther not only will succeed in principally eliminating aesthetics from Protestant theology (at least until Barth), but will also influence Kierkegaard, who in turn dramatically affects not only contemporary philosophy, but theology both Protestant and Catholic as well.

Balthasar's indictment of Kierkegaard is especially pertinent to any philosophical recovery of beauty. For Balthasar, Kierkegaard, in sympathy with Luther's sensibilities, eliminates the aesthetic more concretely in terms of the philosophical subject. Kierkegaard's enthusiasm to "delineate all more clearly the distance and total difference existing between the *agape* of Christ and his followers on the one hand, and human *eros*, on the other" becomes part of the problem. It is here that the Eastern adage "every uncovering is a covering over" applies, so that Kierkegaard's enthusiasm eventually "robs" us of "all joy of the aesthetic" (*GL*, 1.50). Specifically, Balthasar's critique centres on Kierkegard's famous distinction between the three spheres or stages of existential human living: the aesthetic, the ethical, and the religious. In *Either/Or*, Kierkegaard "can no longer achieve a meeting of religion and aesthetics. He is impelled to use the concept of 'the aesthetic' to stake out and define a basic attitude which for the Christian is unacceptable" (*GL*, 1.50). This unacceptable attitude pertains to an unbridled hedonism that is part and parcel of the world of the aesthete. Similarly, in Kierkegaard's *Stages on Life's Way*, a wedge is driven between the aesthetic and the ethical that succeeds in "eradicating from theology all traces of an aesthetic attitude" (*GL*, 1.50).[10]

In view of Balthasar's critique, it may be possible to reconceive Kierkegaard's three spheres as differentiations in human consciousness. Then the spheres would be grounded in the unity of human consciousness and also allow for an interpenetration of the various spheres. I will return to this topic in chapter 4.

Following Kierkegaard, Karl Barth achieves a restoration of the beauty of God. For Balthasar, Barth represents a lone, prophetic voice calling out in a wilderness of modern and liberal theologies that have simply relegated beauty to the realm of aesthetics. Barth brings beauty back to the heart of his theology and conceives beauty as a primary aspect of God.

However, Barth, following a Lutheran tradition, is still suspicious of anything that philosophy or reason (or what Bernard Lonergan would term "general categories") might contribute to a theological aesthetics. For Barth, only the "special categories" of revelation suffice to forge a theological aesthetics. In this view, a separation between philosophy and theology persists. Such a separation would not have been the case with Aquinas, and so we presume that a contemporary philosophy for a theology of beauty will presuppose a complementary relationship between philosophy and theology as well as the inclusion of both general and special categories.

A Post-Kantian Transposition of Thomistic Metaphysics

Balthasar's view of the role of reason in a theological aesthetics is not as extreme as Barth's. By way of indebtedness to Erich Pryzwara, Balthasar affirmed the *analogia entis*, the analogy of being, so that one can extrapolate from the created order to the beauty of God, albeit imperfectly and approximately and with an ever-increasing dissimilarity between the created and the Creator.[11]

Still the question remains, is the *analogia entis* alone sufficient to provide the philosophical basis for a theological aesthetics? One still needs the philosophical foundations for making judgments of beauty. That is, when we affirm an instance of being as real, true, good, and one, how do we make the further judgment that it is beautiful? Certainly beauty is more than just "in the eye of the beholder." The latter statement has become an unreflective, commonly accepted belief that is a symptom of the very thing Balthasar is railing against. There remains a need for a philosophical basis on which we can articulate judgments of beauty, just as we do when we make judgments of fact and judgments of value.

A philosophy for a theological aesthetics would attempt to recapture the achievement of the Thomistic epistemology/metaphysics that contains each of the transcendentals (unity, beauty, truth, goodness). It would be open to both special categories (categories specific to theology) and general categories (categories from other disciplines) and would retain the "balanced" view of the transcendentals that Balthasar saw as essential to a recovery of beauty. In addition, the philosophy would need to account for aesthetic judgments of instances of the beautiful and respond to a Kantian critique of judgment. Armand Maurer attempted such retrieval in his book *About Beauty: A Thomistic Interpretation*. He would agree with Balthasar about the legacy of Kant:

> The subjectivity of beauty and ugliness is a legacy to modern philosophy from Immanuel Kant. Kant is well known for his Copernican revolution in philosophy. In his *Critique of Pure Reason* he proposed a radically new philosophy ... [He] supposed that objects must conform to our knowledge. Knowledge was no longer to be taken as an understanding of things in themselves or as they actually exist but rather of things as they are shaped and determined by our reason ...
>
> In his *Critique of Judgment* Kant extended his Copernican revolution to matters of taste and the beautiful ... The real world offers us no intelligible forms, no radiance, no proportion or wholeness that might delight us. We legislate these to the world of our experience, and so too we legislate beauty to it (*AB*, 25–6).

Interestingly, although Thomas may have philosophical presuppositions that were pleasing for Balthasar, Maurer points out that there is evidence in Thomas of a "relative disinterest in beauty." Thomas offers no systematic treatment of beauty although perhaps it is implicit throughout his thought.[12] Étienne Gilson argues that beauty is inextricably tied up with the good in Aquinas (*AB*, 1–2).[13] These issues need to be clarified and addressed in terms of a transposed Thomistic philosophy, one that has reckoned with Kant and the sceptics, not by going backward to historical Thomism alone, as Maurer and others attempt, but by going forward, providing an integral philosophical basis for beauty through a transposed Thomistic approach in light of the philosophical turn to the subject – intentional consciousness. In Maurer's study, I rely on his scholarship and accept for the most part his presuppositions. But I will be attempting in this book to transpose the fruits of his research and insights into twentieth-century Thomism. Such will provide the foundations for recovering transcendental beauty from a philosophical perspective and the beauty of God as a theological notion. I will examine Aquinas's notion of beauty in the next chapter.

Balthasar was expressly critical of the so-called transcendental Thomism especially as expressed by Karl Rahner, for Balthasar believed that Rahner's thought was simply a product of, rather than an authentic response to and transposition of, Kantian philosophy. One wonders if Balthasar would think such a transposition is even possible. Indeed, there is perhaps a healthy skepticism with respect to the so-called turn to the subject for fear that it leads to subjectivism. We can sympathize with Balthasar when we realize that Descartes, Hume, and Kant all lead to what Michael Polanyi calls a "doctrine of doubt."[14] However, if this is true, then we must reckon with the philosophers of doubt, especially Kant, and transpose them into a philosophically appropriate form that gives way to theology. Balthasar might be expected to oppose such a program, as he rejects "transposing Thomas into the modality of the modern philosophy of identity."[15] However, this need not be the case. Indeed, Balthasar's view of the degeneration of beauty beginning from Scotus/Eckhart may be akin to a cloud with a silver lining. While there is with these thinkers a philosophical demise that leads eventually to what Lonergan describes as a "decadent scholasticism," this demise also signals the decline of what climaxes in Aquinas, namely, what Lonergan identified as the second stage of meaning. However, the decline of the second stage of meaning opens up to the third stage of meaning in the philosophical turn to the subject beginning with Descartes, Hume, and Kant. Yet there remains a need for a philosophy that can respond to the doctrine of doubt that still permeates much of modern thought, including postmodernism. The work of Descartes, Hume, and Kant can be seen as the initial attempt to ground philosophy within interiority, but those attempts are incomplete. Balthasar's analysis of the loss of beauty can be placed into the context of the stages of meaning in order to enable us to further analyse what is going forward in the broader scope of history. Thus we can recover beauty in a transposed way to meet the exigencies of a third stage of meaning. This point will be further elaborated upon in the next section.

Considerations for a Contemporary Philosophy of Beauty

In this section I would like to sketch out some points that will lead us towards a philosophy of beauty that will support and leave open further developments in a theological aesthetics.

First, a philosophy of beauty that could ground a theological aesthetics would need to address the philosophical turn to the subject that comes about as a result of what Lonergan terms the third stage of meaning. In order to elaborate, a brief summary of the stages of meaning is necessary.[16]

The first stage of meaning is called common sense. It concerns the "world of things related to us" and draws heavily on myths in order to provide explanations for the origins of things. In ancient Greece, the myths of Homer, for example, would have provided such explanations. However, from the pre-Socratics up to Plato there begins to emerge what Lonergan calls a systematic exigence. The role of reason begins to replace the role of myth by asking fundamental questions pertaining the nature of things, "the world of things related to one another." Plato's cave allegory exemplifies the limitations of the world of common sense because it restricts knowing to the world of the senses. Plato correctly identifies the priority of reason over knowing through the senses but he is not able to keep the two worlds together and ends up privileging the invisible world of forms to the diminution of the senses. Undoubtedly, this has implications for beauty, in that Plato's the One, the Good, and the Beautiful are separated from the world of particulars and sensible experience.[17]

In theology, the second stage of meaning is marked by the achievement of Aquinas's *Summa Theologica*. The prolongation of the second stage of meaning eventually culminates in the emergence of modern science. Myth is replaced by scientific theories that provide explanations of the universe. Eventually, as the second stage of meaning comes to fruition, a critical exigence emerges. Philosophy becomes differentiated from science so that philosophers begin to ask: How are the worlds of common sense and the worlds of theory related to one another? Where science is concerned primarily with the data of sense, philosophy now becomes concerned with the data of consciousness.

The critical exigence emerges in Descartes's *Meditations* when he turns to his own intentional consciousness in order to ground a differentiation between the world of common sense and the world of theory. Unfortunately his laudable quest for an indubitable leads to a legacy of scepticism that is reinforced in Western philosophy by the further ambitious attempts of Kant and Hume. Again, Polanyi refers to the turn to the subject and the legacy of scepticism and subjectivism that it leaves in its wake as the "doctrine of doubt."

In a more recent attempt, Mary Mothersill engages Kantian aesthetics in order to recover beauty.[18] However, it is doubtful whether one can make beauty a property of being in Mothersill's approach. Therefore, while I am sympathetic to her desire to restore beauty, I cannot help but agree with Paul Guyer, who states, in his review of the book, "there may be even wider room and deeper need for a theory of beauty than Mothersill allows."[19]

In his principal philosophical work *Insight* (1957) Lonergan attempts to bring philosophy into the third stage of meaning, to appropriate the turn to the subject as a transposition of Aquinas's philosophy of mind. Lonergan is more positive in his approach to this turn. It signals for him the emergence of the third stage of meaning where intentional consciousness becomes the philosophical basis for grounding a plurality of worldviews. Lonergan's response to the doctrine of doubt is to complete the attempts of the turn to the subject by clarifying an adequate epistemology. We will go into this in more detail below, but suffice it to say that the epistemology rests on the proper appropriation of one's own operations of consciousness and with the self-affirmation of the knower.[20] It is the recognition that "knowing is not just taking a look"; rather, knowing involves the cumulative, recurrent cognitional operations of *experience*, *understanding*, and *judgment* (and *decision*).[21] Lonergan states: "Objectivity is the fruit of authentic subjectivity," and it is authenticity that makes the difference between knowing, on the one hand, and subjectivism, scepticism, and relativism on the other.[22] The ability of a person to truly affirm him or herself as a knower, to claim "I am a knower!", corrects the previous incomplete attempts of the doctrinaires of doubt and, in the contemporary setting, competes as a dissenting voice especially among postmodern thinkers.

In the third stage of meaning, metaphysics is tertiary, derived from an adequate cognitional theory, which correctly identifies how one comes to know, and an epistemology based on the self-affirmation that one can truly know. In terms of the transcendental properties of being, each is linked to the intention of being as manifested in each of the operations of intentional consciousness. The operation of *decision* intends *value*, or the goodness of being. The operation of *judgment* intends the *true* and, with this, the existence of being. The operation of *understanding* intends being as intelligible. It grasps a unity or a relationship in each incremental act of understanding (which is true insofar as it is affirmed in judgment).

While Lonergan never really factored transcendental beauty and aesthetic judgments into his philosophy, his philosophy does not preclude such a development. In fact, such development is warranted, one that can take into account beholding the beautiful in sensitive experience and affirming the beautiful in aesthetic judgments.

As stated above, Balthasar was expressly critical of attempts by Catholic thinkers to incorporate the philosophical turn to the subject. However, we can respond to his critique by viewing the turn in the context of what Lonergan identifies as the stages of meaning, as a concrete historical heuristic structure of interpretation. Thus Catholic thinkers who attempt to take into account the philosophical turn to the subject are doing so according to a legitimate *zeitgeist*; they are meeting a necessary exigence in contemporary theology. Of course, the success of such attempts will vary. Other attempts have been simply dismissed or ignored due to a context of disillusionment that still permeates the contemporary philosophical scene. This point is particularly relevant to the work of Lonergan. Unfortunately, he is often dismissed by many as a "Kantian" while, in fact, he provides a thorough Catholic response to Kant. He enables an appropriate recovery of the philosophical turn to the subject that may enrich theology.[23]

Hence, just as it may be true that Scotus and Eckhart depart from the achievement of Thomistic metaphysics, so too one can say they signal the decline of the second stage of meaning (which culminated in Aquinas's ontology) that leads eventually to the third stage of meaning. In other words, the "door" of philosophical achievement that hinges on a Thomistic metaphysics swings between the climax of the second stage of meaning and eventually opens up to the third stage of meaning. What may on the one hand constitute a demise on the other hand eventually issues in a development, a third stage of meaning, the stage in which philosophy takes human consciousness or interiority as a starting point.

Christian philosophers have yet to sufficiently grapple with the philosophical turn to the subject, perhaps because of their fear that by doing so they will make truth relative or subjective. Conversely, one of the reasons we have not recovered beauty in philosophy to date is that we have not yet sufficiently grasped a philosophical basis grounded in conscious interiority. Such a basis could comprise a philosophy of beauty for a third stage of meaning, one that takes conscious interiority as a starting point for philosophy. In other words, we need an equivalent to a Thomistic achievement for the third stage of meaning, and I believe Lonergan's philosophy provides that equivalent.

Second, a post-Kantian transposed Thomistic philosophy of beauty à la Lonergan will have to address the fact that throughout his corpus,

Lonergan does not treat the topic of beauty. Indeed, Lonergan scholars must humbly concede that there is a sense in which he is open to Balthasar's indictment of Western philosophy and theology as neglecting beauty. However, this is not because Lonergan did not think beauty was important, but because most of his labours, especially in *Insight*, are devoted to transcendental truth and, to some extent, transcendental goodness (chapter 18 of *Insight*).[24]

Moreover, Lonergan admits that the outline of the structure of knowing that he puts forth in *Insight* is open to minor but not major revisions (*IN*, 591). In this way, a philosophy *for* a theology of beauty based on Lonergan's philosophical foundations will have to provide a basis for beauty, working out specifically how beauty fits within the overall structure of his thought. Undoubtedly, this will include, among other things, aesthetic experience, an aesthetic differentiation of consciousness, and aesthetic judgments. This complex task, one could say, will be a "major-minor" revision of his work, but one that will provide lasting benefits.

Robert Doran has begun such a revision in his attempts to reorient depth psychology in terms of Lonergan's philosophy through his own notion of "psychic conversion." This will be discussed further below; briefly, Doran sees in Lonergan's cognitional theory an avenue for complementing and clarifying what Balthasar means by "seeing" the beauty of God. He explains how this can be appropriately analogized from the created order through the subject as self-transcending. More specifically, Doran's attempt focuses on the sensitive and intellectual apprehension of beauty and will serve as a precursor for establishing aesthetic judgments in Lonergan's theory of consciousness.[25]

Third, a transposed Thomistic philosophy of beauty will have to respond to the Kantian legacy of aesthetic judgments. Recall Maurer's comments on Kantian aesthetic judgments above. An analogous symptom that arises from this philosophy is the commonly held belief that "beauty is in the eye of the beholder." Again, this has become an accepted, unreflective, common sense understanding of beauty. And while it may in some sense be true, to accept it uncritically is to buy into a relativism that eclipses beauty from being. What is needed is a philosophy that can ground aesthetic judgments wherein specific aesthetic judgments affirm something as (or as not) an instance of the beautiful.

Lonergan worked out in precision and detail an account of epistemological judgments in chapters 9 and 10 of *Insight*. Later, in *Method in Theology*, he came to speak of "judgments of value," distinguishing these from judgments of fact. But he gave no account of aesthetic judgments, and one will need to explore how aesthetic judgments could be incorporated into his philosophy as a ground for judgments about beauty. For example, is an aesthetic judgment a judgment of fact, or is it a judgment of value? Or some combination of the two? Or would it have its own independent category as a judgment? These are just a few questions that need to be addressed, and are investigated in chapter 7.

Fourth, a philosophy of beauty for a theological aesthetics will need to address the critique levelled against Kierkegaard by Balthasar and others that Kierkegaard separates the various spheres (aesthetic, ethical, and religious), effectively bifurcating the aesthetic from the ethical and religious. The effects of this bifurcation lead to the separation of beauty from ethics and religion.

By grounding the various spheres within the interiority of consciousness as differentiations of consciousness, the achievement of Kierkegaard's stages could be preserved while any ambiguity surrounding the bifurcation of such stages could be clarified. We would be mainly interested in the aesthetic differentiation of consciousness and religiously differentiated consciousness. Although distinct, their unity lies in human consciousness. Moreover, since various patterns, levels, and differentiations of consciousness can interpenetrate, they need not exclude each other, or the ethical realm for that matter.[26]

Bernard Lonergan distinguishes between the aesthetically differentiated consciousness of the artist and the religiously differentiated consciousness of the mystic. However, unlike Kierkegaard's, these differentiations are not *de facto* separate; rather, they have their ground in the unity of consciousness, which is polymorphic by nature and therefore can flow in various patterns. Consequently, the various differentiations of consciousness can interpenetrate so that the artist and religious mystic may be one and the same person. This topic is addressed further in chapter 4.

Since Lonergan's philosophy of consciousness is the foil against which I attempt to interpret and establish a transpositional Thomistic philosophy of beauty, it is worth providing a brief overview of his philosophy of consciousness and how it functions as a hermeneutic for approaching various aspects of aesthetics.

Lonergan's Philosophy and Hermeneutics: A Brief Overview

In Lonergan's theory of intentional consciousness there are *intentions, operations, patterns/differentiations,* and *transformations of consciousness.*

These are not only interrelated, but provide the basis for a hermeneutics that can ground a philosophy of beauty. In this section I provide a brief overview of Lonergan's philosophy, and in the following chapters I go into more detail as the various topics arise.[27]

Lonergan's philosophy of consciousness begins with a primordial curiosity or Aristotelian wonder that he calls *the unrestricted desire to know*. In Lonergan's book *Insight*, this wonder is restricted to intellectual inquiry. The questions that arise are ordered to particular operations in intentional consciousness. Thomistic in spirit, Lonergan transposes Aquinas's notion of the intellect into the "levels" (a term he invokes metaphorically) or operations of *understanding* and *judgment* (critical reflection). The transposition of Aquinas's notion of will occurs later in his thought when he develops the fourth level of operations, *deliberation* or *decision*.

Two points are important to keep in mind before proceeding. First, Lonergan distinguishes between intentional and non-intentional consciousness. Intentional consciousness involves the four levels of *experiencing* (presentations), *understanding*, *judging*, and *deciding*. Non-intentional consciousness refers to the subject's self-presence, although this self-presence is present to the four levels (*MT*, 8). Second, the levels are related to one another concretely through sublation.[28] Therein, the higher levels subsume or sublate the lower, transcending or adding something to them, while at the same time preserving and retaining the prior elements.

The first level of intentional consciousness is *empirical consciousness*, but it is more often referred to as *experience* and less so as *presentations*, although the latter is more precise. Through this consciousness "we sense, perceive, imagine, feel, speak, move" (*MT*, 9). Presentations occur in two ways: through conscious experience of the data of the five senses and through the data of consciousness, the subject's self-presence through operations, imagination, memories, and so on.

In the process of coming to know at the level of empirical consciousness, it is essential to *attend* to the data of one's experience. Proper understanding occurs in part to the extent that one adverts to the relevant data presented to consciousness. Conversely, the failure to attend to relevant data leads to misunderstanding.

Questions emerge within the subject from the data presented to empirical consciousness. The question for intelligence or understanding asks "What is it?" and is equivalent to *quidditas*, or "whatness" in Aquinas's philosophy of mind. The question can be phrased in a number of ways as long as it is able to get at the intelligible understanding, the essence, the nature of, or the relations within the data of a given inquiry. Some examples are: "What is the problem?," "What is the nature of an eclipse?," or "What is beauty"?

The question "What is it?" pertains to the second level of intentional consciousness, *intellectual consciousness*, or understanding. Intellectual consciousness involves *acts of understanding*, or *insights*, and the formulation of *concepts*. The insight grasps the intelligible unity within the data or the relations among the data. Concepts express acts of understanding, and both are the fruits of inquiry.[29] However, they are further subject to the critical scrutiny of rational reflection that is the next operation – judgment.

Answers to questions for intelligence give rise to further questions for reflection. The former questions anticipate intelligibility and the latter questions anticipate truth, existence, and reality. Questions for reflection pertain to the third level of consciousness, *rational* consciousness or *judgment*. The primary question at this level is "Is it so?" (*IN*, 106). If the judgment is to be true then the answers to questions for reflection must be in either the affirmative or the negative.

When one grasps the necessary conditions to make a true judgment, then the judgment that follows from that grasp is said to be true. The answer to all relevant questions in a given inquiry meets these necessary conditions. Moreover, to make a true judgment also means that the judgment is external to the individual making the judgment. If an object coming over the hill is truly judged to be a horse and not a donkey, then the object truly is a horse and its identity is no longer just a matter for conjecture. One has grasped sufficient evidence to declare the object to be a horse, and the truth of the judgment is now independent of the subject who judges it to be so.

Lonergan's notion of judgment is inextricably linked to his epistemology. The challenge of what he calls *self-appropriation* involves adverting to one's own levels of intentional consciousness as data. One asks: "Am I a knower? Do I make judgments?" Through the process of identifying and affirming the empirical, intelligent, and rational consciousness within oneself, the invariant philosophical framework is discovered not as a mere possibility, but as a concrete reality.[30]

The foundation of Lonergan's philosophy lies in the proper unfolding of the structure of conscious intentionality in questions, understanding, judgment, and decision: "Genuine objectivity is the fruit of authentic subjectivity. Objectivity is to be attained only by attaining

authentic subjectivity" (*MT*, 292). One attains authenticity by allowing
questions to arise, being attentive to the data pertinent to the query,
being intelligent in one's understanding of the data, being reasonable
in one's judgments about the understanding of the data, and being responsible in one's decisions as to what should be done with the knowledge acquired (*MT*, 265).

Finally, each level of intentional consciousness *intends* different aspects of being and so, for the purposes of this study, each level will emphasize different philosophical aspects of beauty. That is, at the level of
experience one intends being as experienced or presented to consciousness, and in this particular study questions at that level will concern
matters of aesthetic perception and aesthetic experience. At the level
of understanding, one intends being as intelligible. In terms of beauty,
this will entail the three conditions of beauty as identified by Aquinas,
to be taken up in the next chapter. At the level of judgment, one intends
being as true and real, which will raise the question of aesthetic judgments of beauty. At the level of decision, one intends being as value or
goodness, which will concern the creation and contemplation of beauty.
In addition, when one undertakes the task of self-appropriation, one
comes to know oneself as a concrete unity-identity-whole, a *being* that
knows.[31] One's knows one judgments of beauty to be true judgments
and not just "in the eye of the beholder." Further, when one falls in
love, one becomes a *being* in love, so the mystery of another person or
of some transcendent Other becomes a locus for the appreciation of
beauty.

Patterns of experience. Human consciousness is polymorphic. There is
a stream to consciousness, but there is also an organizing principle in
which consciousness is directed through "conation, interest, attention,
purpose" (*IN*, 205). Lonergan emphasizes that consciousness flows in
various *patterns of experience*: the biological, aesthetic, artistic, intellectual, dramatic (see *IN*, 202–12), practical, and mystical patterns, to name
a few of the principle ones (*IN*, 410).[32] "These patterns alternate; they
blend or mix; they can interfere, conflict, lose their way, break down"
(*IN*, 410). I will go into more detail in subsequent chapters on these patterns as they pertain to the discussion of beauty and aesthetics.

In addition to the patterns of consciousness, there are also *differentiations of consciousness.* The four basic differentiations of consciousness
Lonergan refers to are: common sense, theory, interiority, and religious
(*MT*, 257). There are other differentiations of consciousness, and like
the patterns of experience, each can mix, blend, or operate in a manifold

ways (*MT*, 272). Moreover, one can conceive of these differentiations in individuals or collectively in communities, societies, and civilizations. As we reviewed them earlier in this chapter, specific differentiations of consciousness can pertain to the different stages of meaning, so that an understanding of the differentiations can account for cultural development (*MT*, 305).

In general, the primary difference between *patterns of experience* and *differentiations of consciousness* is one of degree. In a pattern of experience the flow of consciousness can be spontaneous and fleeting. By contrast, a differentiation of consciousness is the fruit of a deliberate and habitual development within the subject. For example, it is one thing to understand a mathematic equation, although to do so requires that I enter the intellectual pattern of experience. However, in order to advance a mathematical theory in a professional context, I need to have acquired the education, habits, and skills required for a theoretical differentiation of consciousness. This requires a prior commitment to make the intellectual pattern of experience a way of life.[33]

There exists, in addition to the operations, intentions, patterns of experience, and differentiations within human consciousness, the possibility of *transformations within human consciousness.* Lonergan called the three transformations or conversions that occur the intellectual, moral, and religious. There is also a fourth psychological transformation that Lonergan affirmed following its development by his successor, Robert Doran, which we will also include.

Intellectual conversion involves a "radical clarification" of knowledge, existence, and reality. The transformation entails the amelioration of the myth that knowing simply involves "taking a good look" (*MT*, 238). The assumption is false because it fails to distinguish between *the world of immediacy* and the world *mediated by meaning.* The world of immediacy is the world prior to the mediating operations of experience, understanding, and judgment. Intellectual conversion effects the realization that human knowing involves the compound of operations of presentations, understanding, and judgment. The content of these operations is knowledge of a real world mediated by meaning. Intellectual conversion will be important to our argument that beauty is real, a property of being.

Moral conversion "changes the criterion of one's decisions and choices from satisfactions to values" (*MT*, 240). The effects of the transformation enable one to choose more autonomously and responsibly, where one has been previously unable or unwilling to do so because of some obstacle or block in development. Moral conversion involves the choice of the "truly good" over immediate gratification, or sensitive satisfaction, especially when value and satisfaction conflict. In our study, this will be demonstrated in reference to Kierkegaard's theory of the existential spheres, and specifically the movement from aesthetic hedonism to the ethical sphere of taking responsibility for one's actions.

Religious conversion transforms one's living into a dynamic state of *being* in love in an unrestricted manner:

> Religious conversion is being grasped by ultimate concern. It is other-worldly falling in love. It is total and permanent self-surrender without conditions, qualifications, reservations. But it is such a surrender, not as an act, but as a dynamic state that is prior to and principle of subsequent acts. It is revealed in retrospect as an under-tow of existential consciousness, as a fated acceptance of a vocation to holiness, as perhaps an increasing simplicity and passivity in prayer. It is interpreted differently in the context of different religious traditions (*MT*, 240–1).

The response of the subject in love is to surrender and commit wholeheartedly to that love which has content but no apprehended object.

The application of the notion of religious transformation in our study of beauty will help in understanding those individuals who are transformed profoundly by aesthetic experiences. Such transformations bring positive displacements to their personalities, such as in the cases of Sergei Bulgakov and Fyodor Dostoevsky.

In a subsequent development to Lonergan's three transformations, Robert Doran seeks to integrate Lonergan's notion of conversion with insights from depth psychology. He calls this integration *psychic conversion*.[34] This transformation effects the liberation of the human subject from the oppression of psychological wounds and complexes. Doran defines psychic conversion as "a transformation of the psychic component of what Freud calls 'the censor' from a repressive to a constructive agency in a person's development."[35] The censor is like a filter that selects or excludes material or images needed for insight. When it is operating constructively, it "sorts through" the plethora of sensitive data that might otherwise be overwhelming and allows us to receive the images needed for insights. When it is repressive, the censor does not allow select images that might lead to insight to be presented to consciousness. The positive effect of psychic conversion is that it "allows access to *one's own* symbolic system."[36] Obviously the access to the symbolic system will have a positive bearing on the creativity of the art-ist. This dimension of conversion will be also helpful in trying to reap-propriate Nietzsche's binary aesthetics, a topic we address in chapter 3.

Lonergan's philosophy of consciousness as hermeneutic framework. The en-tire range of Lonergan's philosophy of consciousness from the structure and pattern of operations in intentional consciousness, with its poly-morphic nature of patterns, differentiations, and transformations, to one's own successful and habituated appropriation of that conscious-ness serve as the foundations for the hermeneutic structure that enables effective interpretation (*IN*, 590). Lonergan invokes the analogy of a pair of scissors in discussing the structure of interpretation. The "upper blade" refers to the general hermeneutic principles that close upon a "lower blade" of data in a given query (*IN*, 600). This upper blade con-sists of the operations and polymorphic structure of human conscious-ness. When those principles, in this case the cognitional theory, come to bear adequately upon select data of a given query, the closing of the scissors yields a more proximate and accurate interpretation (*MT*, 162).

In a previous work, I demonstrated this through bringing Lonergan's philosophy to bear upon Mircea Eliade's phenomenology of religion.[37] I not only sought to gain a more systematic approach to Eliade's theory through Lonergan's hermeneutics, but also invoked the latter as an or-ganizing principle to address the topics. In a similar way, in attempting to construct a philosophy of beauty based on Lonergan's philosophy, especially in chapters 5 to 8 of this book, I will approach the topics in terms of the patterns of operations (experience, understanding, judg-ment, decision), considering aesthetic experience, the intelligibility of beauty, judgments of beauty, and the creation and contemplation of beauty.

As I stated earlier in the chapter, Lonergan had little to say explicitly about beauty. Hence we have to construct anything he has to say on the basis of his philosophy of consciousness. Therefore, before proceeding, let me echo a warning by another who attempted to interpret Loner-gan's philosophy, namely his successor Frederick Crowe, who stated at the outset of a notable lecture: "I will not distinguish always between what Lonergan says and what I make him mean."[38] A similar confes-sion applies to my exposition and application of Lonergan's thought. Moreover, I recognize that I may need to make revisions in the future, based on feedback I receive from this extended argument. Still, I am convinced of the provocative contribution Lonergan has to make, not only to a philosophy of beauty, but to the foundations for a theology of beauty along the lines Balthasar attempted, and if nothing else I hope to make a good start.

Conclusion

We have been attempting to outline an extensive program to recover beauty as a transcendental property of being. This work aims to provide the philosophical foundations for beauty through a transposed post-Kantian Thomistic philosophy drawing upon the work of Bernard Lonergan. This will entail a minor but needed revision to Lonergan's work that will include, for example, the establishment of judgments as affirming instances of the beautiful. Hopefully, this task will lead us towards a recovery of beauty, so for our part we can one day sing, along with the Diné (Navajo), "from the West beauty has been restored."

2 Every Being Is Beautiful

In this chapter I will conduct a brief survey of the emergence of the doctrine of the transcendentals, examine some questions concerning a Thomistic interpretation of beauty, and then present an overview of Aquinas's thought on beauty. This chapter provides a context for a transposed philosophy of Aquinas in light of Lonergan's engagement and response to modern philosophical trends. Therefore, I conclude by examining some comments on transcendental beauty made by Lonergan.

Beauty as a Transcendental Property of Being

Balthasar is convinced that beauty is a transcendental property of being and that Aquinas's philosophy is a significant development of this doctrine. Balthasar is specifically indebted to Franz Kovach's interpretation of Thomas on this account.

When considering the question of whether beauty is a transcendental property of being, Kovach sees only four possible positions: (1) no being is beautiful, (2) only one thing (specific being) is beautiful, (3) some beings are beautiful and other beings are not, and (4) all beings are beautiful.[1] On the face of it, relying on one's common-sense experience, one may be tempted to opt for number three. However, Kovach opts for number four, that all beings are beautiful. This is not a naïve position for him, but rather one that follows logically and has its roots in a philosophical tradition extending from Greek philosophy to the heights of medieval scholasticism. Therefore, we begin by summarizing briefly the history of the doctrine of the transcendentals, taking Kovach's summary as a starting point while paying special attention to the issue of transcendental beauty in Aquinas.

The roots for the transcendental properties of being begin with Aristotle's notion of "the one" (τὸ 'ἕν). This proposition asserts that every being is one or, rather, a unity as a condition of its individual being (*PB*, 236).

In order to get a better understanding of what a transcendental property of being is, one must distinguish between *logical properties* and *transcendental properties*. A logical property of being follows necessarily from the nature of the being itself; all people have the ability to laugh (risibility). A transcendental property of being, on the other hand, is "a necessary consequence of the property of a thing as being" (*PB*, 237). In the case of Aristotle, unity is a property of any existing particular being. In order for a thing to be a thing, there must be a unity to its existence. "Logical property is confined to a given species or genus; transcendental property transcends all genera and species, and characterizes every kind of being." Aristotle referred to such properties as passions (πάθη) or common properties (κοινά), meaning that they are the first determinations of being. Later thinkers began to refer to them as transcendental properties of being (*PB*, 237).

The characteristics of transcendental properties include (1) *convertibility with being*: "every being is one, every one is a being, every being is good, every good is a being; every being is beautiful, every beautiful is a being"; (2) *convertibility with each other*: every beautiful is true, every truth is beautiful, and so on; and (3) *real identity and a merely logical distinction standing between being and all transcendental properties*: being, the one, the good, the beautiful signify the same thing, but are not exactly the same: being is that which exists, oneness refers to the indivisibility of a being, and so on (*PB*, 238).

The Development of Transcendental Beauty

Kovach divides the history of the "doctrine" of the transcendental properties of being into five periods: (1) pre-Aristotelian (from Heraclitus to Plato); (2) from Aristotle to Avicenna; (3) from Philip the Chancellor to Thomas Aquinas; (4) from Duns Scotus to Francisco Suárez; (5) subsequent scholastic thought (writing in 1974).

In Plato one finds transcendental unity, goodness, and beauty by way of participation in the One, the Good, and the Beautiful. In Aristotle there is the recognition of unity, truth, and goodness, but not beauty. Plotinus, indebted to Plato, emphasizes beauty but at the expense of transcendental truth. Consequently, Augustine affirms the beauty of being and also recovers transcendental truth. Boethius explicitly affirms transcendental unity and goodness, but not beauty. Dionysus the Areopagite, influenced by neo-Platonism, affirms beauty as well as unity, goodness, and truth. Later thinkers like Avicenna add to the Aristotelian list of transcendentals: thing (definiteness) and something (otherness) (*PB*, 240). In the more modern references to the transcendentals, the unity of a being includes the latter two.

A shift occurs in the third period, beginning in the thirteenth century, characterized by an attempt to systematize the transcendentals. Heretofore, up to the eve of the scholastic endeavours, attempts were made at "an aesthetic vision of the universe" derived from various concepts taken from the Book of Wisdom (11:21). Early attempts to systematize the biblical concepts were in groups of triads: measure, number, weight; dimension, form, order; substance, nature, power; and the like.[2] The thirteenth century reveals the need for what Lonergan cálls a systematic exigence, and in this case it occurs when the scholastics attempt to systematize these triads taken from biblical literature (see *MT*, 83) into metaphysical language. Among them, Philip the Chancellor, Alexander of Hales, and Albert the Great make significant attempts to systematize the transcendentals, particularly as this involves accounting for beauty and its effect on the subject.

Philip the Chancellor speaks of the one, the true, and the good in his *Summa de bono*, but he does not address beauty. He was mainly interested in the relationship between truth and goodness, given as he was to responding to the resurgence of Manichaean-like attitudes in the Middle Ages. Still he begins to link the transcendentals with the subject, which will have a subsequent importance. For him, the transcendentals are convertible with being and the distinction between them is one of *secundum rationem*, distinguished in the mind.[3]

The scholastics also inherited the Greek notion of *kalokagathia*, which combines the notion of beauty and goodness; therefore they did not initially distinguish beauty from goodness. One could have been tempted to conclude, as Robert Grosseteste (ca. 1242 AD) does in his commentary on Pseudo-Dionysus, that "If everything desires the good and the beautiful together, the good and the beautiful are the same."[4]

The *Summa* of Alexander of Hales (ca. 1245 AD), while affirming beauty, also contributed to the clarification of the difference between beauty and goodness. Like Philip's *Summa*, Alexander's underscores the difference between the transcendentals by placing the emphasis on the intentionality of the perceiver. One of its authors, John de la Rochelle, distinguished beauty from goodness by claiming that beauty pleases the apprehension while goodness pleases or satisfies the affections (desires). Likewise, as Aquinas also claims, beauty pertains to formal causality (the intelligibility of a being) and the good pertains to final causality (the end or goal of a thing). Hence, when one grasps the beautiful, one grasps the beauty of the form of a specific object, while the good is apprehended in terms of the proper end of a human desire. For example, a chef prepares an aesthetically pleasing meal that looks almost too good to eat. The apprehension of the culinary delight is pleasing; it pertains to beauty. The satisfying of human hunger and the nourishment that follows from eating the meal pertains to the good. One could stare at the prepared meal with delight all day, but it would not satisfy the appetite for food.

Several scholastics began commenting on Pseudo-Dionysus's *Divine Names*, a work with a substantive treatment of beauty in relation to God. In his commentary on the *Divine Names of Pseudo-Dionysus*, Albert the Great affirms beauty as a transcendental and as distinct from the good. Seeking to clarify how beauty is distinguished from the good in an object, Albert focuses on beauty as the splendour of the form: "The nature of the beautiful consists in general in a resplendence of form, whether in duly-ordered parts of material objects, or in [human beings], or in actions." Beauty "does not subsist in material parts, but in resplendence of form."[5] Again, we see here the linking of beauty to formal causality that will be emphasized by his student Aquinas.

This series of developments in the understanding of beauty bring a systematic approach to the questions concerning the triads derived from the Book of Wisdom. This is significant, as Eco points out, because the triads (number, weight, and measure; dimension, species, order) can now be ascribed to form.[6] The splendour of the form becomes a particular aspect for defining beauty. However, according to Eco, Albert's account is too objectivist in the sense that he does not sufficiently account for the knowing subject. His student Aquinas will address the latter concern and hence systematically attempt to account for the full range of beauty in the object and in the subject. Whether Aquinas succeeds is a matter of debate. Scholars differ on whether one can legitimately posit that beauty is a transcendental for him. Given the relevance of this issue for the argument of this book, I turn to a short excursus on the matter.

Aquinas and Transcendental Beauty?

Aquinas's lack of a systematic treatment of beauty and the question of how we understand it in terms of the philosophy of knowing provide a context for ongoing reflection. Kovach accounts for the lack of systematic treatment of beauty in Aquinas's thought in the following way:

> This system of transcendentals, as can be readily seen, does not contain transcendental beauty, since the derivation is to be found in a relatively early work of Thomas Aquinas, the *De veritate* (On Truth). Later on, prob-ably while writing his commentary on Pseudo-Dionysus' *On the Divine Names*, Thomas clearly expresses his belief in the transcendality of beauty by declaring with Plato that every being is both good and beautiful; also, that the beautiful is convertible with the good; and the beautiful and the good are really identical and only logically distinct ... Is there a place in the above Thomistic system for transcendental beauty? ... [T]he truth is that there definitely is room for transcendental beauty in Thomas's sys-tem. (*PB*, 241–2)

Armand Maurer would agree. He states that for Aquinas "Beauty is a transcendental mode of being, accompanying being wherever it is found, so that every being is beautiful insofar as it exists" (*AB*, 34). In his book *Beauty in the Middle Ages*, Umberto Eco states that "Aquinas accepted, implicitly at any rate, the view that beauty was a transcen-dental."[7] In another book on Aquinas's aesthetics, a book singled out by Étienne Gilson for its scholarship, Eco devotes an entire chapter to the question and concludes similarly:

> It is a property of being, not because it appears this way in aesthetic intu-itions of the world, nor in some emotive sense of beauty without rational justification; rather, it is a property of being in a precise and categorical sense of these terms, or, better, in a kind of metacategorical simplification. That is, beauty is identified with being simply as being. This theory is implicit rather than explicit, however; Aquinas never expressly states that *ens* and *bonum* and *pulchrum* are interchangeable. Instead, beauty adheres to being only through the mediation of the good.[8]

In *Art and Scholasticism*, Jacques Maritain, commenting on Aquinas's treatment of beauty, states clearly:

> [B]eauty belongs to the order of the transcendentals ... Like the one, the true, and the good, the beautiful is *being* itself considered from a certain aspect; it is a property of being ... each kind of being *is* in its own way, is *good* in its own way, is *beautiful* in its own way.[9]

However, the exact nature of beauty remains unclear. Is it a constitutive aspect of the form itself, or is it the splendour of the transcendentals together? Maritain states: "Strictly speaking, Beauty is the radiance of all the transcendentals united."[10] Eco is critical of this aspect of Maritain, stating that it does not appear in Thomas or in neo-scholastism.[11] It is reminiscent of the thought of Bonaventure and is even present in Balthasar when he claims that beauty sets a kind of seal upon the transcendentals (GL, 2.38–9). Moreover, it is also unclear from Maritain to what extent beauty is distinct from the good. "The classic table of the transcendentals (ens, res, unum, aliquid, verum, bonum) does not exhaust all the transcendental values, and if the beautiful is not included, it is because it can be reduced to one of them (to the good – for the beautiful is that which in things faces the mind as an object of intuitive delight)."[12] This, of course, remains a question for Thomist scholars who reference Thomas himself:

> Beauty and goodness in a thing are identical fundamentally; for they are based upon the same thing, namely, the form; and consequently goodness is praised as beauty. But they differ logically, for goodness properly relates to the appetite (goodness being what all things desire); and therefore it has the aspect of an end (the appetite being a kind of movement towards a thing). On the other hand, beauty relates to the cognitive faculty; for beautiful things are those which please when seen. Hence beauty consists in due proportion; for the senses delight in things duly proportioned, as in what is after their own kind – because even sense is a sort of reason, just as is every cognitive faculty. Now since knowledge is by assimilation, and similarity relates to form, beauty properly belongs to the nature of a formal cause. (ST, 1.5.4 ad 1)

Again, Aquinas states that beauty and goodness are identical fundamentally but distinct logically:

> The beautiful is the same as the good, and they differ in one aspect only. For since good is what all seek, the notion of good is that which calms the desire; while the notion of the beautiful is that which calms the desire, by being seen or known. Consequently those senses chiefly regard the beautiful, which are the most cognitive … Thus it is evident that beauty adds to goodness a relation to the cognitive faculty: so that "good" means that which simply pleases the appetite; while the "beautiful" is something pleasant to apprehend. (ST, 1-2.27.1 ad 3)

Concerning Aquinas's treatment of beauty, Étienne Gilson states: "[E]verything is beautiful as having a form (through which it has *esse*), and this form is a sort of a participation of the divine clarity." However, the question of beauty remains open. Gilson's reading of Aquinas is that "in the last analysis, beauty is a certain good, but a good distinct from all other classes."[13] Hence, on the face of it, it would appear that beauty is a transcendental, but a closer inspection suggests that for Gilson, it is a subdivision of the good.

The good pertains to what the appetite desires (*id quod omnia appetunt*). Drawing upon Aquinas, Gilson agrees "beauty relates to form as known, whereas goodness relates to form as desired."[14] Moreover, he points out that Thomas also speaks of beauty as that which pleases when it is seen (*id quod visum placet*). He notes that "sight" refers more broadly to intellect as well as sense "provided real knowledge is involved."[15] What Gilson does not clarify is that if beauty pertains primarily to formal causality, and if the good pertains to final causality (that which is desired), how can beauty be a particular aspect of the good?

> The beautiful is a variety of the good. It is the particular kind of good to be experienced, by a knowing power [grasping the form], in the very act of knowing an object eminently fit to be known. The pleasure experienced in knowing the beautiful does not constitute beauty itself, but it betrays its presence. It testifies to the excellence of the commensuration there is between a certain power of knowing and a certain known object.[16]

G.B. Phelan is also convinced of the transcendentality of beauty in Aquinas, but not as a subdivision of the good:

> One of the most distinctive characteristics of St. Thomas's conception of beauty is its realism. The objectivity of beauty is asserted and reasserted, and always with such clearness that misunderstanding on this score becomes impossible. Beauty dwells in the very heart of things that exist. It reveals itself to the admiring gaze of those who look for it as coming from the depths of reality itself. The beautiful is unequivocally objective. Nothing is beautiful which is not in some sense real; and all that is, is in some sense beautiful. The very actuality which all real things possess is the source and origin of whatever is beautiful in them. All things are beautiful because they exist; and the degree of their beauty is in precise proportion to the perfection

of their being ... There is throughout [Aquinas's] whole doctrine on beauty that underlying conviction that beauty is real and the real is beautiful.[17]

By contrast, Jan Aertsen argues clearly against the transcendentality of beauty in Aquinas. His is a dissenting voice (although he is not the sole dissenter) among a chorus of Aquinas scholars of significant repute who affirm that beauty is a transcendental for Aquinas.[18] Aertsen's main contention is the absence of beauty in Aquinas's *De Veritate*, where he systematically treats the transcendentals but not beauty. Nonetheless, Kovach's argument that Aquinas reckons with beauty later in his commentary on Pseudo-Dionysus is provocative. Moreover, if transcendental beauty does have a kind of unique or different status from the other transcendentals, then this might explain in part the lack of treatment of beauty in *De Veritate*. Still, it is one thing to admit a lack of clarity in how Aquinas conceived transcendental beauty, and quite another entirely to deny a place to transcendental beauty in his thought. In his work on beauty in Aquinas, Piotr Jaroszynski explains: "[O]ur grasp of all reality in the dimension of the transcendental properties, including beauty, is the foundation, and ferment of our assimilation of reality within us in terms of wisdom, and for determining our human place in the world and in culture ... [D]isregard for transcendental beauty leads to the sterilization of culture."[19]

While it is quite reasonable to presume that Aquinas affirmed transcendental beauty, it is equally true that his treatment was not systematic, at least not in the way that his treatment of the transcendentals was in *De Veritate*. This lack of systematic treatment has too often been the grounds for its dismissal when what is called for is a more precise understanding of how beauty is a transcendental. While I agree with Kovach that Aquinas arrived at beauty later in his career, I also think that if beauty is a transcendental, it may well be a different type of transcendental, in the way Bonaventure perhaps was suggesting when he speaks of beauty as the splendour of the transcendentals together. The possibility of beauty being a different sort of transcendental could further explain why it is missing in Aquinas's *De Veritate*.

The Fourth Period

The fourth period of the history of the transcendentals according to Kovach extends from Duns Scotus (1265–1308) to Francisco Suárez (1548–1617) and is represented in a shift from metaphysics to the logical order.

Both of these thinkers "considerably increased the logical character of Aristotle's completely metaphysical theory of the transcendental properties of being" (*PB*, 245). Scotus accepts the Aristotelian properties (truth, unity, goodness), which he calls categorical transcendentals, and then he adds a second group called disjunctive transcendentals. In terms of the latter he posits that some properties of being can only be predicated of being disjunctively (e.g., being is finite or infinite, necessary or contingent). The result is that the "innovation clearly moves the transcendentals out of the realm of reality and into the realm of thinking" (e.g., conceptualism) (*PB*, 243). Hence, the achievement of Aquinas is eclipsed because the transcendental properties of being are no longer necessarily actual properties but are conceptualized.

Suárez continues the move from metaphysics to logic, but he goes further than Scotus by eliminating the transcendentals of definiteness (*res*) and otherness (*aliquid*). He further distinguishes between transcendentals and properties of being. The implications of this for beauty perhaps set the stage for the modern loss of beauty in scholastic thought: "the concept 'beautiful' is not formed by the direct addition of one logical note to 'being,' unlike the 'one' (undivided + being) or the 'good' (= desirable + being), but rather by the addition of a logical note to the transcendental concept 'good.' As a consequence of this logical formation, the concept 'beautiful' may be transcendental in the sense that is truly predicable of all being but it is not a genuine 'property of being'" (*PB*, 255).

Aesthetics as a distinct discipline emerges in the eighteenth century by way of Alexander Baumgarten (1714 – 1762). Post-medieval reflection developed an emphasis on the triad "true-good-beautiful."[20] This culminates in the tri-fold work of Kant: *Critique of Pure Reason* (truth), *Critique of Practical Reason* (goodness), and *Critique of Judgment* (beauty). As we pointed out in the first chapter, Balthasar's trilogy is a deliberate response to this view.

The fifth period Kovach describes is the renewal in scholastic and Thomistic thought beginning in the middle nineteenth century. This renewal was prompted by Leo XIII's encyclical *Aeterni Patris*, promulgated in August 1879. While no new transcendentals were postulated during this period, a resurgence of the discussion of transcendental beauty emerges:

> The number of those scholastic thinkers who hold the transcendality of beauty seems to be ever-growing, thereby representing a reaction to the

fourth period that, from Duns Scotus on, tended to move away from the ideas of transcendental beauty. (*PB*, 243)

Given these comments, one can see why Balthasar would posit a decline in metaphysics after Aquinas specifically as it pertains to beauty subsequent to Scotus, reliant as Balthasar was on Kovach's interpretation of the loss of beauty.

A number of Thomists inspired by Pope Leo's call to Thomistic renewal engaged the question of beauty. Already cited among them are Étienne Gilson, Jacques Maritain, Franz Kovach, Armand Maurer, and Piotr Jaroszynski. However, they all had one thing in common: their attempts to recover beauty were strictly in terms of historical Thomism. In other words, they did not attempt a recovery of beauty based on a transposed philosophy of Aquinas following the turn to the subject – one that would, in the spirit of Thomas, engage the crucial insights of the day, yet try to respond to and appropriate them in accordance with the writer's own intellectual and faith tradition.

By contrast, as we argued in the previous chapter, in his book *Insight: A Study of Human Understanding* Lonergan responded to the Kantian legacy of doubt left in the wake of the *First Critique*. However, Kant's *Third Critique* remains to be adequately engaged by Lonergan's philosophy, and this is what I am proposing in this work. Before delving into that more deeply, however, I turn to a brief summary of Aquinas on beauty based on Maurer's approach, which provides a context for this work.

Beauty: A Thomistic Interpretation

In his book *About Beauty*, Armand Maurer attempts to explicate the philosophy and theology of beauty that he believes is implicit although scattered throughout Aquinas's writings. Maurer's reading of Thomas insists that beauty is a transcendental property of being: "Every being is beautiful insofar as it is, just as it is true and good" (*AB*, 1).

Maurer emphasizes the metaphysical revolution or turning point that occurs in Aquinas when the metaphysics of essence is transposed into one of existence. For Aquinas, being is that which *exists*. This means that if is something is true or good, then it exists as true and good (*AB*, 3). Likewise, if it is beautiful, then it exists as beautiful. In other words, beauty exists qua being. Maurer concludes: "The translation of beauty into the language of existence was not made very explicitly by St. Thomas, but he left hints and suggestions as to how it could be done" (*AB*, 4).

The Conditions of Beauty

Beauty is apprehended by the intellect as form through the senses. Existence is often presupposed since it is so deeply bound up with all life. Existence is "the secret source of all the perfection and actuality of a being, including its beauty" (*AB*, 9.). Much of the determination of beauty lies in the notion of form. Form makes something distinctively what it is, its own "species" so to speak. Traditionally this is referred to as substantial form. Each form has its own radiance or luminosity (*claritas*) that is either pleasing to the senses, such as a beautiful flower, or pleasing to the intellect, as in the clarity of a successfully deduced mathematical equation.[21] The difference between the two is analogous. Likewise, darkness and obscurity are the opposite of beauty except for those occasions when they lend to beauty, as in the use of contrast in a painting, for example.

In addition to form and clarity, harmony (*consonantia* – "sounding together") or due proportion (*debita proportio*) is an essential aspect of beauty. The harmony/proportion of any being pertains to its form (*ST*, 1.5.4 ad 1). However, since forms depend on existence for their perfection, so it is that beautiful objects exist (*AB*, 12).[22]

Third, a beautiful thing needs wholeness or integrity (*integritas*). Integrity connotes two senses. The first sense reflects the perfection of a being in its existence. However, in addition to the integrity of existence (one cannot be split in two) there is integrity of operation and action.

> Natural beings, like animals, birds, trees, have their own integrity or wholeness, dependent on their own natural forms. The notion of wholeness is thus analogous, like the notions of radiance and proportion. The wholeness of a dream is not the same as the wholeness of a novel or painting, and the completeness of a natural being is judged differently from that of a work of art. A living woman without arms is hardly counted beautiful; the Venus of Milo in the Louvre can give intense enjoyment as a beautiful statue. (*AB*, 13)

In the moral sphere, integrity would be a consistency in knowing the good and choosing the good.[23]

In sum, existence as embodied in form is the ground of beauty. The beauty of a form consists in (1) radiance, splendour, luminosity, or clarity (*claritas*), (2) harmony (*consonantia*) or due proportion (*debita proportio*), and (3) perfection, wholeness, or integrity (*integritas*). As Aquinas states:

> For beauty includes three conditions, "integrity" or "perfection," since those things which are impaired are by the very fact ugly; due "proportion" or "harmony"; and lastly, "brightness" or "clarity," whence things are called beautiful which have a bright color. (*ST*, 1.39.8)[24]

Each of these three conditions is linked to the form for Aquinas. As Eco states, "[A]nything he says about beauty indicates that it is grounded in form, and if an object is to be experienced as beautiful it must be considered from the point of view of its formal cause."[25] In other words, a form that is well proportioned, integral with all its constitutive parts, and possesses luminosity is beautiful.

This intimate relationship between beauty and existence is related to Aquinas's interpretation of creation. In Maurer's words, "Cosmogenesis (the birth of the universe) is at the same time calogenesis (the birth of beauty)" (*AB*, 44). "St. Thomas's interpretation of Genesis is of interest to us, not because of its scientific view of the universe, which is now outmoded, but because it shows us how his metaphysics of beauty can be used in a theology of creation" (*AB*, 56).

Maurer notes how Aquinas's three conditions of beauty are implicit in his account of the creation and beautification of the universe: light as radiance of the form (as visible and as intelligible), order (proportion) and harmony, and wholeness or integrity (*AB*, 51). God's work of artistic creation begins with the first day and the creation of light; it proceeds to ordering the creation by separating the elements into harmonious interrelations, establishing them in their proper places. The stars, plants, and creatures are the "last stroke on the canvas of his creation." "From an original state of formlessness and confusion the universe gradually became a fully formed and beautiful world, in short, a cosmos" (*AB*, 53). On the sixth day, God reflects upon the entire whole or integrity of his creation and declares that it is good.

The beauty of the human body pertains to the form of the individual's physical constitution with its radiance (complexion), the harmony of its proportion, and its integrity or wholeness. Presumably there is conceptual room for variation of judgment across individuals, times, and cultures .

For human beings, beauty is not just skin deep. The unique spiritual beauty of the human being lies in the reason or mind (*ST*, 2-2.116.2 ad 2). Human beings are comprised of two kinds of beauty: the beauty of the body, which is beautiful insofar as the proportion, integrity, and clarity exist in the physical form; and more importantly, a spiritual beauty that refers to human intelligence and will instantiated in the body. Aquinas states:

> I answer that, as may be gathered from the words of Dionysus (Div. Nom. iv), beauty or comeliness results from the concurrence of clarity and due proportion. For he states that God is said to be beautiful, as being "the cause of the harmony and clarity of the universe." *Hence the beauty of the body consists in a man having his bodily limbs well proportioned, together with a certain clarity of color. On like manner spiritual beauty consists in his conduct or actions being well proportioned in respect of the spiritual clarity of reason.* Now this is what is meant by honesty, which we have stated (1) to be the same as virtue; and it is virtue that moderates according to reason all that is connected with man. Wherefore "honesty is the same as spiritual beauty." Hence Augustine says (Q83, qu. 30): "By honesty I mean intelligible beauty, which we properly designate as spiritual," and further on he adds that "many things are beautiful to the eye, which it would be hardly proper to call honest." (*ST*, 2-2.145.2)

Beauty pertains to morally upright individuals, as stated in the above quote, when one's actions are in harmony with one's knowledge and affirmed values. There is a special beauty in the virtue of temperance or that of allowing reason to order the passions. Of this Thomas states: "[B]eauty is in the moral virtues by participation, insofar as they participate in the order of reason; and especially is it in temperance, which restrains the concupiscences which especially darken the light of reason" (*ST*, 2-2.180.2 ad 3).

For Maurer, Thomas presents an understanding of beauty that lies beyond just sensible beauty and includes the notion of spiritual beauty. Although even spiritual beauty as intelligibly grasped by the light of the intellect is mediated through the senses, although not directly. One can think of the beauty of mathematics or of a clear and ordered demonstrated argument, or even of an insight that intelligibly orders heretofore disparate clues in the data. The light of understanding that comes from such beauty is pleasing to the intellect. "Beauty still consists in actuality, but in an intelligible and spiritual actuality that only the mind can properly apprehend and enjoy. The components of beauty are still clarity, order and completeness, but now these must be understood in the intelligible and not in the sensible order" (*AB*, 68).

Finally, the three conditions of beauty are linked to the contemplative life. This is perhaps an extension of Aquinas's analogy of the sixth day of creation where God delights in his own creation.

> Beauty, as stated above (145, 2), consists in a certain clarity and due proportion. Now each of these is found radically in the reason; because both the light that makes beauty seen, and the establishing of due proportion among things belong to reason. Hence since the contemplative life consists in an act of the reason, there is beauty in it by its very nature and essence; wherefore it is written (Wisdom 8:2) of the contemplation of wisdom: "I became a lover of her beauty" (*ST*, 2-2.180.2 ad 3).

While this passage does not include a specific reference to integrity, it is presupposes an integral form. This presumption is evidenced by other references in Aquinas such as when he speaks of the human body with well-proportioned limbs (see *ST*, 2-2.145.2).

Further Questions

There are several questions that arise concerning Aquinas's three conditions of beauty: (1) the extent to which Aquinas is consistent in his references to the three conditions, (2) the question of ugliness and the three conditions, and (3) the relationship between beauty and goodness.

Mark Jordan addresses two principal issues in Aquinas: the three conditions of beauty (*ST*, 1.39.8) and the distinction between beauty and goodness. Beauty and goodness are the same insofar as they both pertain to form; however, they differ in notion (*ratione*) – in that beauty pertains to formal causality and goodness pertains to final causality (*ST*, 1.5.4 ad 1). The good is the object of desire, which is the term of an appetite; the beautiful is an intelligible form, possessing the three conditions, that is pleasing when apprehended. "On these two pillars of text," states Jordan, "stand most edifices of Thomistic Aesthetics."[26]

Jordan claims, however, that "the definition of beauty in terms of three features ought not be treated as canonical."[27] He cites various inconsistent references in Aquinas's corpus in support of his case, and states: "If we were to proceed by textual frequency alone, then the typical Thomist definition of the beautiful would contain only two terms, *'claritas'* or *'splendor'* and *'consonantia'* or *'proportio.'*"[28] Jordan proceeds to emphasize the importance of *claritas* in Aquinas's treatment of beauty, and while I will make reference to his careful scholarship in my own work, still I think two considerations are in order to support the three conditions of beauty for Aquinas as foundational for his aesthetics.

First, it is important to note that a significant passage in which Aquinas invokes the three conditions of beauty concerns the second person of the Trinity: "Species or beauty has a likeness to the property of the Son" (*ST*, 1.39.8). This is because the Son is an expression of integrity (wholeness, perfection) – the Son perfectly expresses the *nature* of the Father. Second, the term *consonantia* (harmony-proportion) is fittingly applied to the Son because he perfectly expresses the *image* of the Father. Third, *claritas* is befitting of the Son as the word, "which is the light and splendor of the intellect" (*ST*, 1.39.8). Aquinas is not explicitly speaking about the Son as Incarnate Word here, but one can surmise that the analogy with beauty is quite fitting because the secondary act of existence of the Incarnation, the Word's assumed humanity, as God's greatest act of creation, would exemplify the three principles of beauty.

We must also keep in mind that, as indicated by G.B. Phelan, philosophy is not Aquinas's central concern: "His primary concern was to expound and elucidate the teachings of divine revelation."[29] Since he is first and foremost a Christian theologian, and given the priority of the dogma concerning the second person of the Trinity, a central tenet of the faith, Aquinas's application of the three aesthetic features to the Son makes them appropriate as foundational aesthetic principles.

Second, I would argue that the fact, as Jordan claims, that *claritas/splendor* and *consonantia/proportio* are most frequently coupled together in Aquinas's textual references to beauty further supports rather than contradicts the importance of the three conditions. For one can always ask: To what do *claritas/splendor* refer? To what do *consonantia/proportio* refer? It would make no sense to speak of these two without reference to or the presupposing of *an integral species or intelligible form*. The fact that

Aquinas does not always mention the three together does not mean that they are not always presumed. In order to presume *claritas/splendor* and *consonantia/proportion*, an integral species or form must be presumed; further, this would be in keeping with Aquinas's claim of beauty as formal causality.

The second question that emerges is, what is one to make of ugliness in this schema? "Ugliness is the lack of beauty, as error is the lack of truth and evil the lack of goodness" (*AB*, 13). Ugliness refers to the lack of integrity, proportion, and clarity. What lacks integrity or perfection of a form, what lacks proportion or harmony, and what lacks luminosity or some combination thereof contributes to its ugliness. It is the difference between cacophony and symphony, where cacophony is a lack of harmony. Ugliness arouses feelings of displeasure and even revulsion. And just as there is sensible ugliness, there can also be spiritual ugliness, such as those acts which bluntly affront human reason, for instance deception or blatant acts of violence. While some modern theorists have given ugliness a more positive characteristic, in the Thomistic sense this cannot be because beauty as a transcendental property of being exists, and ugliness is a lack.

Another related question concerning beauty is its relationship to the good. They are very closely related; some scholars even identify them. Of the relationship between goodness and beauty Thomas declares:

> Beauty and goodness in a thing are identical fundamentally; for they are based upon the same thing, namely, the form; and consequently goodness is praised as beauty. But they differ logically, for goodness properly relates to the appetite (goodness being what all things desire); and therefore it has the aspect of an end (the appetite being a kind of movement towards a thing). On the other hand, beauty relates to the cognitive faculty; for beautiful things are those which please when seen. (*ST* 1.5.4 ad 1)[30]

The good is that which the will desires, and the beautiful is that which pleases when it is seen or apprehended. As Maurer states, "The beautiful also catches our eye [like the good], arouses our attention, not to take possession of it, but to enjoy the sight of it" (*AB*, 17). The call of beauty (from the Greek *kalos*) is different from the good in that the beautiful attracts us to look at it. Beauty is in a sense "disinterested." That is, we are not compelled to *do* something with it; rather we seek simply to appreciate and contemplate it. And this very experience of beauty is a fleeting one. We listen to our favourite song repeatedly until we are satiated; then we withdraw and later return to appreciate its beauty, but never to the extent that we originally appreciated it. Hence, just like our hunger for knowledge is insatiable, albeit abating temporarily, provided we are open to ever-increasing knowledge, so the call of beauty is both bittersweet and continuous. It is bittersweet in the sense that Maritain declares because we are aware that beauty will fade, but the call of beauty is also continuous in that our contemplation of beauty is never completely fulfilled. Even the masterpieces of art can exhaust their admirers. In terms of the continuous call of beauty, Maurer cites Plato's *Symposium* where the ultimate contemplation of beauty begins with the beauty of created bodies, and gradually takes one beyond the created order to essences and ultimately to the contemplation of absolute beauty (*AB*, 19). Platonic metaphysics aside, I suspect what Maurer is emphasizing here about beauty can be analogized with what Bernard Lonergan says about the *detached, disinterested, unrestricted desire to know,* in that the desire for beauty will be ultimately fulfilled only with the beatific vision. But I will return to this in a later chapter on aesthetic experience.

The Perception of Beauty

As stated above, for Aquinas the distinction between the good and the beautiful can be understood by virtue of their respective effects upon the subject. The good is what the will desires; the beautiful is that which pleases when seen or apprehended. The beautiful is the same as the good, and they differ in aspect only.

Certain phenomenological approaches to aesthetics emphasize the perception of beauty but often at the expense of bracketing it within the field of perception and not asking the further question concerning the ontological status of beauty. For Thomas there is a sense in which beauty would be in the eye of the beholder, insofar as the beautiful pleases when it is seen or apprehended, and presumably the variances in the subjective perception of beauty will depend to some extent upon people's backgrounds, education, and openness to it. However, for Thomas the perception of beauty does not *create* the beauty in the object, but rather is a response to an object as beautiful: "Beauty is the shining forth of being, with its fullness, radiance and harmony, and perception is the means by which we open ourselves to its splendor" (*AB*, 31).

Aquinas's emphasis that "those things are beautiful which please when they are seen" (*pulchra sunt quae visa placent*) was a development to counter the purely objectivist notions of beauty that were a part of his context.[31] However, it also creates problems. Eco suggests it is difficult to know how important this notion is and how it would fit into his broader system. Second, if this statement concerning the pleasantness of beauty is true, then questions arise concerning how to relate the subjective and objective aspects of beauty, and how to interpret the *visio* so that beauty is not just directly linked to the senses.

There is no doubt that Aquinas's use of *visio* implied the visual perception of the eye. However, Eco makes reference to the following passage from Aquinas:

> Any word may be used in two ways – that is to say, either in its original application or in its more extended meaning. This is clearly shown in the word "sight," originally applied to the act of the sense, and then, as sight is the noblest and most trustworthy of the senses, extended in common speech to all knowledge obtained through the other senses. Thus we say, "Seeing how it tastes," or "smells," or "burns." Further, sight is applied to knowledge obtained through the intellect, as in those words: "Blessed are the clean of heart, for they shall see God" (Matthew 5:8). And thus it is with the word light. In its primary meaning it signifies that which makes manifest to the sense of sight; afterwards it was extended to that which makes manifest to cognition of any kind. If, then, the word is taken in its strict and primary meaning, it is to be understood metaphorically when applied to spiritual things, as Ambrose says (*De Fide* ii). But if taken in its common and extended use, as applied to manifestation of every kind, it may properly be applied to spiritual things. (*ST*, 1.67.1)

Therefore, Eco concludes that the term *apprehensio* (from *ST*, 1-2.27.1 ad 3) as identified with *visio* may be defined as "a kind of seeing or looking which is mediated by the senses but is of an intellectually cognitive order, and which is both disinterested and yet produces a certain kind of pleasure."[32]

Moreover, this perception of the beautiful for Aquinas is more complete in the sense of sight and hearing than in taste, touch, and smell because the senses of sight and hearing are more cognitive than the other senses. Even in ordinary language we are more apt to speak of beautiful sights and sounds than we are of beautiful tastes, smells, and tactile sensations; the latter three serve more the biological exigencies of human beings (see *AB*, 33 and n. 21).

Human beings are embodied intellects; all of our understanding comes through the senses, beginning with the data and proceeding through the cognitional operations of understanding and judgment. In this way, one can say our knowledge is mediated through the senses. Maurer elaborates:

> When an object is presented that floods the senses and *mind* with the splendor of its form, and which they find well proportioned and whole in itself and also well suited to their own capacities, the person responds to the apprehension of the object with pleasure and delight. We call this peculiarly human mode of experiencing beauty an aesthetic experience. (*AB*, 32; emphasis added)

When aesthetics emerges as a separate science or discipline with Baumgarten, the emphasis in aesthetics begins to restrict itself to the perception of beauty, just as the word itself is derived from the Greek verb *aisthanomai* (I perceive).

In contrast, for Aquinas beauty is *being*, and therefore it properly belongs to metaphysics rather than to a narrow discipline called aesthetics. Beauty is both sensible and intelligible so that one must view it more generally in terms of an ontology of being rather than simply as perception.

Maurer further acknowledges that those grasps of intelligible objects mediated through the senses but not directly linked to sense perception, such as mathematical equations, abstract ideas, or moral conduct, can also be beautiful. While the intellect is dependent on sense data for all knowledge, the beauty of these intelligible objects is not grasped directly by the senses; in the latter examples they are based upon the "radiant intelligibility to the intelligence, awaking in the will a delight and joy in the apprehension of these objects" (*AB*, 39).

Finally, Maurer addresses aesthetic judgments or judgments of beauty in Aquinas. To judge that a rainbow is beautiful is to say that the rainbow actually exists as beautiful. In judgment, Thomistic thought refers to the existence of something, so to make a judgment of beauty is to say that the beautiful thing in question actually exists. Nevertheless, the aesthetic judgment for Maurer is quite distinct from regular cognitive judgments of fact. An aesthetic judgment is "a consequence

of adopting an aesthetic stance towards beautiful things. It is not a conclusion arrived at by a reasoning process, but it is the expression of an
immediate, intuitive experience of something beautiful ... [I]t concerns
the particular beautiful object of that experience" (*AB*, 40). In chapter 7
I will address these issues in terms of Lonergan's notion of judgment,
one that will clarify the judgment of beauty more extensively and will
avoid the language of an "intuitive epistemology."

Beauty and Art

Traditionally art can be thought of as either the beautifying of practical
objects or, in the case of the fine arts, the expression of beauty solely for
the sake of appreciation and contemplation. Just as God is the source of
natural beauty, the artist is the source of art. And the goal of the artist,
from a Thomistic point of view, is to create beautiful objects. An artist
would not deliberately make something ugly, unless the object that the
art represents is itself ugly, but in that case even the represented image,
a gargoyle for example, would retain its own beauty. The truth of the
representation would reveal the beauty of the artwork (*AB*, 87).

Maurer clarifies the beauty of art and distinguishes it from spiritual
beauty of the intellect:

> The beauty of a work of art, like the beauty of nature, depends on its ra-
> diance, or clarity, proportion and wholeness, which are given to it by its
> form. The form of the artwork is always a sensuous form, one that attracts
> the senses, and so too are the clarity, proportion and wholeness of the art-
> work. As we have seen, there are forms in the intelligible or spiritual order,
> but these do not belong to the world of art ... nor would their forms be
> called artistic forms. The realm of art belongs to the realm of the aestheti-
> cally beautiful, i.e. beauty that primarily appeals to the sense, though not,
> of course, to the neglect of the intellect. (*AB*, 88)

Maurer proceeds to raise three pertinent questions with respect to art
from a Thomistic point of view: Is the work of art the expression of the
artist? Is the work of art a representation or imitation of nature? In other
words, is art copy? Finally, to what extent does the work of art manifest
or reveal nature? These questions are still asked today in the art world.
Maurer offers his response from a Thomistic point of view:

> The work of art does express the artist's self; it tells us something about
> him [or her], but only in an obscure way. The work of art also depends

on nature and often represents it, though it need not do so, as in the case of abstract art. Even when it represents nature it does not simply copy or picture it. The artwork also helps us to take a new perspective on nature; but its essence lies elsewhere. (*AB*, 94)

The essence of a work of art lies not in nature or in God but in the novel form of the work of art itself and its specific participation in beauty. Art may be inspired by nature, but each work is "a new entity in the world, with its own fresh form and existence." It is "the added decoration of the world after God's creation of it" (*AB*, 94).

But what about the source from which art originates? Fine art requires a skill or *habitus* for creating beautiful things, or to put it another way, for successfully communicating meanings through various artistic media. As a *habitus*, it involves the uses of one's reason in the creative activity that entails *recta ratio factibilium*, "reason rightly disposed for making objects." Thomas contrasts the latter notion with the virtue of prudence as *recta ratio agibilium*, reason disposed to right action. It differs from the making of art in that art, unlike prudence, does not presuppose a "rectitude of the appetite" (*ST*, 1-2.57.4).

It is worth noting here that Jacques Maritain and Étienne Gilson disagree with each other on how this theory of art is worked out. For Maritain, the essence of art lies in the intellect of the artist, and the source or "soul" of a work of fine art is in the *creative intuition* of the practical intellect.[33] The inspiration of the artist lies in "the intellective flash" "by which one obscurely grasps his own subjectivity and the objective reality of the world in its singularity" (*AB*, 96). The artist grasps the possible form immanent in what is to become the work of art. The artist proceeds to manifest the creative intuition within the artistic medium. The greatness of the work of art lies in the intelligibility of the creative intuition in the finished work of art and less so in the effectiveness and skill of the artist.

Gilson concurs that the source of art lies in the mind of the artist, but he emphasizes that it also lies in the hands or skill of the artist.[34] He especially references painting: "In painting it is impossible to distinguish between art itself and execution, as if art were wholly in the mind and execution wholly in the hand."[35] In other words, the skill of the artist is just as important as the his or her creative inspiration.

This inability to distinguish between the "art itself and execution" reflects in part what Lonergan refers to as *elemental meaning* – an experience common to the artist where the distinction between the subject/ object is not clear (see *MT*, 63). Lonergan would not construe it as

creative intuition, however. For him, the genius of the artist would reside in both the creative inspiration and the practical skill to carry it
out. Art embodies the artist's insights into the experience of elemental
meaning where one encounters ulterior significance. We address this issue in more detail in chapter 8 on creating beauty, where I argue that art
is the expression of the creative intellect of the artist in her/his attempt
to skilfully express elemental meaning within various artistic media.

Beauty: A Lonergan Approach?

Concerning the lack of a synthetic treatment of beauty in Thomas Aquinas, Jordan cautions: "Such scattered remarks must be treated, not
as fragments of an accidentally missing whole, but as specimens of a
variegated language that might have been reworked by Thomas into
a single account."[36] With this as background as we approach the role
of beauty in Lonergan's thought, we will keep in mind six principal
aspects from Aquinas on beauty: (1) "Nothing exists that does not participate in beauty" (*De Divinis Nominibus*, 4.5);[37] (2) "Everyone loves the
beautiful" (*Super Psalmo*, 25.5);[38] (3) the beautiful is pleasing when it is
seen (apprehended) (*ST*, 1.5.4 ad 1; *ST*, 1-2.27.1 ad 3); (4) the three conditions for beauty (*ST*, 1.39.8); (5) beauty pertains to formal causality
(goodness to final causality) (*ST* 1.5.4 ad 1; *ST*, 1-2.27.1 ad 3); and (6) the
relationship between contemplation and beauty (*ST*, 2-2.180.2 ad 3).

Before proceeding to some preliminary comments on Lonergan and
beauty, let us mention a context in which Lonergan might contribute to
a renewed Thomistic-like interpretation for our time. Because beauty is
inextricably connected with light, Eco identifies two ways in which the
philosophy of light was construed during the period of the medieval
discussion of the transcendentals. The first path was taken by Robert
Grosseteste and St Bonaventure, and the second by Albert the Great
and Thomas Aquinas. Grosseteste and Bonaventure articulated light in
a kind of "physico-aesthetical cosmology." As the first medieval thinker
to identify beauty as a property of being, Bonaventure is noteworthy for
his attempt to understand the transcendentals in terms of causality by
relating unity to efficient causality, truth to formal causality, goodness to
final causality, and beauty (*pulchrum*) as the "splendour of all the transcendentals together."[39] With this path one observes, first, the emphasis
on the "object" as beautiful and, second, the suggestion that beauty is
a *different type* of transcendental, in that Bonaventure does not link it
singly to a specific causality but as the splendour of the whole object.

The second path, taken by St Albert the Great and St Thomas Aquinas, concentrates on *light* (splendour) as part of the ontology of form.[40] Of course one should be careful not to overemphasize the differences between these two paths. The ontology of the form cannot be separated from the entire universe nor its participation in the ground of all beauty.

The splendour of the form shining through it as integral and well proportioned is pleasing when apprehended (*ST*, 1-2.27.1 ad 3). This emphasis is on the subject's apprehension of beauty. And it has caused some Thomists to deny the transcendental nature of beauty because they take this passage in Aquinas to reveal a subjective character of beauty.[41] I agree with Jaroszynski's refutation of these claims when he states that "the subjective moment is accented (although not in separation from the object)."[42]

Moreover, in light of Eco's statements above, I suspect that Bonaventure and Aquinas are approaching transcendental beauty from two different emphases. The former focuses on beauty more as an object and the latter on the effect of beauty on the subject. To the extent that this is the case, there is a further complication with Balthasar's attempt to recover beauty. Given his suspicion of those philosophers who "turn to the subject," and in spite of his praise of Aquinas's metaphysics for a recovery of beauty, I suspect Balthasar is not able to take full advantage of the aspect of Aquinas that focuses on beauty as apprehended by the subject. That is, he does not grasp how the effect on the subject might be construed epistemologically without succumbing to the subjectivism that can result from the turn to the subject.

In the following chapters, I will argue that Lonergan's philosophy of intentional consciousness, especially his epistemological claim that "objectivity is the fruit of authentic subjectivity," can bring a potential resolution to the ongoing debate surrounding the subjective/objective character of beauty. I believe it can avoid the relativist notion of beauty on the one hand and the essentialist notion of beauty on the other.

Furthermore, in light of Bonaventure's claim that beauty is the "splendor of the transcendentals together," one of the few comments Lonergan makes concerning beauty when asked directly about it seems to suggest something similar to Bonaventure's claim *but* from the side of the subject. Lonergan states:

> [Beauty] is, as it were, *a total response of the person to an object*. The other transcendentals are what articulate the type of knowing that is mediated by meaning, by words and so on. Beauty is something that *evokes a response*

from the whole person – it may be through meanings, as in poetry or drama, but it may be apart from meanings in any ordinary sense.[43]

However, in this passage Lonergan does not seem to distinguish between metaphysical beauty and aesthetic beauty – a topic we return to in chapter 5 on aesthetic experience.

Still, in earlier lectures on method, Lonergan answers the same question put to him in the following manner and seems to have a more metaphysical notion of beauty in mind:

Beauty as a transcendental, yes. But it's in terms of developing consciousness, and consciousness at a level in which the higher reaches, the higher concerns, such as truth, reality, value are apprehended through the sensible and are, as it were, a sort of plus to the harmony, the unity, the balance, and so on, that is found in the sensible or the denial of them. The pure desire to know: that is the transcendentals generally or the first one and then moving on to the second and then moving on to the third. Really, that desire is value as opposed to satisfaction – that is what makes it pure. To know value you have to know reality; and to know reality you have to know truth; to know truth you have to grasp intelligibility; and to grasp intelligibility you have to attend to the data; and so it is all one thrust. Beauty is self-transcendence expressed through the sensible ... it is the whole put together.[44]

These comments are not the product of Lonergan's deliberate thinking on the topic, but rather are impromptu. In the earlier Regis lecture he is indicating that beauty pertains to the world mediated by meaning and is motivated by value in that beauty is the *plus* to the grasp of truth and value. However, in the later Dublin lecture, Lonergan indicates that beauty is experienced prior to the mediation of operations that would specifically anticipate truth and value. In other words, it seems he has in mind here what he refers to later as *elemental meaning*.

In both cases Lonergan invokes the language of the "whole" when referencing transcendental beauty. Although in the Dublin Q&A he has in mind the whole person as involved in the aesthetic experience and with a special emphasis on the artist, in the Regis Q&A, by contrast, he has in mind the whole structure of conscious intentionality and its unrestricted orientation towards the intelligible, the true, and the good. Beauty pertains to this whole orientation: "beauty is self-transcendence expressed through the sensible."

It is interesting to contrast this with Bonaventure, who focuses on beauty as the splendour of the transcendentals from the side of the object. Lonergan focuses on the involvement of the whole person in response to beauty, and also as the "whole thrust of self-transcendence." In other words, as he suggested in his treatment of aesthetic value in *Topics in Education*, beauty shines through when the fruits of attentive, intellectual, and rational consciousness pervade the good of order in a society (see *TE*, 37). This seems consonant with Bonaventure.

Further, in the Dublin Q&A he repeats that beauty is a transcendental but of a "different kind." By this presumably he means it does not easily correlate with the levels of intentional consciousness as do intelligibility, truth, and goodness.

A comparison of the two statements indicates that Lonergan has not thought through the matter of transcendental beauty thoroughly. However, as he comes from the tradition of Albert the Great and Thomas Aquinas, we can presume he would favour their emphasis on the link between transcendental beauty and the subject. To this extent an adequate philosophy of beauty from Lonergan's perspective could complement such emphases as Bonaventure's on the objectivity of beauty. This is to say, both Lonergan and Bonaventure focus on beauty as the fruit of the transcendentals together, the latter from the side of the object and the former from the side of the subject. There is precedent in both to establish beauty as a different kind of transcendental. These observations may give us some clues as to how to proceed.

Finally, if we presume that Bonaventure and Aquinas (and Lonergan) are approaching the issue of transcendental beauty from different emphases, Bonaventure starting from the object and Aquinas from the subject (although we still need to reckon with Aquinas's claims concerning beauty as a formal cause), then in attempting to decipher what Lonergan has to contribute to the notion of beauty, we can look to *Insight* for a methodological presupposition. In the Introduction to that text, Lonergan emphasizes that he is not going to dispute whether truth actually exists; he will presume that it exists and ask instead "How [do] we come to know?" (*IN*, 13). In a similar way, I will presume that beauty exists and attempt to articulate in the subsequent chapters of this book how beauty would be construed in terms of Lonergan's philosophy of intentional consciousness. How is it that beauty is experienced at the first level – presentations? How is it to be understood in terms of the second level – intelligibility? How is it to be affirmed as true and existing at the third level – judgment? How is it to be valued or lived out at the fourth level – decision? Finally, what is it to say, "We love beauty"?

Before proceeding to address these questions explicitly, however, we must first engage the aesthetic legacies of Nietzsche and Kierkegaard respectively in the next two chapters. Although each has contributed to the loss of beauty, each contains valuable insights for its recovery.

3 Violence and the Loss of Beauty

Violence is ugly.

– Grace Janzten, *Foundations of Violence*

As we saw in the introduction to this book, for Balthasar the loss of one transcendental leads to the loss of them all. Inevitably this leads him to ask, "What will happen to Being itself?" (*GL*, I, 18–19). Although Balthasar does not elaborate on this, it is possible to flesh out the destructive implications for the loss of transcendental beauty. In this chapter we explore these implications in terms of the perpetuation of violence that is related to the loss of beauty through its displacement and distortion. We will emphasize this with reference to Nietzsche's aesthetics through the critique offered by René Girard. This treatment will not exhaust the topic, but I hope to get to the heart of the matter, thus further providing a context for a transposed Thomistic philosophy of beauty.

Displacement and Distortion of Beauty

If Dostoevsky is right that beauty will save the world, what does the reverse of this statement indicate? Does the lack of beauty signal the condemnation of the world – the perpetuation of violence and ugliness?

Following the Thomistic scholar Franz Kovach, Balthasar argues that the epistemological and metaphysical philosophy appropriate for beauty is no longer tenable due to its steady decline from the heights of the philosophical achievement of Aquinas. Balthasar traced this decline from Duns Scotus and Meister Eckhart to our present-day intellectual context. Whether or not one agrees with Balthasar's analysis, his critique is independently matched, specifically in art, by Hegel and Heidegger, both of whom bemoan the loss of beauty in the contemporary art of their time. In more recent times, the title of the philosopher Arthur Danto's volume of essays on art sums up the situation nicely – *The Abuse of Beauty*.

As stated previously, from its inception the field of aesthetics, identified by Baumgarten in the eighteenth century, has been confined strictly to perception, thus preventing further questions concerning the intelligibility and existence of beauty. As long as aesthetics is confined to sense perception, the locus of beauty remains external rather than embedded within a deeper value; for example, it remains in the physicality rather than in the *being* of a person. Although he did not construe the problem in these terms, Lonergan addressed this issue when he spoke of the degradation of the symbol. The latter is indirectly related to the loss of beauty in that such degradation is a symptom of rationalism, which for Balthasar is related to the loss of transcendental truth. This overemphasis on human reason, according to Lonergan,

> did not eliminate the symbols or their concrete efficacy in human living, but simply led to a degradation and vulgarization of the symbol. Hera and Artemis and Aphrodite were replaced by the pinup girl, and "Paradise Lost" by "South Pacific." But symbols remain necessary and constant in human experience whether we attend to them or not. (*TE*, 221)

The violence that flows from such degradation, as feminist authors point out, is often directed towards women.[1] The shift of the locus of beauty to the physical, as reflected in the quote from Lonergan above, entails a loss of the fuller notion of beauty that includes more profundity and depth. For example, Milo's *Venus* is beautiful in a way that a photograph of a contemporary cover model is not. This is because in the latter the focus is strictly on the physical beauty and not on the richer aspect of the feminine as communicated through Milo's sculpture, and this despite the lack of arms on the statue. In contrast, the magazine cover does not do justice to the model's fuller beauty, something not reducible to her physical beauty. Such objectification is likely an offshoot of the relegation of aesthetics and beauty to sensible perception.

The distortion of beauty can also lead to a fetishism of sorts, as when the foot binding of women in China became a measure of a woman's beauty.[2] This is not to say that there are not culturally diverse attitudes towards beauty. Foot binding reflected a social and institutionalized notion of beauty that was forced on women and did violence to their bodies. The phenomenon of foot binding is not unrelated to certain Western practices that reflect attitudes towards beauty. For example, Shelia Jeffreys declares that Western distorted notions of beauty have increasingly violent effects on women, and she sees this illustrated by a "high heel" fetish that disables women. Concerning these and other practices she states:

> In the last two decades the brutality of the beauty practices that women carry out on their bodies has become much more severe. Today's practices require the breaking of skin, spilling of blood and rearrangement or amputation of body parts. Foreign bodies, in the form of breast implants, are placed under the flesh and next to the heart, women's labia are cut to shape, fat is liposuctioned out of the thighs and buttocks and sometimes injected into other sites such as cheeks and chins.[3]

For Jeffreys, these practices are an indication of the oppressive standards of beauty imposed on women by male-dominated social structures rather than practices of true beauty. These standards, she argues, promote violence to women's bodies in another way: they influence the pornographic and prostitution industries, which not only objectify women but in turn promote new beauty practices that pressure women to conform, for instance breast implants.

While the above is a matter of debate among feminist philosophers, it is nevertheless commonly accepted that distorted images of beauty in Western culture can lead to violence. This is evident, for example, in the obsession with weight and eating disorders that particularly afflict young women and can lead to their death.

In her uncompleted trilogy on beauty, Grace Janzten argues for an ongoing dialectic in the West between the lust for death (necrophilia) versus the desire for birth and creativity (natality):

> What I wish to show, also, is how the attraction of beauty can inspire resistance and creative response, and can draw forward desire that is premised not upon lack or death but upon potential for new beginning. Preoccupation with death requires a refusal of beauty, or its displacement into some less threatening sphere. Conversely, response to beauty reconfigures consciousness towards creativity and new life. Beauty, creativity, seeks to bring newness into the world, a newness that is at odds with violence.[4]

Jantzen argues that a pattern of violence is inscribed in the collective *habitus*, what in Lonergan's terms might be construed as a collective *bias*, and this includes dramatic and group biases against women. For example, the genderizing of aesthetics by Edmund Burke (1729–1797), where he distinguished between the sublime (male) and beautiful (female), would be symptomatic of this bias – the beautiful was small, delicate, pretty, and the sublime was strong, powerful, destructive.

Jantzen argues for a recovery of beauty, creativity, and natality that will act as a kind of macro-therapy at the cultural level to bring society as a whole to a transformation beyond an obsession with death and violence. While we will have more to say about Lonergan's notion of cultural value in a subsequent chapter, it is worth noting that for him the fine arts, as they pertain to cultural value, at their best can promote the macro-therapy that Janzten suggests. The arts can direct a culture to reflect on its meanings and values with the hope of moving society into a more humane sphere that is consonant with the goals of self-transcendence.

Unfortunately Jantzen completed only the first volume, dealing with the dialectic between beauty and violence in ancient Greece. Therefore, we are not privy to her analysis of Nietzsche. While Nietzsche's aesthetics are binary in structure, they are not binary in the same way as the genderizing aesthetics of Edmund Burke. However, given the influence of Nietzsche's thought on German national socialism in the past century, and given his own self-destructive tendencies, which at the very least are indirectly related to the Dionysian pole of his aesthetics, a summary and critique of his contribution is necessary. It is in Nietzsche's aesthetics that we can identify most clearly the link between aesthetics and violence, and it is René Girard who shines the light on the nature of this violence.

Finally, it can hardly be doubted that the loss of beauty is inextricably related to violence to the planet. The ecological crises, exploitation of natural resources, and extinction of species are related to an attitude of dominion expounded by some Christian theologies and in those (implicit and explicit) philosophies based on a will to power or, in the past few centuries, on a predominance of utilitarian philosophies.

Nietzsche's Aesthetics

Friedrich Nietzsche (1844–1900) is a tragic yet very influential figure in the history of Western philosophy. While not an anti-Semite himself, his thought was appropriated by the Nazis as a source of inspiration for their comprehensive agenda, and his legacy was tainted by his sister, who was sympathetic to the Aryan ideology. He was self-destructive and, while he would probably not approve of the fascist appropriation of his thought, he nonetheless left a legacy of violence in part due to his preference for Dionysus over the Crucified – a choice, as we will see, of violence over peace.

At age twenty-seven Nietzsche published *The Birth of Tragedy*. It was highly praised by Richard Wagner (1813–1883) and simultaneously sharply criticized by the leading philologist in the German speaking academy at the time, Ulrich von Wilamowitz-Möllendorff (1848–1931).

Let us closely examine his argument in this book. There are those, Bruno Snell for example, who argue that a significant development occurs between the Greek myths and the emergence of the Socratic embrace of rationality – a movement commonly described as one from *mythos* to *logos*.[5] In other words, in ancient Greece there is a transition from an explanatory account of the world based on mythology to one based on reason and nature. This latter presupposition has been widely taken for granted and viewed as the cornerstone of the Western intellectual tradition. However, Nietzsche examines this presupposition critically. Like an archaeologist he seeks to recover what he calls the Dionysian spirit that was lost in the emergence of Greek rationality. He juxtaposes the Dionysian element against Apollonian form. In aesthetics, the Dionysian pertains to music and the Apollonian to visual art. "Through Apollo and Dionysus, the two art-deities of the Greeks," he states, "we come to recognize that in the Greek world there existed a sharp opposition, in origin and aims, between the Apollonian art of sculpture, and the non-plastic, Dionysian, art of music."[6] However, these binary principles have much broader application, scope, and implications.

Nietzsche elaborates further on these two by distinguishing them in terms of *dreams* and *drunkenness*. Dreams pertain to the world of Apollo, since in many of the Greek myths dreams are a source of divine revelation. The dream-world is the source of inspiration for artists' creations, specifically the embodiment of form, not only in sculpture but also in poetry, which one could call a linguistic sculpture. "Thus the esthetically sensitive man stands in the same relation to the reality of dreams as the philosopher does to the reality of existence."[7]

Dionysus is associated with drunkenness, which should not be surprising given his status as the god of wine. During the ecstasy of

Dionysus, "the slave is free; now all the hostile barriers, which necessity, caprice or 'shameless fashion' have erected ... are broken down." Reconciliation, universal harmony, and a feeling of oneness prevail among neighbours. "The veil of Maya" is torn away, and one experiences a "Primordial unity." Dance, music, and spontaneity are the order of the day. Perhaps most significantly, the Dionysian ecstatic feels like "a god," like the ones encountered within Apollonian dreams. Therein, the individual, rather than being simply an artist, becomes "a work of art." [8]

These two creative energies of the Apollonian and Dionysian are rooted in the world of nature and "without the mediation of the artist."[9] Again, they are antithetically related to one another, so much so that throughout history their harmonious synthesis, according to Nietzsche, can be found only in the achievement of Greek Attic tragedy. However, such a historic synthesis cannot last. As the age of ancient myths gives way to the Socratic turn to reason, the Apollonian energy begins to dominate the Western tradition. By itself, Dionysian energy is blinding; by itself Apollonian energy is rigid, empty form. Form at the expense of fluidity becomes the prevailing factor. While the balance or integration of the two remains the ideal, Nietzsche beckons the pendulum to swing back in the direction of the Dionysian.

The influence of Schopenhauer on Nietzsche perhaps predisposes the latter to prefer the aesthetic of music, and likewise to identify personally with Dionysus against Apollo. However, in his later writings, when his mental health becomes questionable, one sees an almost complete identification with Dionysus, one that accompanies not only his own self-destructive tendencies but his growing antagonism towards Christianity. While the Apollonian aesthetic is linked to the dream world, one can ask whether the world of Dionysian frenzy also has a questionable basis in reality. More important, one can wonder whether or not these two aesthetic energies can be construed in a way that lifts them out of the purely aesthetic realm and so grounds them philosophically in a more solid manner. I will return to this topic after first addressing René Girard's critique of Nietzsche's aesthetics and its relation to violence.

Girard's Critique of Nietzsche

René Girard's theory of violence brings to light the notion of *interdividual* psychology, that is, competitive relations, mimetic envy, and how these relate to the cycle of violence. He has become well known in academic circles for his insights into this cycle, although he is also controversial. At the heart of his theory is the belief that human history is replete with examples of the victim mechanism. By this he means the cycle of violence that culminates in the collective sacrifice of an innocent person in order to distract rivalrous participants from the scandal of their own mimetic relations. I summarize Girard's theory with specific reference to his work I *See Satan Fall Like Lightning* because it offers a good overview of his theory, and because he concludes it with a chapter on Nietzsche's aesthetics.[10]

Girard develops his theory in the context of his professional life as a prolific literary critic, but his theories are supported by a major school in modern psychology, the social learning theory as developed by Albert Bandura.[11] The latter corroborates the positive aspects of modelling and imitation that are integral to human development and learning. Girard's assumptions are rooted in an anthropology that presumes mimesis or mimetic désire to be foundational in the establishment of religion and culture. His theory focuses on the negative or darker side of imitative desire.

The Decalogue provides a religious proscription against unfettered mimetic desires that can lead to conflict and violence. On the one hand, wanting what another possesses is part of the developmental process: "Of course, the chief neighbors, the 'near ones,' for the infant are its parents. This desire that comes into being through following models of desire is not bad."[12] On the other hand, imitative desire "does lead to conflict and violence."[13] James Alison, a theologian and a follower of Girard, makes a further elaborate argument that mimetic envy is the "original" sin.[14]

Societies contain milder forms of mimesis such as those manifested in competition in the workplace and in the sports world. The more dramatic forms of mimesis usually involve a triangular desire between two parties desiring the same thing that a model possesses. In their race to obtain what the model has, increasingly they try to imitate the model. Eventually, the rivalry takes precedence over the coveted object and relations become increasingly conflictual between the competing parties. A rival can become so obsessed with the competitor that he or she becomes the other's mimetic double, mimicking whatever he or she does in an increasingly obsessive manner.

Mimetic rivalries are also animated and perpetuated by scandals. By "scandal" Girard means "specifically a situation that comes about when a person or a group of persons feel themselves blocked or obstructed as they desire some specific object of power, prestige, or property that their model possesses or is imagined to possess."[15] The contagion of mimetic rivalry and the increasing tensions of accumulating scandals will lead to the desire to unleash that tension upon an innocent victim. "The whole process of a scandal developing to a breaking point is an unconscious one."[16] This "single victim mechanism" climaxes in a collective murder, a communal release, due to the build-up of a psychic contagion vented upon an innocent victim or scapegoat. The murder of the scapegoat provides the community with a cathartic discharge of their conflicting relations and brings about a temporary peace among them. However, the participants seem oblivious to their guilt as they revel in their new-found peace that unfortunately was achieved by doing the Devil's bidding.

For Girard, the Judeo-Christian tradition represents God's intervention into human history in order to reverse the cycle of violence. In ancient Israel, this begins with God taking the side of the victim by freeing the Israelites from Egypt. In Christianity God takes the place of the victim as the crucified. Consequently from an eschatological point of view, the resurrection marks the beginning of the end of the cycle of violence in human history.

While Nietzsche's aesthetics are not central to Girard's thought, the latter's emphasis on mimetic envy is probably anticipated by the former's emphasis on *ressentiment*. Moreover, Girard identifies aspects of the myth of Dionysus that parallel and simultaneously diverge from key aspects of Christianity, such as Christ and the death of God, among others.

Dionysus and the Crucified

Nietzsche's aesthetics constitutes what Girard calls "a two-fold heritage." On the one hand, Nietzsche's myth of Dionysus identifies for the first time in the history of philosophy "the vocation for the concern for victims." On other hand, Nietzsche is not able to see that the collective violence against innocent victims is unjust. Conversely, for Girard the Jewish-Christian traditions reveal that God is on the side of the victims and intervenes in history to overcome such oppressive structures. But such views only antagonize Nietzsche, who views taking the side of the victim as a manifestation of resentment against "pagan aristocrats."[17] In fact, Nietzsche is "obliged to justify human sacrifice, and doesn't hesitate to do so, resorting to horrifying arguments." This includes the suggestion that societies get rid of the vulnerable and the marginal.[18] Girard explains this aspect in Nietzsche's thought in the following way:

> A culture has to pay a price in order to breed a higher class of [human beings]. It has to assume even the worst forms of violence. Time and time again, Nietzsche tells us that Dionysus accommodates all human passions, including the lust to annihilate, the most ferocious appetite for destruction. Dionysus says yes to the sacrifice of many human lives, including, not so paradoxically, those of the highest type that is being bred in the process.[19]

It is ironic that Nietzsche, who so often set himself against mob mentalities, paradoxically provides an intellectual basis for them. This is evidenced subsequently by the Nazis' appropriation of his ideas for their own purposes. Yet Nietzsche's inability to rise above his Dionysian commitment, which in Girard's reading supports the victim mechanism, takes him to the brink of madness. This leads Girard to conclude concerning the second aspect of the twofold heritage that "By insanely condemning the real greatness of our world, not only did Nietzsche destroy himself, but he suggested the terrible destruction that was later done by National Socialism."[20] Robert Johnson, a member of the inaugural class of Jungian analysts in Zurich and a student of Jung, links National Socialism directly with the Dionysian energy. He summarizes as follows:

> I happened onto some little-known articles that Jung wrote between 1921 and 1945 about an archetype that was bubbling up in the psyche of the German people. Every German patient he saw, young and old, intelligent and unintelligent, seemed to be carrying a new archetype. He called it "the Blond Beast," because it often appeared that way in the German unconscious. By 1930 it had surfaced enough so that he was able to identify it as a reemergence of Wotan, the berserker god of wisdom and war in Germanic and Norse mythology. Wotan is, in many ways, parallel to Dionysus in Greek mythology. He's the ecstatic, attractive one – with boundless energy – who overturns so much. By the early 1930s the movement of which Wotan was the archetypal force had a name, Nazism, and it was overtaking Germany. By 1940 it was rampant, and by 1945 it had left most of Europe in wreckage.[21]

Indeed, according to Girard the key to Nietzsche's madness stems from his adherence to and identification with the Dionysian myth. In

Greek mythology, Dionysus, son of Zeus, was begotten on the mortal Semele. She was not aware of Zeus's identity. Zeus's wife Hera was jealous of Semele and tricked her by coaxing her to persuade Zeus to reveal his true identity. Zeus obliged Semele's request, and his mortal lover was incinerated by the power of Zeus's self-manifestation. However, Zeus saved Dionysus from Semele's womb and stitched him into his thigh.

Threatened by Semele's offspring, Hera incites the Titans (their leader was Kronos, father of Zeus) to dismember and consume Dionysus. They carry out the task. Sorrowing for the misfortune of Zeus's son, the goddess Rhea raises him from the dead. Dionysus then wanders the world promoting the Bacchaean rites of frenzy.

In his analysis of Nietzsche's aesthetics Girard specifically references Euripides' play *Bacchae* (ca. 405 BC). In the latter, Dionysus disguises himself as a drifter in order to exact revenge against King Pentheus. The king is obsessed with the Bacchean rites and wishes to gain control over them and perhaps even to abolish them. Dionysus tricks the king into participating in the rites, and consequently Pentheus ends up being ritually dismembered by his own mother.

In directing the reader's attention to this play, Girard points out that despite any parallels that Dionysus's martyrdom may have with the death of Jesus Christ, Dionysus, unlike Christ, becomes an advocate and perpetuator of revenge and violence:

> In all other episodes of the Dionysian cycle, there is a collective *diasparagmos*, a martyrdom similar to the martyrdom of Dionysus at the hands of the Titans. In all of these, however, the god is not the victim but the instigator of the mob lynching.
>
> Every time Dionysus appears, a victim is dismembered and is often devoured by his or her many murderers. The god can be the victim and he can also be the chief murderer. He can be victimized and he can be victimizer.[22]

It is not that Nietzsche is so much an advocate of this type of violence, but that he sees it as an inevitable part of life with these two conflicting energies. The Dionysian and the Apollonian dimensions are inextricably intertwined in the same way as are chaos and stability. Nevertheless, in holding fast to this view, Nietzsche effectively and unwittingly consents to the ongoing cycle of collective violence and does so in contradistinction to Christianity.

In *Will to Power* Nietzsche identifies the main divide between "The Two Types: Dionysus and the Crucified [Christ]":

> Dionysus versus "Christ"; here you have the contrast. It is not a difference in regard to the martyrdom, – but the latter has a different meaning. Life itself – Life's eternal fruitfulness and recurrence caused anguish, destruction and the will to annihilation. In the other case, the suffering of the "Christ as the innocent one" stands as an objection against life, it is the formula for Life's condemnation. – Readers will guess that the problem concerns the meaning of suffering; whether a Christian or a tragic meaning be given to it. In the first case it is the road to a holy mode of existence. In the second case, *existence itself is regarded as sufficiently holy* to justify an enormous amount of suffering. The tragic man says yea even to the most excruciating suffering: he is sufficiently strong, rich and capable of deifying, in order to do this; the Christian denies even the happy lots on earth: he is weak, poor, and disinherited enough to suffer from life in any form. God on the cross is a curse upon Life; a signpost directing people to deliver themselves from it; – Dionysus cut into pieces is a *promise* of Life: it will be forever born anew, and rise afresh from destruction.[23]

For Girard, Nietzsche is correct in his recognition that the difference between Dionysus and the Crucified is not the events per se but the meaning ascribed to them; this meaning ascribed also runs counter to the late nineteenth- and early twentieth-century positivist anthropologies that tended to equate the "murder of the god" in pan-mythology with the death of Jesus. Contra to the positivists, Nietzsche's brilliance lies in the fact that he sees the main difference. Stijn Latré explains:

> For Girard as for Nietzsche, the difference between pagan mythology and Christian faith resides in their different account of collective violence. Nietzsche adheres to the tragic vision of life. This vision accepts life in all its dimensions – also in its negation by means of extreme violence. Or, to put it more exactly, destruction is inherent to the existence of life. Without destructive forces and sacrifices, life can never reach its fullness. Nietzsche almost entirely unmasks the scapegoat mechanism. But he does never [*sic*] mention its moral injustice. Doing so would reveal too much and threaten the mechanism of violence and hence the fullness of life. Becoming conscious of scapegoating ends up in the impossibility of maintaining that practice.

At this point of his theory, Girard becomes, we might say, the Hegel of anthropology. Myths reflect and justify the scapegoat mechanism unconsciously. Tragedy almost uncovers this mechanism, but at last chooses a mythical solution in order to preserve the "eternal recurrence" of scapegoat violence. Girard is the Hegel of history as he is the first to understand fully the mechanism of violence as revealed in the Bible. Girard argues that Nietzsche's tragic account of life explains his vehement repudiation of Christianity. As it is known, the Bible reveals the scapegoat mechanism and its moral untenability. Hence the Bible is a threat to the tragic vision of life. So Girard congratulates Nietzsche with his insight in the fundamental difference between pagan religion and Christian faith, but accuses him of having chosen the wrong side.[24]

As he has chosen the "wrong side," one is not surprised to see Nietzsche's antagonism towards Christianity expressed in his treatment of *ressentiment*. Girard sees this as an expression of the mimetic complex: "*Ressentiment* is really a thwarted and traumatized desire. The very word evokes the image of an immovable obstacle against which the initial 'sentiment' did in fact collide and to which it keeps obsessively coming back, only to be frustrated again and again."[25] The immovable obstacle, the *scandalon*, is that which propels the mutual rivals to eventually channel their energy onto an innocent victim. The will to power expresses the competitive urge to triumph over one another. However, only a few can be victorious. Those who cannot compete resent the victorious and the powerful. This collective resentment manifests within Christianity as slave morality; Nietzsche views the Christians as justifying their own plight as inferior and therefore raising up the marginalized in a sustained and resentful protest. Still, Nietzsche gets the difference: Christianity denounces the violence against the victim. Dionysus demonstrates that violence against the victim is inevitable and so perpetuates it.

Culpability in the Collective Murder

In another article, Girard addresses Nietzsche's aesthetics in more detail, focusing on the idea of the collective murder. Girard had an intuition that something in Nietzsche's philosophy resonated with his own theory of violence, but he puzzled over what aspect of it that might be. He discovered it in one of the significant aphorisms of Nietzsche's *The Gay Science*: the idea that God has been killed. The aphorism depicts a "madman" who runs into the town desperately seeking God. His queries are met by ridicule and sarcasm by the crowd:

Haven't you heard of that madman who in the bright morning lit a lantern and ran around the marketplace crying incessantly, "I'm looking for God! I'm looking for God!" Since many of those who did not believe in God were standing around together just then, he caused great laughter. Has he been lost, then? asked one. Did he lose his way like a child? asked another. Or is he hiding? Is he afraid of us? Has he gone to sea? Emigrated? Thus they shouted and laughed, one interrupting the other. The madman jumped into their midst and pierced them with his eyes. "Where is God?" he cried; "I'll tell you! *We have killed him* – you and I! We are all his murderers. But how did we do this? How were we able to drink up the sea? Who gave us the sponge to wipe away the entire horizon? What were we doing when we unchained the earth from its sun? Where is it moving now? Where are we moving to? Away from all suns? Are we not continually falling? And backwards, sidewards, forwards, in all directions? Is there still an up and a down? Aren't we straying as though through an infinite nothing? Isn't empty space breathing at us? Hasn't it got colder? Isn't night and more night coming again and again? Don't lanterns have to be lit in the morning? Do we still hear nothing of the noise of the grave-diggers who are burying God? Do we still smell nothing of the divine decomposition? – Gods, too, decompose! God is dead! God remains dead! And we have killed him! How can we console ourselves, the murderers of all murderers? The holiest and mightiest thing the world has ever possessed has bled to death under our knives: who will wipe this blood from us? With what water could we clean ourselves? What festivals of atonement, what holy games will we have to invent for ourselves? Is the magnitude of this deed not too great for us? Do we not ourselves have to become gods merely to be worthy of it? There was never a greater deed – and whoever is born after us will on of this deed belong to a higher history than all history up to now!"

Here the madman fell silent and looked again at his listeners; they too were silent and looked at him disconcertedly. Finally he threw his lantern on the ground so that it broke into pieces and went out. "I come too early," he then said; "my time is not yet. The tremendous event is still on its way, wandering; – it has not yet reached the ears of men. Lightning and thunder need time; the light of the stars needs time; deeds need time, even after they are done in order to be seen and heard. This deed is still more remote to them than the remotest stars – *and yet they have done it themselves!*"

It is still recounted how on the same day the madman forced his way into several churches and there started singing his *requiem aeternam deo*. Led out and called to account, he is said always to have replied nothing but: "What then are these churches now if not the tombs and sepulchres of God?"[26]

For Girard, the fuller meaning of the famous aphorism remains hidden from those who simply extract the popular phrase "God is dead!" Some of the crowd in the aphorism presume that God has simply died of old age, echoing the smug attitude of secularism that society has outgrown the need for religion.

According to Girard two components are neglected in the popularization of Nietzsche's phrase "God is dead": (1) God has not simply quietly passed away but has been murdered; and (2) all are responsible for this murder.[27] For Girard, this neglect is partly due to the misappropriation of this aspect of Nietzsche's thought. Still, these two aspects reveal the collective murder. The madman [Nietzsche] cries: "*We have killed him* – you and I! We are all his murderers." The popular aphorism, in lacking the latter sentence, is missing its most essential component – the fact that all are culpable for the collective murder. Girard argues: "The natural death of God is the alibi of the murderers who deny the reality of their murder. How could we have killed the biblical God, they repeat, since He died without help from anyone, in the last stage of senility?"[28]

Worse than mere atheism, Girard emphasizes the "vulgar atheism" of the crowd – vulgar precisely because they deny that God has been murdered and that they are collectively culpable. It is not that we have simply outgrown the need for God in a post-Enlightenment context, but rather that the death of God is a violent one. Therefore, we can anticipate in the prophetic words of the Madman that the results will be violent. The result of this collapse of ultimate meaning leaves a void further predicted in the question raised by the madman: "Must we not becomes gods ourselves to become worthy of such a deed?" Hence, in the wake of the death of God, the door is open for the *Übermensch*, the human *will* to power, and an ethics *beyond* good and evil.

The death of God in Nietzsche's famous aphorism contains all the elements of the bloody ritual sacrifice and collective murder of typical "primitive" mythologies. However, this time, perhaps due to advances in technology and the proliferation of weapons of mass destruction, the situation is more serious. Girard summarizes the seriousness in the following way, referencing the Dionysian frenzy:

It is indeed the sacrificial crisis described a thousand times, but no longer quite the old carnival masquerade, the inversion of roles and hierarchies during a brief festive period, strictly delimited. The affair appears more serious; all guideposts are gone, in time as well as in space. There is no longer either difference or deferral, no more horizon, no more fixed point anywhere to provide sense or direction. It is on the former God that the *humanization* of the real rested, and what little remains of this is in the process of rotting.[29]

The violent death of God, the dissolution of opposites, the inability to discern the difference between good and evil perpetuate a collapse of the meanings and values that were heretofore associated with religious belief. Secularism cannot fill the void, and far too often ideology steps in to fill it.

Dionysus as a Mimicked Distortion of Christ

Girard's interpretation of the collective murder of God construes Nietzsche more as a prophet of the dead end of secularism than as an advocate of atheism. Nietzsche is the first one to speak the truth concerning the death of God. Still the words of the madman are: "I have come too early; my time has not come yet. The tremendous event is still on its way ..." One cannot help wondering if this statement contains predictions of the twentieth century with its mass bloodshed, collective murders, and genocide. Eerily, Nietzsche's madman is like a mirrored distortion of John the Baptist; instead of anticipating the Messiah, the madman anticipates the anti-Christ – the escalation of violence evidenced by the titles of his last two works, *The Anti-Christ* and *Ecce Homo*.

In a previous work on Girard and Lonergan I have argued that evil functions as a mimicked distortion of the good.[30] In a similar way, there is an aspect of Nietzsche's Dionysian aesthetics that mirrors Christianity, yet diverges from it and radically distorts one of its most essential features – the concern for victims. Ironically, both views are "christocentric" in that "the real point of departure for both is the Crucified as the center of history."[31] However, for Nietzsche this marks the end of Christianity, and with it, an era *beyond* morality. For Girard, on the other hand, it marks the beginning of the overcoming of violence through love.

Indeed the mimicked distortion of the true meaning of the Crucified is the dividing line between the way of peace and the way of violence – a violence psychologically prepared for by Nietzsche's aesthetics, demonstrated in his personal demise by virtue of his own psychological identification with Dionysus over and against Apollo.

There is a further psychological component in Nietzsche's preference for Dionysus. It concerns his own performative identification with the god. For example, Girard sees Nietzsche's relationship with Richard Wagner as triangular in the mimetic sense. Nietzsche has a complicated life-long relationship with Wagner that swings from uncritical praise to outright disdain.

In his early work on aesthetics, *The Birth of Tragedy*, Nietzsche identifies Wagner with Dionysus and in so doing deifies him. However, in his last work, *Ecce Homo*, the triangle has shifted, Wagner is now a rival, and Nietzsche rails against him. In turn, Nietzsche now identifies with Dionysus although he remains enmeshed with the Crucified.[32] Girard explains:

> It is not a matter of indifference, of course, that the megalomania of Nietzsche is presented under the title of *Ecce Homo* and that he signs both as Dionysus and the Crucified. Each time Nietzsche feels like a god for a little while, he must pay for it dearly and becomes the Crucified. The would-be god is really a victim. Here, finally, and only here, the self-defeating process at work everywhere in Nietzsche becomes manifest. The confusion between the god and the victim is the climax of the manic-depressive oscillation. In the shift from Dionysus *against* the Crucified to Dionysus *or* the Crucified, in the collapse of that supreme difference, we have the collapse of Nietzschean thought. [33]

Nietzsche's progressive insanity leads to an inability to clearly differentiate in his own psyche between Dionysus and the Crucified. He consciously identifies with Dionysus and unconsciously identifies with the victim on the cross. The result is tragedy, not only his own self-destruction, despite his brilliance, but an intellectual legacy that justifies emerging secularist attitudes and further aspects that will be appropriated by totalitarian regimes in justifying, not only collective murders, but collective victims.

A Reorientation of Nietzschean Aesthetics?

Is there a way to preserve Nietzsche's aesthetics and avoid the destructive Dionysian perpetuation of violence? Probably not altogether.

However, there is a distinction in Lonergan's philosophy that might offer an analogy for appropriating the Dionysian and Apollonian elements. The analogy concerns Lonergan's distinction between "the world of immediacy" and "the world mediated by meaning and motivated by value."

Lonergan draws this distinction from his study of Piaget's theory of childhood development. The world of immediacy is the world of the vulnerable infant whose experience of the world is always immediate. The mother leaves the room and the child wails because the child does not know if the mother will return. As the child develops, the cognitive sets of operations begin to differentiate. The child gradually becomes aware of her separateness from the mother; the child's world differentiates and complexifies according to an identifiable developmental pattern. As the child matures into early adulthood, the world is no longer one of undifferentiated experience, but is mediated to her through the compound operations of knowing (experience, understanding, and judgment) and motivated through values (decision).

For the most part, we live our lives in the world mediated by meaning and motivated by value. One might think that this world is analogous to the world of Apollonian form. However, any direct correlation with the Apollonian is remote, because among other things, he views the world of Apollo as giving primacy to the dream world, whereas for Lonergan the world mediated by meaning and motivated by value is oriented to the concrete world of living but includes the world of imagination and dreams. Still, insofar as the world mediated by meaning and motivated by value brings an intelligibility and order through a differentiation of the world of immediacy, one can say that it functions in a way analogous to the Apollonian as a counterweight to Dionysian frenzy.

The world of immediacy, for Lonergan, is also the world of surplus and ulterior significance. While we can never return to the world of the infant, we are all capable of "mediated returns to immediacy" (MT, 77). This most frequently occurs in aesthetic and mystical encounters. For example, it may happen when a person dances and then is swept up by the moment – time stands still. It occurs in those experiences when the whole person is present in such a way that the subject-object distinction recedes. The dance, the music, and circumstances mediate the dancer to the world of immediacy, of surplus and ulterior significance. Hence, there is a way in which the Dionysian frenzy is analogous to this world of immediacy. But for Lonergan, the notion of Dionysian frenzy as a return to some amoral pattern "beyond good and evil" would not be acceptable. True, there may be a sense in which Dionysian frenzy retains elements of *coincidentia oppositorum*, but I suspect that for Lonergan, the coinciding of contrary opposites would be one thing, the coinciding of contradictory opposites another.[34] The latter would perpetuate the destructive aspects of myth of which Girard is critical. Moreover, the danger of Dionysian frenzy is the return to lower animal instincts. Again, in this way the Apollonian form brings a counterweight and structure to this world, but as Nietzsche points out, the dominance of the Apollonian can prevent one from access to the Dionysian altogether.

Hence, the issue becomes one of integration, which for Lonergan refers to the ability to move between the various "worlds" or differentiations of consciousness. Nietzsche's performative identification with Dionysus reflects a lack of integration on his part and coincides with his increasing mental instability. Whether his mental deterioration was due to syphilis, alcoholism, or to other underlying organic processes does not concern us. What I would highlight is the aspect of Lonergan's notion of transformation of consciousness that heals the blocks to a more integrated consciousness. The block is the inability to move between the two worlds – in the language of Nietzsche's aesthetics, to move between the worlds of Dionysus and Apollo without drowning in the world of the former or being strangled by the latter. I will comment briefly on how intellectual, psychological, moral, and religious self-transformation facilitate the integration of consciousness and behaviour. My discussion will be suggestive only but I hope will reveal some provocative avenues for further development.

Intellectual Conversion. Recall from chapter 1 that intellectual conversion facilitates a transformation of the belief that knowing is taking a good look.

> [T]here are two different realisms, ... there is an incoherent realism, half animal and half human, that poses as a halfway house between materialism and idealism, and on the other hand ... there is an intelligent and reasonable realism between which and materialism the halfway house is idealism. (*IN*, 22)

Lonergan's intellectual conversion establishes a horizon of critical realism that responds to the philosophical distortions of materialism and idealism. It responds to materialism in its recognition that knowing is not just taking a good look. Human knowing is more than animal knowing. However, it also responds to the distortion of idealism, which separates itself from the concrete world of experience. Intellectual conversion offers the dramatic clarification that knowing is a matter of the compound operations of experience, understanding, and judgment – the world mediated by meaning.

> The world of immediacy is the sum of what is seen, heard, touched, tasted, smelt, felt. It conforms well enough to the myth's view of reality, objectivity, knowledge. But it is a tiny fragment of the world mediated by meaning. For the world mediated by meaning is a world known not by the sense experience of an individual but by the external and internal experience of a cultural community, and by the continuously checked and rechecked judgments of the community. Knowing, accordingly, is not just seeing; it is experiencing, understanding, judging, and believing. The criteria of objectivity are not just the criteria of ocular vision; they are the compound criteria of experiencing, of understanding, of judging, and of believing. The reality known is not just looked at; it is given in experience, organized and extrapolated by understanding, posited by judgment and belief. (*MT*, 238)

There is a sense in which the overemphasis on the Dionysian world is analogous to the materialist emphasis and likewise tends to overemphasize the world of immediacy in the same way that an excess of wine can "mediate" one to the world of immediacy. In contrast, rationalist idealism embodies an overemphasis on the Apollonian world. Hence, critical realism as the fruit of intellectual conversion offers the potential for an integration of the Apollonian and the Dionysian – the ability to situate adequately and philosophically the world of immediacy and the world mediated by meaning, and the ability to move between the two worlds.

Psychic Conversion. Robert Doran developed Lonergan's general empirical method to include the psychological self-appropriation of the human subject. Lonergan viewed it as a legitimate extension of his thought. The fruit of psychic conversion is intimately related to the aesthetic-dramatic subject and the recovery of symbolism that is part and parcel of creative expression. Doran has explicitly attempted to link this with the recovery of beauty:

> [W]hat I have called psychic conversion may be the bridge between Balthasar's forgotten transcendental (the beautiful) and the transcendentals that Lonergan has retrieved in interiorly differentiated consciousness (the intelligible, the true, the real, and the good).[35]

Psychic conversion addresses the healing of what Freud identified as the "psychic" censor from a repressive to a constructive functioning. The fruit of the healing of the censor is the recovery of the creative aesthetic-dramatic dynamism in the psyche. "Psychic conversion is the transformation of that censorship from a repressive to a constructive functioning, thus releasing the aesthetic and dramatic operator into freedom from repression that is required if it is to form its proper function."[36]

Another fruit of psychological transformation pertains to the healing of dramatic bias, the bias that often brings about violence to oneself and others. In his summative comments on Girard's theory of violence James Williams states: "The whole process of a scandal developing to a breaking point is an *unconscious one*."[37] Those involved in the scapegoat mechanism and cycle of violence are not fully aware of what they are participating in. Hence, one begins to see the concrete need for a psychic conversion, not only for the proper appropriation of aesthetic-dramatic creative living, but to challenge individuals to authenticity – to confront and ameliorate the objects of their dramatic biases that, when left unchecked, can sweep them up into the contagion of the mimetic cycle. The *drama* in Lonergan's dramatic bias is rooted in antipathy, fear, and frustration. In this way, it gives rise to *ressentiment* in the sense that Nietzsche spoke of and that Max Scheler expounded upon.[38]

In terms of Nietzsche's aesthetics, psychic conversion can bring about the healing of the psyche in such a way that an integral aesthetics arises – one that does not have to choose between the visual arts (Apollonian) and music (Dionysian), but a fuller aesthetics that expresses (mediates) the richness of the world of immediacy in a variety of ways. This includes ways that reflect the integrity of the polymorphic flow of human consciousness and the excess of meaning expressed by various artistic media.

Insofar as Nietzsche's aesthetics fosters mimetic mania and the scapegoating of individuals or groups, to that extent the dynamic of psychic conversion challenges people to look at their own feelings of self-doubt, their own envy, jealousy, rivalries, and the targets of their own dramatic hatred. It can facilitate the healing of the distortions that lead to the perpetuation of the mimetic cycle and scapegoat mechanisms.

In terms of *moral self-transformation*, the shift in the criteria of one's decisions from satisfactions to values functions to mitigate the amoral aspects of Dionysian frenzy. Nietzsche's nihilistic ethics as exemplified by the title of his book *Beyond Good and Evil* do not enable one to adequately distinguish contradictory versus contrary differences within the *coincidentia oppositorum* that accompanies Dionysian frenzy.[39] It is one thing for a rich person to portray a destitute person during a Dionysian frenzy; it is another thing for a rich person to scapegoat a destitute person. The lack of moral compass in Nietzsche's "ethics" does not enable one sufficiently to discern the instances of evil within the Dionysian dynamic. As Girard has pointed out, the murder of Dionysus leads to subsequent murders and dismemberments orchestrated by Dionysus himself. An ethics beyond good and evil leads individuals to rely solely on the brute force of the will for moral decision making.

Lonergan's moral conversion emphasizes the need to discern true value in accordance with a preferential scale of values (vital, social, cultural, personal, religious) over mere satisfaction. It enables one to discern between the light and the dark that are often intermingled. It also enables one to discern true value over the excesses of Dionysian frenzy. One can discern the true liberation that gives rise to beauty and creativity over the liberation of licentiousness and release from the responsibilities of social and personal norms and expectations. This issue is also pertinent to the topic in the next chapter on Kierkegaard, specifically with regard to the hedonistic aesthete.

Finally, *religious conversion* is "being grasped by ultimate concern." It is the "dynamic state of being-in-love in an unrestricted manner" (*MT*, 106). In terms of beauty, it is the apprehension (but not comprehension) of the ultimate ground of beauty. It is Apollonian and Dionysian at their best as expressed in religious iconography and sacred music and worship – as each strains to express the ulterior significance of transcendent meaning. Moreover, the fruit of religious conversion is the habit of charity. There is a vertical and horizontal alterity guided by self-sacrificing love as a first principle. There is a love of justice that resists scapegoating in all its forms – that defends the vulnerable out of the duty of a transformed conscience.

Conclusion

In this chapter we have explored the relationship between the loss of beauty and violence. It is a relationship suggested in Balthasar's critique but not fleshed out. Specifically, we highlighted the aesthetics of Nietzsche as critiqued by Girard to single out how Nietzsche's aesthetics reflects and feeds an aesthetic stance that supports the perpetuation of violence. This is seen not only in Nietzsche's own demise, accompanied by his own increasing performative identification with Dionysian aesthetics, but further in the appropriation of key aspects of his thought by the German National Socialists. This legacy of violence is exacerbated in the distorted mimicry of Dionysus over and against the Crucified.

To counter this tendency and to preserve the genius of Nietzsche's aesthetics, we have suggested how key aspects of Lonergan's philosophy, the transformations of consciousness, can be invoked to offer an interpretation that embraces the aims and goals of self-transcendence. On this interpretation the distinction between the two aesthetics can be preserved and the cycle of violence avoided.

4 Recovering Beauty in the Subject

The recovery of beauty as a transcendental property of being will be inextricably linked to the recovery of beauty in the human subject, specifically within human intentional consciousness. According to Hans Urs von Balthasar, Søren Kierkegaard is partly to blame for the loss of beauty in the modern era. At times Balthasar's rhetoric is pointed: "What right has this Protestant tearing apart of the aesthetic and the ethical-religious dimensions, appealing to a sense of tragedy, to exist in our domain, which is the domain of Augustine, of Dante, of Fra Angelico, of Mozart?"[1] A loss of beauty in the subject indicates the loss of beauty in the object and vice versa. This might explain why Balthasar lodged such an indictment against Kierkegaard.

Valentine Tomberg, author of the *Meditations on the Tarot*, summarizes succinctly what happens when transcendental goodness is separated from transcendental beauty:

> But the good from which the beautiful is lost from sight hardens into principles and laws – it becomes pure duty; the beautiful which is detached from the good and loses it from sight becomes softened to pure enjoyment – stripped of obligation and responsibility. The hardening of the good into a moral code and the softening of the beautiful to pure pleasure is the result of the separation of the good and the beautiful – be it morally, in religion, or in art. It is thus that a legalistic moralism and a

This chapter was published as John D. Dadosky, "Recovering Beauty in the Subject: Balthasar and Lonergan Confront Kierkegaard," *American Catholic Philosophical Quarterly* 83, no. 4 (2009): 509–32, DOI: 10.5840/acpq200983443; it has undergone some minor editorial revisions.

pure aestheticism of little depth has come into existence. This has, at the same time, also engendered corresponding human types: on the one hand, the "stiff as a pig" human type, who was at his height during the reign of Puritanism in England – this form of life and religion without any joy and without art – as also in the shape of Huguenot ennui in a large part of France and Switzerland, and on the other hand the human type of the bearded "artist", of shabby appearance with a mop of tufted hair, and with licentious morals, who is in full flower now [1966] all over the place.[2]

His consonance with Balthasar on this point might explain why Balthasar wrote an afterword to the tome. Tomberg speaks to the negative aspects of Kierkegaard's separation of the aesthetic and ethical spheres.

There are obviously different senses of the aesthetic, and not all of them include beauty. One could speak of ontological beauty, aesthetics, the beauty of art, or, as Kierkegaard suggests, aesthetics as an existential sphere or stage. Kierkegaard's treatment of the aesthetic is psychological rather than metaphysical. He designates it as the first of three spheres of existential consciousness; the other spheres are ethical and the religious. The latter, in turn, is divided into two spheres. The spheres pertain primarily to the consciousness of the subject, and contrary to Balthasar's critique, they can overlap and interpenetrate within the subject's conscious intending.

In this chapter, I will argue that Balthasar's critique of Kierkegaard applies to the latter's use of tragedy, or his "negative aesthetic," but not to his delineation of the aesthetic, ethical, and religious spheres. Indeed, a more positive aesthetic is needed, one that includes the contemplation of beauty as subsumed by the ethical and religious spheres, yet leaving behind the negative features of the aesthetic stage, tragedy, as meaningless or negative existence. Furthermore, I will show that an interpretation of Kierkegaard's stages in terms of Lonergan's theory of consciousness can offer a remedy for the separation of the aesthetic from the other spheres by interpreting Kierkegaard's stages within the polymorphic unity of consciousness expounded by Lonergan from within his philosophical anthropology. Moreover, I shall suggest the possibility of recovering the desire for beauty as part of authentic human striving, thereby moving beyond the merely negative sense of the aesthetic while retaining some of Kierkegaard's rich insights.

For Lonergan, one of Kierkegaard's philosophical achievements lies in the latter's differentiation of what Lonergan calls the fourth level of operations – *responsible decision*. Balthasar and Lonergan would both agree that the value of Kierkegaard remains permanent because he turns the criteria of true Christianity away from one strictly of external and nominal affiliation and towards an inward authentic deciding for God.

Kierkegaard's Spheres of Existence

Kierkegaard divides the sphere of the aesthetic into three aspects.[3] With each aspect he associates a personage from the literary world: Mozart's Don Juan with sensuality, Goethe's Faustus with doubt, and Ahasuerus, the legendary "Wandering Jew," with despair. I will summarize his treatment of the first two, since the third represents the culmination of the other two within an aimless, despairing wandering.

The first aspect of the aesthetic, *pleasure*, deals with music because it pertains to the immediacy of experience. "At all times I am dealing with the immediate in its total immediacy ... sensuous love is disappearance in time, but the medium that expresses this is indeed music."[4] Likewise, this stage is epitomized by the life of the hedonist, and this is represented by Don Juan, specifically as portrayed in Mozart's musical interpretation *Don Giovanni*. The hedonist embraces the immediacy of the present moment as a form of escape and is not concerned with the future or with taking responsibility for it. Don Juan embraces many women, not as individuals but rather as the collective *woman*:

> Don Juan, however, is a downright seducer. His love is sensuous, not psychical, and, according to this concept, sensuous love is not faithful but totally faithless; it loves not one but all – that is, it seduces all. It is indeed only in the moment, but considered in its concept, that moment is the sum of moments, and so we have the seducer.[5]

The Don enjoys the power of seduction as conquest, at least initially, but subsequently the enjoyment shifts to the desire simply to seduce with less emphasis on the results. The intoxication of the pursuit flows from an illusion of power giving the hedonist reprieve from an otherwise "boring" existence. The association of this stage with the musical version of Don Juan is intentional. For Kierkegaard music is like a fleeting energy that one enjoys in the present moment, and once it has passed, there is silence. Nevertheless, while the Don may be living his life casually and carefree, his predicament is deadly serious: "Don Juan, then, is the expression for the demonic qualified as the sensuous."[6]

Eventually the excess pleasures of the moment are not sufficient to quell the existential thirst of the hedonist, and so the pursuit of pleasure becomes mired in boredom. The existential subject's situation becomes more serious. At this deeper level, the aesthete moves into a more sober existential stance – that of doubt. For Kierkegaard, the personage characterizing this aspect is Goethe's Faust.

In Faust there is a transition from doubt to boredom. Faust seduces, but his seduction is in some ways more dangerous and has more dramatic effects on his victim than that of Don Juan. The latter seduces thousands, the former seduces only one – Margaret (Gretchen). Unlike the Don, Faust does not attract women in a spirit of fun and conviviality; rather, he "scares them to himself."[7] Indeed, whereas both are hungry for sensuous delights, Faust is particularly motivated by his need for distraction from doubt:

> Faust is a demonic figure, just like a Don Juan, but a superior one. Sensuousness does not acquire importance for him until he has lost a whole previous world, but the consciousness of this loss is not blotted out; it is always present, and therefore he seeks in the sensuousness not so much pleasure as distraction. His doubting soul finds nothing in which it can rest ... His pleasure, therefore, does not have the *Heiterkeit* (cheerfulness) that characterizes a Don Juan. His visage is not smiling, his brow not unclouded, and joy is not his escort ... What he is seeking, therefore, is not only the pleasure of the sensuousness but the immediacy of the spirit. Just as ghosts in the underworld, when a living being fell into their hands, sucked his blood and lived as long as this blood warmed and nourished them, so Faust seeks an immediate life whereby he will be rejuvenated and strengthened.[8]

Likewise, boredom and the failure of a present or finite "fix" to distract one from his or her existential condition results in despair: "Boredom is the root of all evil."[9]

In choosing despair one really chooses oneself. Therefore, one enters into a new horizon of knowing and choosing – the *ethical* sphere or stage of existence. This sphere is dominated by a mood of seriousness with one's choices.[10] One could say there are two aspects of this sphere – choice and character – and each is reciprocally related to the other. On the one hand, one becomes more responsible for one's choices, and on the other hand, this responsibility flows from the fact that one's decisions are self-constituting. This stage pertains to the kind of fundamental choices that alter, direct, and guide one's subsequent choices. Kierkegaard gives three examples of such ethical choices, which, according to George Price, represent the seriousness of the mood in which ethical choices are made. The choices are marriage, friendship, and vocation, and each of the choices is self-constituting.

Marriage.[11] The marriage commitment transforms the fleeting inclinations of the aesthete into a stable, permanent relationship. Eroticism and sensuousness are reordered and reorientated in the context of a more meaningful relationship, where commitment is implied by a responsibility to the other. Lonergan would employ here the Hegelian notion of *Aufhebung* or "sublation" to describe this transition, although he would also qualify it: "This omits, however, the Hegelian view that the higher reconciles a contradiction in the lower."[12] Applying this analogously to Kierkegaard's stages, by "sublation" we presume that the contradictory aspects of the aesthetic stage are shed in the transition to ethical while an implicit desire for beauty is retained. The notion is not only consonant with Kierkegaard's thought but can be seen throughout the stages. In the next section, however, I will apply it differently: I will show that in the transition between the stages the subsequent supersedes but simultaneously retains aspects of the previous stage, at least those aspects that contribute to the subject's authentic development. And to speak of the difference between the spheres as authentic and inauthentic, one must recognize that there is a gulf between them that can only be bridged in those limiting situations by a free constitutive decision on the part of the subject.[13] For example, the aimlessness of the drifter is replaced in marriage by stability and anchorage.

In marriage, individual character is refined as one becomes more responsible. "Marriage is a school for character; one marries in order to ennoble and cultivate one's character."[14] Marriage involves a fundamental self-constitutive choice that includes a public vow. The only reason one should marry is for love. Marriage is never imposed but rather is a choice that paradoxically gives one freedom.[15] The choice in this context is simultaneously a choice of oneself. This freedom to be oneself includes the ability to reveal all of one's secrets. Hence, Kierkegaard declares that one should not marry a person to whom one cannot confide one's secrets.[16] Price summarizes Kierkegaard's thoughts about marriage as follows: "the ultimate human issue is whether there is a complete openness of mind, of freedom to be oneself, and whether or not there exists at least one relationship in which one can live without pretence, and, finally, whether or not one is committed to be what one is not and to be fearful of being any other."[17] The choice for marriage is an either/or but it is also a preserving of the aesthetic. The stability that marriage offers provides an avenue for freedom of self-expression. The spouses become more themselves in the commitment. The loss of freedom that the aesthete fears is only an illusion; the stability of marriage brings freedom.

Friendship. The adage that you can choose your friends but you cannot choose your relatives applies to Kierkegaard's notion of friendship. A friend is more than a mere acquaintance who happens to drift into the horizon of one's intersubjective relations; a friend is deliberately *chosen*. Analogous to marriage, the choice of one's friend is a choice made in a mood of seriousness. It entails a permanent or long-term commitment, and allows one the freedom to be oneself. In this way it provides sustained mutual affection, consolation, and identification.[18] One chooses a friend on the basis of a similar "life-view," one that is linked with the ethical: "[F]riendship requires a positive life-view. But a positive view of life is unimaginable unless it has an ethical element in it."[19]

Vocation. "Every human being has a calling."[20] It can be distinct from a job, which provides merely for one's vital necessities. "A vocation requires an inward preparation, a seriousness of mind without which it cannot succeed … it bestows moments of freedom, of deep pleasure and of a sense of personal meaningfulness."[21] There may be moments of boredom, but the boredom is temporary and redirected by a deeper sense of purpose that reflects the basic commitment embodied in the vocation. A vocation is inextricably linked to a person's fundamental identity while the choice thereof implies a direction and a commitment to the actualization of one's identity. Finally, the choice of a vocation may collide with the expectations of others, but the faithful adherence to one's vocation builds character.

In all three of these examples, the primary impetus lies in a deliberative committed choice that is self-constitutive of the person. To put it in Lonergan's terminology, the operative intention of Kierkegaard's ethics is the transcendental imperative to "be responsible." However, this would be only a partial sense of the meaning for Lonergan, for whom being responsible entails an integrity between one's knowing and choosing and also the consideration of short-term as well as long-term aspects in one's decision making. For Kierkegaard the ethical implies a responsibility relative to the life of the aesthete, one demanding commitment to the social order – the ethical absolute. In the religious stage, responsibility will imply something fuller – a commitment to God, which may in turn include a critique of the social order.

The difference between the aesthetic and the ethical is not so much a choice against the aesthetic; rather, the difference is between the one who evades responsibility in favour of fleeting moments of pleasure and the one who takes responsibility for his or her choices as constitutive of the self. In other words, it is the difference between the "drifter" and the "anchored."

It is important to note that the choice of the ethical does not abrogate the aesthetic or slough it off completely. For Kierkegaard, the ethical alters the aesthetic, transforming it into a higher integration of authentic subjectivity. Price concurs: "It is most important to note that Kierkegaard insists that the ethical does not destroy the aesthetic. It rather transforms it … [He] never preaches the abrogation of the aesthetic as such."[22] Kierkegaard insists that "consciousness integrates" and this integration occurs in the choosing of oneself.[23]

"No one is ever enfeebled by the ethical, for the ethical as self-responsibility never robs life of its beauty and strength but rather bestows them: it saves the self from 'vain enthusiasms' and from floating away into nothingness."[24] The aesthetic is preserved although it is construed as relative to the ethical: "In choosing itself, the personality chooses itself ethically and absolutely excludes the esthetic; but since he nevertheless chooses himself and does not become another being by choosing himself, all the esthetic returns in its relativity."[25]

Eventually the person in the ethical sphere succumbs to the various ambiguities of life that challenge it. This occurs on two levels: (1) the clash of the universals between the individual and society, and (2) the clash within the individual alone. The individual in this stage is torn between the conflicting demands of his or her sense of duty to work, family, and society. The complexities of life often force the individual to compromise; moral tensions and conflicts erode his or her sense of confidence in the ability to live out these ideals. This is illustrated by Judge William's high elevation of marriage in Stages on Life's Way: "Marriage I regard, then, as the highest τέλος [goal] of individual life."[26] His ideal for marriage seems to replace the religious. But a single person or union of persons cannot take the place of or fulfil the desire for God. Hence, Kierkegaard has paved the way for part three of his work Stages on Life's Way in which he describes the religious sphere.

Eventually the ethical gives way to the increasing inner conflicts between the actualizing self in the concrete world and the ideal self that one realizes is impossible to actualize. Right and wrong are not just utilitarian choices but speak of a deeper sense of mission. However, guilt increases as one becomes aware of the impossibility of living out the ethical life. One gradually realizes that it is impossible to be free of one's own biases, prejudices, and shortcomings. Even the most faithful husband at times feels lust for another woman. Since ethics involves conforming to the norms of the universal, an irresolvable paradox emerges: on the one hand, to assert one's individuality over and above the universal, or the concrete social order, is to go against the ethical, and thus one experiences guilt. On the other hand, to fail to assert one's individuality is also to go against the ethical, and thus leads to guilt.

People in this stage cannot save themselves. Virtue alone will not resolve the existential crisis; the solution is found only in *faith*, and this implies another sphere of existence. For the religious person, this paradox simply underscores the sinful nature of humankind, but for the non-religious person, the increasing frustration and guilt resulting from this situation lead to deeper despair.

Kierkegaard divides the religious spheres into *religion A* and *religion B*. Religion A pertains to the human fascination with the numinous and the vague sense of the spiritual within nature. It also pertains to those who affirm some kind of transcendent reality, but such belief has little bearing on their ability to constitute and actualize themselves.

He sees three forms for religion A. There is the *romantic religiousness* of his day, which includes the Rousseauian "back to nature" romanticism as well as the Kantian moral imperative. Second, there is the *philosophical religiousness* that the philosophical heritage of Hegel exemplifies. Third, there is *Christian religiousness*, the fusion of church and state that he believed led to the watering down of authentic religiousness, especially in Denmark during his time. In each of these expressions, the underlying feature is that the individuals do not constitute their own authentic inner religious striving – they do not choose themselves. Price emphasizes that the tragedy lies not in what these philosophies/theologies say about God, but rather the effects they have on "the degradation of the individual."[27]

In the limit, despair, disgust, and guilt all lead to the jumping-off place where one can either plummet to one's death in suicide or take the leap of faith. Religion B calls for such an act of faith as an intentional act of the will. In order to understand the latter sphere, especially in its distinction from the ethical, Kierkegaard draws on the story of Abraham and Isaac. Abraham finds himself in a deep existential dilemma where he is asked to sacrifice his son to the very God who gave his son to him. In the ethical sphere, this amounts to Abraham becoming a murderer. However, Abraham's willingness exemplifies his faith in the God who gave him the gift of his son in the first place. The results are that Abraham's relationship with God is deepened and he gets his son returned to him. Indeed, the chief result is "to be able to lose one's understanding and along with it everything finite ... and then to win the very same finitude again by virtue of the absurd."[28] Whereas the aesthetic sphere pertains to the sphere of immediacy and the ethical to the sphere of requirement (commitment), the religious sphere pertains to fulfilment.[29] The fruit of faith is life abundant.

There is a paradox in the fact that everyone is expected to respect the "laws" but simultaneously one must become an individual; to do so is to "individuate" oneself from the universal. Becoming an individual in the religious sphere involves choosing God absolutely before anything else. Therefore, the truly ethical task is religious because God is the ground of all goodness and therefore the ground of all ethics.

Whereas Abraham is prevented at the last moment from sacrificing his son, God does not spare his own Son. According to Kierkegaard, it is Christ the paradoxical God-human who elicits and preserves faith. Kierkegaard's Christ comes as *Incognito*, as the hidden revelation in the world, not even known among his closest followers.[30] He also comes as *Offence*, or as an irresolvable paradox to human reason, who two thousand years later still offers the only recourse from rationalism – faith. Encountering this paradox "offends" the rational: "This means that such a [person] possesses no category, and hence it was possible for him to think that he believed an individual [human being] to be God, without stumbling at the offence. But then the same person will stumble at the offence of lowliness."[31] Finally, Christ comes as *Atonement*, the offer of forgiveness and the command to accept it.[32] "There is a comfort which did not exist so long as Christ lived ... the comfort of His death as the atonement, the pledge that sins are forgiven."[33]

Kierkegaard often uses the term "repetition" instead of "forgiveness" because the forward-looking condition of repetition offers the possibility of likeness to God effected in Christ, which is more than just the pardon for individual sins. Having become now a Knight of Faith, one's task is to imitate Christ. Kierkegaard offers a kind of lay spirituality wherein the follower of Christ works incognito in the world alongside non-believers, but with an internal stance that is unabashedly directed towards God through faith.[34]

Balthasar's Critique: A Closer Examination

In his essay "Revelation and the Beautiful" Balthasar begins by citing an anecdote about the occasion of Kierkegaard's royal reception where he was congratulated by the queen on the publication of *Either/Or*. The queen mispronounced the title as *"Either and Or."*[35] The irony of this mishap indicates Balthasar's fundamental problem with Kierkegaard. The very work where the Danish thinker outlines the difference between the aesthetic and ethical dimensions constitutes for Balthasar their untenable separation. However, just because the two spheres are different does not mean that they are completely separate. Therefore the solution lies precisely with the queen's addition of "and"; the word "and" keeps the two spheres together, and that is what Balthasar proposes in his essay.

The question remains: Does Kierkegaard intend to and does he actually separate the three spheres? It seems clear that he has no intention of separating the spheres. George Price explains:

> It must be protested that this question comes up only because Kierkegaard is never properly read. He himself answers it clearly. He says, *Nothing is ever lost. Nothing that we have experienced, loved and treasured is ever thrown away.* What is discarded in the Leap from one level to another is not the content of experience but the mood, the existential attitude, in which we hold it. What is changed is the quality, not the content of the self. For example, the aesthetic as an attitude towards life must inevitably disappear, but the ethical, which replaces it, does not annihilate its content, it simply transforms it, gathers it up and redirects it.[36]

Geza E. Thiessen concurs that the aesthetic stage is illusory insofar as one flees the responsibility and suffering by fleeing it in immediate sensitive experience. However, the religious stage retrieves the "subjective inwardness" of the aesthetic and reorients it towards the absolute – a new horizon is established in the Leap of Faith. "Kierkegaard did not deny the aesthetic attitude in favor of the religious attitude."[37] The mistake is to view the aesthetic strictly as a means of salvation.

Because it seems so clear that Kierkegaard has no intention of separating the aesthetic from the ethical and religious spheres, we must wonder if Balthasar has misunderstood Kierkegaard. Nevertheless, he may still have a legitimate concern regarding Kierkegaard's view of the aesthetic. Balthasar uses the term "tragedy" in order to describe it, but might we ask accordingly, where is the pursuit of beauty in Kierkegaard's aesthetic stage? Is his aesthetic lopsided in terms of the tragic? Can it even adequately account for beauty in the first place? In this way, Balthasar may have a legitimate criticism, that Kierkegaard separates beauty from the life of the aesthetic. Moreover, to complicate matters further, it must be acknowledged that Kierkegaard's writing is performatively aesthetic: he *writes* beautifully. He is using this creative writing as a medium to communicate his philosophy. Does Kierkegaard perhaps have an appreciation of beauty that facilitates the transitions between the stages? It may be said that the aesthetic as an existential stage does not exhaust his full understanding of aesthetics and the beautiful – although this provides a basis for further study, one beyond the scope of this chapter.

Kierkegaard, following a Lutheran tradition, is suspicious of any attempt to analogize from the created order to that of God. This helps to understand why there is a leap involved rather than any rational assent to one achieving the religious sphere. If we consider that Kierkegaard was influenced by Luther in the way Balthasar describes ("Luther's attack on the 'whore' Reason, which aesthetically attempts to achieve a harmony between divinity and humanity," *GL*, I, 47), then for Kierkegaard the beauty of this world can offer no image for the beauty of God.

Balthasar holds that aesthetics emerges as a science of the beautiful "liberated" as it was towards the end of the Enlightenment although the seeds of the liberation began to sprout in the Renaissance. Heretofore, he writes, the beautiful had been "embedded" with the true and the good. Presumably he is referring to the Middle Ages and the epistemology/metaphysics of Aquinas. Indeed, it may be that the lack of consensus among scholars as to whether beauty is a transcendental for Aquinas lies precisely in the fact that beauty was not completely differentiated from the true and the good.

However, the situation changes with the birth of modern science. The true becomes differentiated from the good, and likewise the beautiful becomes an autonomous field of knowledge – aesthetics. The development is a mixed blessing: on the one hand, beauty "takes on a certain independence" from the true and the good; on the other hand, the development is "perilous" because it leads to an aestheticization of the beautiful. The beautiful will not be able to survive in a context conditioned by historicism, materialism, and psychoanalysis. In other words, beauty becomes simply in the eye of the beholder. The immanence of the sciences replaces the possibility of the immanence of the beautiful. "The critical state we have reached may be summed up by noting that whereas previously there was a generally accepted metaphysics establishing a living bond between the immanent sciences and the transcendent Christian revelation [Aquinas], it [the bond] has now become quite unreal and ineffectual and has been abandoned in favor of the immanence of the sciences."[38]

In Balthasar's view Kierkegaard's separation of the aesthetic and religious is symptomatic of this critical state where reason is now devoid of any bearing on the religious – the created order is an utterly separate sphere from the transcendent. It follows that the beauty of this world is disjointed from the possibility of participation in the Divine Beauty. Kierkegaard can no longer achieve a meeting of religion and aesthetics. He is impelled to use the concept of "the aesthetic" to stake out and define a basic attitude that, for the Christian, is unacceptable. The original "harmony" after which he had strived – the "equilibrium" between the aesthetic and the ethical – yields in *Stages on Life's Way* to an inexorable succession in which the "apostle" and the "martyr of truth" are sharply distinguished from the "genius," thereby eradicating from theology all traces of an aesthetic attitude (*GL*, 1, 50).

Kierkegaard anticipates ("passed judgment in advance") the "renewed dominance of the aesthetic element in the liberal theology of the nineteenth and early twentieth centuries with their heavy dependence on Schleiermacher and Hegel" (*GL*, 1, 50). However, the term "aesthetic" now acquires pejorative connotations. It "automatically flows from the pens of both Protestant and Catholic writers when they want to describe an attitude which, in the last analysis, they find to be frivolous, merely curious and self-indulgent" (*GL*, 1, 51). This is what Balthasar finds most objectionable in Kierkegaard. Balthasar is not so concerned with differentiating the ethical from the religious, so he will attempt to show how revelation contains the aesthetic and the "ethico-religious."

I suggested in chapter 1 that there is a need for a transposed Thomistic philosophy that can also provide the proper philosophical foundations and general categories for beauty. It is as if Balthasar is content to praise Aquinas for his epistemology and metaphysics while ignoring the possibility of any contemporary philosophy fulfilling the task of a recovery of beauty in an analogous manner. I am more optimistic that such a philosophical endeavour is possible not only for a transcendental recovery of beauty, but also for an account of Kierkegaard's existential spheres in terms of human intentional consciousness as expounded by Lonergan. In short, aesthetic, moral, and religious consciousness existentially orients us, like the restless heart of Augustine, towards a Beauty that he finds "so ancient and so new."

The Existential Spheres and Intentional Consciousness

This section offers a reading of the existential spheres in terms of intentional consciousness as understood by Lonergan. By understanding the spheres as such, one can insure that nothing essential is lost between the various stages. This is because the spheres, as patterned consciousness that can interpenetrate, are subject to sublation. Still, while Balthasar's critique of the separation of the spheres may be unfounded, the critique concerning Kierkegaard's negative aesthetic (i.e., tragedy) requires a complementary component that leads to a fuller philosophical rendering – one that can account for the individual's orientation to the beautiful and the existential desire to create a work of art out of one's life. In other words, if Aquinas is correct when he states, quoting Dionysus, that everyone loves the beautiful,[39] then we are justified in presuming that everyone, at least at some rudimentary level, desires the beautiful.

As we discussed in chapter 1, human consciousness with its unity in the subject is multifaceted. It is possible to speak of a stream of consciousness, but there is an organizing principle in which consciousness is directed through "conation, interest, attention, purpose" (*IN*, 205). As such, consciousness flows within various dynamic *patterns of experience* within a particular subject. In *Insight* Lonergan specifically identifies the biological, aesthetic, intellectual, and dramatic patterns of experience (see *IN*, 202–12).[40] The variety of patterns of consciousness reflects what he calls the polymorphic nature of human consciousness: "For human consciousness is polymorphic ... these patterns alternate; they blend or mix; they can interfere, conflict, lose their way, break down" (*IN*, 410).

The *aesthetic pattern of experience* refers to the flow of consciousness that directs the subject's attention to the liberation and joy of experiencing for the sake of experiencing. In many ways this pattern characterizes the world of the artist; I will have more to say about that in the next chapter. For Lonergan, art is "an expression of the human subject outside the limits of adequate intellectual formulation and appraisal" (*IN*, 208).[41] The aesthetic pattern of experience acknowledges that our existence is more than biological; "one is led to acknowledge that experience can occur for the sake of experiencing, that it can slip beyond the confines of serious-minded biological purpose, and that this very liberation is a spontaneous, self-justifying joy" (*IN*, 208). When this pattern is operative it promotes creativity and spontaneity within the subject. Later, in *Topics in Education*, Lonergan will approach a description of this pattern from a different angle. He will speak of it in terms of a freedom from instrumentality. In other words, in the aesthetic pattern, one is not operating in another differentiation of consciousness such as the world of theory or interiority. Even later, in *Method in Theology*, he will speak of this in terms of elemental meaning where the aesthetic encounter is one where the subject/object distinction is not clearly differentiated. Hence, in a preliminary way, one could say that, as with Kierkegaard's first sphere, the aesthetic pattern of experience is orientated to the immediacy of our experience.

While not everyone is called to be an artist, no one can avoid the drama of life and the challenge of creating a work of art with one's life. The *dramatic pattern of experience* is the pattern of ordinary living in the concrete world (*TE*, 188). Ordinary living is "charged emotionally and conatively" in such a way that human beings are "capable of aesthetic liberation and artistic creativity." Lonergan emphasizes that human beings' "first work of art is [their] own living" (*IN*, 210). "The dramatic pattern," as Robert Doran elaborates, "is the pattern in which we live the greater part of our lives, the pattern in which we relate to others on the dramatic stage of life, with ulterior concern of making our lives, our relations with others, our world, a work of art."[42] That is, people who are operating within the dramatic pattern of experience seek to accomplish the tasks of daily living with a creative style (*IN*, 212). This potential flair for style and creativity that human beings possess differs from that of the artist. Whereas the latter seeks to express meaning and form creatively in works of art, those operating in the dramatic pattern make creative expressions out of their own living. This is to say that human beings shape and create the drama of life with their own individual contributions, and they in turn are shaped by the drama of life. Indeed, this is consonant with Kierkegaard's fundamental anthropology insofar as he declares that our only true task in this life is to be ourselves – to make ourselves. Likewise, assuming that human beings' vital needs are met, and they are not struggling for survival, a fundamental impetus in human beings is the drive to create a work of art with their lives. Of course, this is not how ordinary people would think of it, but in fact this language captures their efforts to live out a unified narrative.

Is it not appropriate to call this a kind of operator in Lonergan's sense of the term, that is, a kind of dynamism of the human spirit that seeks to create and whose first task is to create a beautiful life? In *Insight*, Lonergan speaks about the pure detached unrestricted desire to know as the fundamental drive, or operator, for human understanding. This desire manifests itself within the human spirit through natural human curiosity, what Aristotle calls "wonder," in questions for intelligence, questions for reflection, and, to some extent, questions for deliberation. However, this impetus or operator, the desire to know, is primarily intellectual: it does not account explicitly for the affective dimension of the human spirit. Later, Lonergan begins to speak of a quasi-operator that he describes at times as a symbolic operator, with a tidal movement, a mass and momentum, or *élan vital* manifesting within the various levels of human intentional consciousness – sensitive, intellectual, rational, and rational self-consciousness – and moving beyond them. This quasi-operator retains the achievements of each of these levels and allows one to find rest in love, and ultimately in unrestricted loving.[43] However, he never works out the quasi-operator with the precision he employs for the unrestricted desire to know. This affective kind of dynamism may be implicitly present, as when, for example, Augustine claims that his heart is restless, and this implies that his mind is restless as well. A read through the *Confessions* reveals that Augustine's insatiable intellectual appetite is matched or corresponds to his pre-conversion desire to fall in love with God. The rest he finds in Book 10 is indicated in the Beauty prayer, which ends "and I have burned for your peace." This can be interpreted as Augustine's ability to contemplate beauty from the standpoint of religious loving.

I would interpret Lonergan's *élan vital*, as it manifests within the dramatic pattern of experience, as the desire to make oneself, to create a work of art with one's life. In this way, insofar as one is not restricted from allowing free rein to this existential impulse, then one is able to take up the challenge to create oneself. The making of one's life as a work of art is consonant with the fundamental anthropology of Kierkegaard, but it also allows for an alternative view of the life of the aesthetic – one that can account for beauty. The ordinary person lives in the aesthetic sphere in the attempt to give free rein to the unfolding of this "mass and momentum" creativity of their everyday living. Just as Erik Erickson claims[44] in his theory of psychological development that those in the twilight of their lives reflect on themselves and discern either a consolation yielding a sense of integrity or desolation leading to despair, so we can say that people can reflect upon their lives and discern whether they have lived a beautiful life or its opposite, an ugly one. In this way, we are presented with an alternative to the strictly pejorative sense of the aesthete as someone who is locked into seizing the fleeting moments of pleasure in the immediate experience with no sense of responsibility for past or the future.

Does this alternative reading threaten the profound analysis of Kierkegaard's existential spheres? I think not, especially if we view the analysis as aided by Lonergan's interpretation of psychological, moral, and religious self-transcendence.

With respect to psychological transformation, we draw upon Doran's notion of *psychic conversion*.[45] As we noted previously, this conversion concerns the liberation of the human subject from the oppression of psychological wounds and complexes. Often, the repressive censor results from the victimization or oppression and the dramatic bias that results.

By "dramatic bias" Lonergan means the prevention of dramatic artistry that can stem from a psychic wound. Dramatic bias causes the censor to become repressive as a form of psychic defence from the feelings associated with the trauma.[46] It is common during sleep that the censor relaxes and allows the repressed images to surface into one's consciousness.[47] In the context of psychotherapy, dreams may provide the seeds for psychic conversion. In addition, the fruit of psychic conversion "allows access to *one's own* symbolic system" because it facilitates internal communication within the subject.[48]

In terms of dramatic artistry, it could be said that the release of repressed images through psychic conversion allows for the insights that lead to creative expression for the artist and dramatic artistry for everyday living.[49] In this view, it becomes difficult to separate aesthetic subjectivity from moral and religious self-transcendence because the aesthetic enables the proper unfolding of moral and religious subjectivity. Not only does the religious sublate the moral, but both in turn sublate the aesthetic. By "sublation" is meant that the later stages transform the earlier stages, directing the individual towards a more authentic living while simultaneously leaving behind the negative features of the earlier stages. Moreover, because these spheres exist concretely rather than abstractly in the existential subject, the spheres can interpenetrate and blend, such as when someone is driving a car and having a meaningful conversation at the same time.[50]

In addition, the access to one's own symbolic system and the unobstructed internal communication that are the fruits of a constructively functioning psychic censor effect not only the constitutive factor as characteristic of artistic creativity and the dramatic artistry of everyday living, but they also enable a general sensitive orientation to the beautiful.[51] This would corroborate Aquinas's claim that beauty belongs essentially to the contemplative life.[52] The transcendental precept for the level of presentations (experience), "be attentive," enables one to contemplate the beautiful. Insofar as dramatic bias prevents such attentiveness, the constructively functioning censor allows this disposition to the beautiful.[53]

Symbols are inextricably connected to feelings and to values. A constructive functioning censor enables internal access to images and symbols. In this way, there is a connection between dramatic artistry and ethics and religion. As Doran states: "If values are apprehended in feelings, aesthetic subjectivity lies at the basis of existential subjectivity, of morals and religion."[54]

In terms of the moral self-transformation of the subject, I would argue that what Kierkegaard determines as the transition from the aesthetic to the ethical sphere is analogous to, if not harmonious with, Lonergan's notion of a *moral conversion*. For the latter, moral conversion enables one to choose autonomously and responsibly where one was previously unable or unwilling to do so. Moral transformation "changes the criterion of one's decisions and choices from satisfactions to values" (*MT*, 240). It occurs to the extent that one is able to choose the "truly good" over immediate gratification or sensitive satisfactions, especially when values and satisfactions conflict. Questions for moral deliberation rest on an apprehension of value that occurs in feelings. However, feelings as intentional responses to objects can be of two different kinds for Lonergan. There are feelings that pertain to whether an object is pleasing or displeasing, satisfying or dissatisfying. There is also a range of feelings that pertain to self-transcendence. The latter involve the apprehension of values in what Lonergan identifies as a scale of preference: vital, social, cultural, personal, and religious (*MT*, 31). It is noteworthy that of the few references Lonergan makes to beauty in his corpus of writing, one appears here. That is, the apprehension of value in feelings can range from "the ontic value of persons or the qualitative value of beauty, understanding, truth, virtuous acts, noble deeds" (*MT*, 31).

The agreeable and the disagreeable alike can reveal the presence of the truly good or the apparently good. "What is agreeable may very well be what also is a true good. But it also happens that what is a true good may be disagreeable" (*MT*, 31). Thus, it could be argued that Kierkegaard's aesthete is solely attached to the agreeable, so that he or she is not able to choose a particular good insofar as it is disagreeable. Persons who are in need of moral self-transformation cannot on their own accord effect such a transformation that would enable them to choose values over satisfactions. Hence, a moral self-transformation is analogous to the movement Kierkegaard identifies from the aesthetic to the ethical sphere of life in that the morally unconverted person is constrained to choose satisfactions over values. It may be that Lonergan had this in mind, judging from his comments in the 1958 Halifax lectures, *Understanding and Being*. He had engaged Kierkegaard by this time and had thought about Kierkegaard's work in reference to his own: "[S]o there is the moral development of the subject from an *aesthetic sphere* that is concerned with objects of appetite ... There is the reversal, the conversion, the transformation of that type of organization in the subject, to bring him into harmony with the objective good of order."[55]

One of the effects of moral self-transformation is the ability to ask questions pertaining to value: "There is the moral self, advancing from individual satisfactions to group interests and, beyond these, to the overarching, unrelenting question, What would be really worth while?"[56] An apprehension of value in feelings can lead to a value judgment – the affirmation that "this is good," or "this good is better than that good," or "this good is only apparently good." Hence, moral deliberation must involve discernment in order to identify and distinguish within oneself the self-regarding feelings from those of self-transcendence, or, in other words, so one can clarify that a value has indeed been apprehended, to affirm it as such, and to act in accordance with that affirmation.[57]

Likewise, the first fruit of moral self-transformation is the ability to take responsibility for one's life.[58] Invoking the examples of Kierkegaard, marriage involves taking responsibility and committing to another and to one's familial obligations as opposed to fleeting sensual relations. Friendship involves a commitment and responsibility for the other rather than just "what's in it for me." Vocation gives the wandering drifter a sense of purpose, even a sense of destiny in some circumstances where one takes responsibility for the future and gives something back to the community.

Again, the fruit of moral conversion does not preclude the aesthetic. Doran states that "[i]f values are apprehended in feelings, aesthetic subjectivity lies at the basis of existential subjectivity, of morals and religion … Ethics is radically aesthetics, and the existential subject for whom the issue is one of personal character is at base the aesthetic subject, the dramatic artist."[59]

My interpretation of Doran's comments is that the ethical sphere of moral self-transcendence sublates the aesthetic so that good moral living embodies dramatic artistry. On this account, it is fruitful to invoke the three principal qualities of beauty in Aquinas, *integritas* (wholeness-perfection), *consonantia-debita proportio* (harmony-proportion), and *claritas* (clarity-luminosity).[60] Moral people possess *integrity* or wholeness of character if their actions are consistent with their knowing and the values they affirm. Such wholeness of character speaks also to another characteristic of beauty for Aquinas, that of proportion or harmony insofar as actions are harmonious with or proportionate to the goods one affirms. Further, acting in accordance with goodness for the sake of the good-virtue (*honestum*) is suggested by Aquinas to reflect "spiritual beauty."[61] Similarly, to be honest is not to obstruct the *claritas* of truth regardless of what the consequences of doing so may be. Another application of *claritas* with respect to moral deliberation and beauty pertains to the radiance of the person possessing authentic moral character. Such radiance is analogous to the reputation one acquires in a community for being honest and responsible. Conversely, a dishonest person becomes seen as untrustworthy. In this way, we can agree with Doran that perhaps the most significant drama in which one participates, the attempt to creatively use one's native talents in order that one's own living becomes a work of art, is the struggle for one's own authenticity and the withdrawal from inauthenticity.[62]

With respect to religious self-transcendence, Kierkegaard and Lonergan place different emphases on the role of faith. For Kierkegaard, the ethical person increasingly encounters the impossibility of adhering to moral absolutes. In the limit, the person experiences ever-increasing levels of guilt that culminate in a dramatic jumping-off point or "leap" into the merciful hands of God. Faith is the act wherein one abandons oneself to the bliss of an irresolvable paradox and, instead of resisting or denying, one simply surrenders and relishes. For Lonergan, on the other hand, religious transformation occurs by way of a dynamic state of being-in-love in an unrestricted manner. Faith is knowledge born of religious love.

Religious self-transcendence is a part of Lonergan's basic anthropology insofar as human beings inevitably raise fundamental questions of ultimate meaning. The question of ultimate meaning arises from within our intentional consciousness at some point. Of course one can ignore or simply brush the questions aside. Nevertheless, the search for the answer to such a question is not simply to satisfy intellectual curiosity, although it might include this. The answer comes by way of fulfilment of this basic questioning, which is found in the dynamic state of being-in-love in an unrestricted manner, and this answer must be given as a gift. This dynamic state would be analogous to Kierkegaard's religious sphere, insofar as it redirects our knowing and choosing through a "transvaluation of values," a phrase Lonergan deliberately borrows from Nietzsche. That is, the dynamic state of being-in-love in an unrestricted manner becomes the first principle in which all our previous knowing and choosing is reoriented towards the One with whom we are in love. In other words, religious self-transcendence transvalues the aesthetic and ethical spheres towards a religious orientation. The ethical implies that one's freedom is directed towards the object of one's love. As Lonergan explains, "Since loving him is my transcending myself, it also is a denial of the self to be transcended. Since loving him means loving attention to him, it is prayer, meditation, contemplation. Since love of him is fruitful, it overflows into love of all those that he loves or might love" (MT, 109). Freedom is redirected to acts of charity and the desire to live life according to God's will. This includes a continued need for discernment. Note that loving attention to the object of one's love in this dynamic state involves contemplation. The sublation of aesthetic subjectivity into this dynamic state of religious self-transcendence implies that the content one contemplates is the beauty of the beloved.

In Lonergan's references to Friedrich Heiler, he specifically mentions "supreme beauty" as one of the seven common areas that Heiler identifies in his phenomenological descriptions of the world religions (MT, 109). While Heiler's work may be out of fashion because of the prevalence of specialized methodologies in religious studies, Lonergan's reference to Heiler's work at least indicates for us that the One with whom one is in love in this dynamic state is supreme beauty, since Heiler includes supreme beauty as one of the seven common areas. This is important considering that beauty is not mentioned as one of the aspects of God in Lonergan's Insight, chapter 19. One also begins to clue in that, for Lonergan, beauty is a value that exists by way of participation in the "originating value" or God. Hence, one of the essential aspects of religious self-transcendence is to contemplate the glory or beauty of God's creation (see MT, 116–17). Again, this is consonant with

Aquinas's claim that beauty belongs essentially to the contemplative life (*ST*, 2-2. 180. 2. ad 3).

Moreover, aesthetic subjectivity continues to play a functional role in religious self-transcendence since religious expression is bound up with aesthetic expression. This agrees with Doran's position that aesthetic subjectivity lies at the basis of religious self-appropriation: "The interpretation of symbolic religious expression can proceed from the self-knowledge of a consciousness that similarly expresses its orientation into the known unknown in symbolic manifestations."[63] In other words, the aesthetic dimension of the subject is dispositive and assists in the expression of the dynamic state in religious symbols, as for example in religious art and iconography. Because symbols can express multivalent meanings, they are appropriate for expressing in an approximate manner a mysterious reality that is not easily expressed in ordinary language.

Finally, at the fourth level of intentional consciousness (responsible decisions), and from within the dynamic state of being-in-love in an unrestricted manner, the proper unfolding of aesthetic subjectivity has far surpassed the life of the hedonist, the seducer, and the drifter. This can occur at the fourth level both passively and actively (or constitutively). Passively, one can contemplate the beauty of God by reflecting on the creation that participates in God's beauty. Actively, one can express this unrestricted loving aesthetically in dramatic acts of artistry with one's life, in works of art such as iconography, music, and architecture and, religiously, in works of aesthetic ritual and liturgy, all of this in order to express praise and thanksgiving to the Beauty that Augustine finds "so ancient and so new," the One in whom he ultimately finds his rest.

Religious self-transcendence also sublates the ethical sphere so that the criterion of one's moral deliberation is transposed and reoriented in terms of unrestricted being-in-love. The sense of duty that grounds the ethical sphere for Kierkegaard is transvalued at the level of religious self-transcendence for Lonergan. For Lonergan, the dynamic state of being-in-love is frivolous without the response of the beloved to the lover. This assent establishes a new horizon of deliberation by way of the habit of charity, where one seeks to love God with one's heart, mind, and strength and to love others as oneself. Ethical deliberation from the standpoint of religious self-transcendence includes love of God, love of neighbour, and love of one's enemies. Moreover, the three examples Kierkegaard provides for the ethical sphere – marriage, friendship, and vocation – are transposed and reoriented as a result of the dynamic state of being-in-love. Marriage becomes mystical marriage as demonstrated by the dramatic examples from the mystical tradition, including the experiences of Catherine of Siena. Friendship becomes friendship with God as expressed by the Belgian priest Fr Egide Van Broeckhoven: "My entire life has been dedicated to teaching people the depths of mystical friendship."[64] Vocation becomes the specific calling that God wills for human beings to creatively use the individual talents given to them. In such a way, they become co-artists with God in order to help create, in an eschatological sense, the Reign of God on Earth.

Conclusion

We are endeavouring to recover beauty within the subject by responding to Balthasar's critique of Kierkegaard. Balthasar blames Kierkegaard for the separation of the aesthetic sphere from the ethical and the religious. A closer inspection reveals that Balthasar's claim is only partially applicable. The real problem of Kierkegaard's anthropology is his emphasis on a negative aesthetic, that is, an aesthetic that emphasizes tragedy and does not fully account for the human being's desire for beauty and creativity. In a religious sphere, this would include a desire for the beauty of God in which all created beauty participates.

Finally, we have been speaking about various senses of the aesthetic. There is the delineation of the aesthetic as an existential category, and its authentic and inauthentic expressions. The inauthentic refers to the habitual attachment to sensual pleasures of the temporal moment and the lust for immediate gratification that leads to despair. The authentic expression of the existential attitude is expressed in the human desire to create a work of art with one's life in the world of everyday living and in the realm of moral self-transcendence. Further, there is the recognition of beauty at the sensitive level of consciousness with the psychic flow including the imagination – one that occurs in the aesthetic pattern of experience. This pattern, differentiated in the consciousness of the artist, gives way to expressions of elemental meaning objectified symbolically in various artistic media. Philosophically, questions can be raised about the beauty of existence or of the splendour of being. Religiously, one can raise the question about the beauty of God and the created order's participation in that divine beauty. Finally, one can speak of the performative aesthetic in which Kierkegaard engages while paradoxically providing us with an incomplete aesthetic.

I have argued that interpreting the existential spheres of Kierkegaard in terms of aspects of Lonergan's theory of polymorphic consciousness enables a response to Balthasar's critique while also preserving the genius of Kierkegaard's anthropology. By viewing the existential spheres in terms of different patterns of and transformations of consciousness, we avoid the separation of the aesthetic, the ethical, and the religious and preserve the potential for beauty as integral to authentic human striving on all levels of existence. Again, Balthasar and Lonergan would both agree that the value of Kierkegaard remains permanent because he turns the criteria of true Christianity away from external and nominal affiliation and inward to the subject's authentic deciding for God.

5 The End of Aesthetic Experience?

The aesthetic attitude engages us both as knowers and as lovers.

– Armand Maurer

Once a potent embodiment of art's sense and value, aesthetic experience is now "hermeneutered."

– Richard Shusterman

I am endeavouring to transpose a philosophy for a theology of beauty for a third stage of meaning by incorporating the philosophy of Bernard Lonergan. As noted previously, in many ways I am following a path clearly delineated by Armand Maurer in his book *About Beauty: A Thomistic Interpretation*. Maurer eschews those Thomistic scholars who conclude that Thomas did not take beauty to be a transcendental property of being. By contrast, Maurer takes the existence of beauty as a starting point and proceeds to offer a clear overview of Aquinas's philosophy of beauty. I proceed in a similar manner to Maurer, in that Lonergan's thought rests heavily on the shoulders of Aquinas but Lonergan also engages the Enlightenment philosophical turn to the subject. I presume the existence of beauty and ask how we can construe beauty in the various levels of Lonergan's philosophy of consciousness.

I argued in chapter 1 that Balthasar's philosophical approach had stopped well short of modern philosophy. He believed that the philosophy of beauty reached its acme with Aquinas's metaphysics only to decline shortly thereafter through the dual legacy of Scotus and Eckhart, and even further via what he believed to be a "wrong turn" in the turn to the subject. I began in the previous chapter to show the provocative nature of Lonergan's contribution in providing a hermeneutic reading for Kierkegaard, whom Balthasar also blames for much of the modern loss of beauty. To the extent our rereading of Kierkegaard through Lonergan's philosophy is adequate, we have made an important step towards recovering beauty in the subject. In this chapter we will continue that recovery by focusing on how aesthetic experience can be construed from Lonergan's philosophical consciousnesses.

The title of this chapter is taken from an essay by a contemporary philosopher of aesthetics, Richard Shusterman, who asks, Has the notion of aesthetic experience been "hermeneutered"?[1] On the one hand, there is the shift that occurs in Kant, where truth is relegated to the conceptual realm and subsequently leads to a privileging of scientific method over and above other approaches to truth. On the other hand, there are the contributions of Heidegger and Gadamer, who bring a priority back to aesthetic experience, associating aesthetic encounters with the concealment/unconcealment of truth.

We proceed with a brief synopsis of the loss of aesthetic experience, an overview of some major post-Kantian attempts to retrieve it, a presentation of Lonergan's notion of aesthetic experience, and a dialogue with Shusterman. In addition we address the question of aesthetic perception in a more contemporary Thomistic context and, finally, the notion of the sublime as experienced.

The Loss of Aesthetic Experience

If Hans Urs von Balthasar is correct in decrying the loss of beauty in Western philosophy and theology, is it any wonder that this leads to the questioning of the existence of aesthetic experience? When adverting to the possibility of aesthetic experience we find that Kant has set the horizon, not only for aesthetic judgments, but for aesthetic experience as well. Armand Maurer states: "The subjectivity of beauty and ugliness is a legacy to modern philosophy from Immanuel Kant."[2] If this is the case, following Kant, the legacy of aesthetic experience will be reduced to sensitive pleasure in the subjective field. The accusation is well established in Gadamer, who states concerning Kant: "In taste nothing is known of the objects judged to be beautiful, but it is stated only that there is a feeling of pleasure connected with them a priori in the subjective consciousness."[3] This is further exemplified by Hume when he states: "Beauty is no quality in things themselves; it exists merely in the mind which contemplates them. One person may even perceive deformity, where another is sensible of beauty; and every individual ought to acquiesce in his own sentiment, without pretending to regulate those of others."[4]

Summarizing this movement, the philosopher of aesthetics Shusterman states: "Once modern science and philosophy had destroyed the classical, medieval, and Renaissance faith that properties like beauty were objective features of the world, modern aesthetics turned to subjective experience to explain and ground them."[5]

Major Post-Kantian Approaches to Aesthetic Experience

For Arthur Schopenhauer (1788–1860), aesthetic experience becomes an antidote to the dregs of ordinary existence; in the words of Robert Wicks, "Schopenhauer's violence-filled vision of the daily world sends him on a quest for tranquility."[6] Schopenhauer had a significant influence on Western notions of aesthetic experience. Experiences of aesthetic contemplation offer moments of freedom from the constraints of the Will and sufficient reason wherein Ideas are made manifest. In those experiences, the "individuality so entirely disappears" and one is privileged to contemplate the absolute.[7] Schopenhauer states:

> [T]he scope of the subjective element in aesthetic pleasure; the deliverance of knowledge from the service of the will, the forgetting of self as individual, and the raising of the consciousness to the pure will-less, timeless, subject of knowledge, independent of all relations. With this subjective side of aesthetic contemplation, there must always appear as its necessary correlative the objective side, the intuitive comprehension of the Platonic Idea.[8]

The types of experiences he refers to are fleeting for the average person, but developed in the mind of the artist, who for Schopenhauer is a genius because the artist relies on a differentiated aesthetic consciousness that enables him or her to perceive this "will-less" realm on a regular basis. Living in such close proximity to this aesthetic realm enables the artist not only to communicate these Forms in works of art, but to invite others into the aesthetic realm insofar as the artist's work successfully communicates the Forms. For Schopenhauer, of all the artistic media, music remains the highest expression. While the other arts, such as the visual or plastic arts, seek to imitate or copy the Ideas, as manifestations of the Will-in-Form, music copies or imitates the Will itself and so is a higher achievement.[9]

The dissolution of the individual in the aesthetic experience is an idea probably influenced by Schopenhauer's study of Indian philosophy.[10] However, in Lonergan's notion, which I will discuss below, this dissolution would not mean that the individual dissolves ontologically; rather it would pertain to an *elemental meaning* of consciousness where the distinction between the subject and object "dissolves," or the two are not differentiated, so to speak, at least for the duration of the experience.

While the epistemological and metaphysical aspects of Schopenhauer's theory are problematic, his emphasis on the *liberating* component of aesthetic experience is perhaps a permanent achievement in its recovery.

George Santayana (1863–1952), whom Arthur Danto describes as "deeply taken with Schopenhauer," emphasizes the subjectivity of aesthetic experience as an internal projection of pleasure.[11] "Beauty is constituted by the objectification of pleasure. It is pleasure objectified."[12] Beauty is a value, but a subjective one, a product of perception rather than an object. He states: "Beauty, as we have seen, is a value; it cannot be conceived as an independent existence which affects our senses and which we consequently perceive. It exists in perception, and cannot exist otherwise."[13] Nevertheless, even though Santayana encourages a subjectification of beauty, his emphasis on aesthetic perception as a disposition may help in a recovery of aesthetic experience. Danto explains:

> What Santayana must be credited with is the recognition that the aesthetic sense is a disposition to respond to rather than a more passive disposition to receive sensations, and in this regard if there is an aesthetic sense, which as we saw he came to doubt, it does not function quite like the other senses, preeminently the sense of sight, but is rather more like senses in that wider meaning according to which we speak of a sense of humor. It is as I suggested more like a sexual than a merely perceptual way of relating to the world.[14]

John Dewey (1859–1952) seeks to emphasize the primacy of aesthetic experience over other types of experience, "[f]or esthetic experience is experience in its integrity." Dewey hesitates to describe it as "pure" experience because he thinks the word has been overused.[15] He aims to free the aesthetic experience from isolation relative to other patterns of experience and to bridge the "chasm between ordinary and esthetic experience."[16] To avoid this, I will argue for a response to this "chasm" by integrating the creative impulse into the flow of ordinary living. On this note, Lonergan speaks of the dramatic artistry of the subject, as stated previously, whose first work of living is to create a work of art with his or her own life.

The phenomenological movement, which emerged in general from the Kantian distinction between the phenomena and the noumena, continued historically to emphasize the subject's aesthetic experience. The Polish phenomenologist Roman Ingarden (1893–1970) acknowledges the object of an aesthetic experience, but he maintains that the aesthetic experience per se pertains to the subject's experience: "The essential mistake of the views about an aesthetic experience consists in the opinion that the object of such an experience is *identical* with the element of the real world and the object of our activities or cognition."[17] We may have an aesthetic experience with respect to a flower, but what is "aesthetic" about it are the feelings that one brings to the object. A scientist would approach the same object from the perspective of her methodological inquiry. For Ingarden, there is an activity with respect to the aesthetic experience that is constitutive in some way of the aesthetic encounter. He states:

> However, it should not be supposed on this basis, that an aesthetic experience is purely passive and noncreative "contemplating" of a quality ... as opposed to an "active" practical life. On the contrary, it is a phase of a very *active*, intensive and creative life of an individual, that these activities do not evoke any changes in the surrounding real world.[18]

Ingarden emphasizes an important aspect of aesthetic experience, that it combines an active dimension with an element of passive repose: "the whole process of aesthetic experience includes, on the one hand, *active phases*, on the other hand, again, the fleeting phases of a passive experiencing, the moments of turning motionless and contemplative."[19]

In contrast to Ingarden, Mikel Dufrenne emphasizes that the perception of an aesthetic object does not constitute it per se, but rather the perception reveals the aesthetic object as such. The perception and the object are inextricably intertwined. Dufrenne states: "The aesthetic object bears its own signification within it, and by entering more profoundly into communion with the object, one discovers its signification, just as one understands the being of others only by virtue of friendship. The communion is indispensable. Without it, the aesthetic object is inert and meaningless."[20]

Monroe Beardsley (1915–1985) emphasizes the "intercourse" between the observer and the aesthetic object in the encounter, whatever the object may be insofar as it is "sensuously presented or imaginatively intended."[21] He states:

> I propose to say that a person is having an aesthetic experience during a particular stretch of time if and only if the greater part of his mental activity during that time is united and made pleasurable by being tied to the form and qualities of a sensuously presented or imaginatively intended object on which his primary attention is concentrated.[22]

Concerning Beardsley's postulate, John Fisher elaborates: "Such an experience is unusually coherent, possesses a high degree of intensity, and tends to be complete in itself."[23] Nor is the experience confined to the world of art.

In his presidential address to the APA in 1978, Beardsley proposed the following five characteristics, four of which are sufficient to delineate an aesthetic experience: (1) object-directedness, an intentional fixing of attention to the object; (2) felt freedom, from the dominance of other concerns; (3) detached affect, sense of a surplus beyond the mediating object; (4) active discovery, engaging the aesthetic object for coherence and insights; (5) a sense of wholeness, a sense of integration.[24]

In sum, there is a legacy of philosophical thought seeking to reckon with the questions of aesthetic experience and how it is to be understood. Whether these attempts sufficiently escape the subjectivization of such experiences is another matter.

Shusterman: "The End of Aesthetic Experience"

The philosopher Richard Shusterman takes up this concern about the loss of aesthetic experience. He responds to many of the tendencies of those listed above, and in his article "The End of Aesthetic Experience" raises the following questions:

> Does aesthetic experience then name the central blunder of modern aesthetics? Though long considered the most essential of aesthetic concepts, as including but also surpassing the realm of art, aesthetic experience has

in the last half-century come under increasing critique. Not only its value but its very existence has been questioned. How has this once vital concept lost its appeal? Does it still offer anything of value?[25]

He proceeds to offer a reason for the demise of aesthetic experience in the contemporary situation and to advance an argument for reasserting its importance and validity.

The key to preserving the notion of aesthetic experience involves highlighting "four features that are central to the tradition of aesthetic experience and whose interplay shapes yet confuses twentieth-century accounts of this concept":

> First, aesthetic experience is essentially valuable and enjoyable; call this its *evaluative dimension*. Second, it is something vividly felt and subjectively savoured, affectively absorbing us and focusing our attention on its immediate presence and thus standing out from the ordinary flow of routine experience; call this its *phenomenological dimension*. Third, it is meaningful experience, not mere sensation; call this its *semantic dimension*. (Its affective power and meaning together explain how aesthetic experience can be so transfigurative.) Fourth, it is a distinctive experience closely identified with the distinction of fine art and representing art's essential aim; call this the *demarcational-definitional dimension*.[26]

These four aspects of aesthetic experience can be further understood in terms of three poles or "axes of contrast": (1) To what extent is the aesthetic experience "intrinsically honorific" (valuable) and to what extent is it "descriptively neutral"? (2) To what extent is aesthetic experience "robustly phenomenological or simply semantic?" and (3) To what extent is aesthetic experience understood as a distinct experience and to what extent can it be expanded to include other human experiences?[27] As an example concerning the latter, Shusterman has raised the question of whether sexual experiences can be aesthetic experiences.[28]

Aesthetic experience as pleasurable and valuable – the evaluative dimension. In a follow-up essay to "The End of Aesthetic Experience," Shusterman delineates the aspect of aesthetic experience as "pleasurable and valuable" and even uses the word "hedonic." In other words, in an aesthetic encounter one experiences pleasure and/or one apprehends value. This is reminiscent of Aquinas's comment that beauty is pleasing when seen or apprehended. However, Shusterman is quick to clarify that one need not conflate pleasure and value because the two can be quite distinct.

Further, he acknowledges that an aesthetic experience need not be plea-surable, as it can include feelings of "shock, fragmentation, disorienta-tion, puzzlement, horror, or even revulsion."[29] Here we encounter the question of the sublime versus a beautiful experience, which I address in the final section of this chapter.

Phenomenological character. Shusterman speaks of a twofold dimen-sion to the phenomenological aspect of aesthetic experience. First, aesthetic experience is "distinctively felt (and, when positive, appre-ciatively savoured)."[30] Second, the experience is not merely subjective, but intends an aesthetic "object" or content. This intentional content, for Shusterman, indicates the experience as one of "meaningful percep-tion."[31] Consequently, he is not convinced by those who would empha-size the objective pole of the experience or those who might argue for an aesthetic experience that may occur unconsciously.

Demarcation versus transformation. In considering aesthetic experience, Shusterman identifies a tension between those theorists who would re-strict the aesthetic experience to a specific range of presentations such as those appropriate to the fine arts, on the one hand, and those who favour expanding the notion to include other types of human experi-ences, on the other. In the case of the latter, he is interested in expanding the notion of aesthetic experience to include sexual experience.

Shusterman takes Dewey as his inspiration with respect to "trans-forming" the notion of aesthetic experience (although I would prefer the term "expanding") to include a broader range of human experiences. Dewey favoured the distinctness of aesthetic experience but simultane-ously sought to articulate this in terms of the various aspects of human living. To express this tension in the words of Lonergan, to what extent is aesthetic experience a reflection of a distinctive aesthetic conscious-ness, and to what extent does it interpenetrate with other patterns and differentiations of consciousness? On this matter, I think Lonergan's philosophy of consciousness may have something to contribute.

Other issues. Shusterman raises some other philosophical questions pertaining to aesthetic experience. One of these concerns the percep-tion of an object in aesthetic experience and knowledge of the object. Granted that one apprehends an object in an aesthetic experience, how does one react when one misconstrues the object? "[C]an an experi-ence be genuinely aesthetic but misconstrue the object it claims to be about?"[32] His position is that it is possible to have a "genuine aes-thetic experience" based on a misperception. The question as raised seems to reflect the problematic phase in the history of philosophy that

Lonergan speaks about in chapter 14 of *Insight*, when philosophers pine for a more explicit metaphysics. But in this case, it would first require an epistemology: "Aesthetic experiences range from veridical perceptions to gross misunderstandings, but also extend to encounters or 'graspings' that precede the explicit formulation of a judgment that could be true or false." Lonergan would agree with Shusterman when the latter states: "There is more to experience than the knowledge of experience."[33]

Related to the question of the distinctness of aesthetic experience is the unity of the experience. In this respect, Shusterman recognizes that some basic unity in the experience is required in order to distinguish the aesthetic experience from the otherwise "unattended flow of humdrum experience."[34]

Closely related to this question is the role of feelings in an aesthetic experience. On the one hand, there is agreement that such experiences commonly involve intense feelings. On the other, there are also encounters that invoke more quiet and "dispassionate" responses. Further, one would need to consider the frame of reference, for example, the difference between the art appreciator and the art critic.

While I cannot hope to address all of the philosophical questions in a comprehensive and satisfactory way, I hope to at least show how Lonergan's philosophy might engage in a general way the three axes that Shusterman articulates.

Lonergan and Aesthetic Experience

For Lonergan, not unlike others such as Heidegger and Gadamer, the notion of aesthetic experience is closely linked to his views on the philosophy of art. In this section I will emphasize the characteristics of aesthetic experience rather than Lonergan's philosophy of art per se, which I will address in chapter 8. I have divided the topic into five features, although there is obvious overlap: the unrestricted desire for beauty, non-instrumentalized consciousness, elemental meaning, ulterior significance and surplus, and the transformative and/or distortive potential of aesthetic encounters.

Aesthetic experience for Lonergan can be construed from several perspectives: (1) the potential for aesthetic experience in all human beings, (2) the creative work of the artist in trying to objectify or express the aesthetically patterned experience symbolically in works of art, and (3) the mediation of the artwork to the observer in order to bring him/her into an experience of the surplus and ulterior significance communicated in the work.[35] I will focus on the first perspective, the potential for aesthetic experience in all human beings, since the second and third pertain more properly to a philosophy of art that I will deal with in chapter 8 on fourth-level operations and aesthetic creativity.

The Unrestricted Desire for Beauty

Shusterman's recognition of an evaluative dimension to aesthetic experience presumes that one can potentially apprehend value in an aesthetic experience. Such apprehension is often pleasurable, although this occurs in different ways and not strictly at the level of sensitivity. Such a dimension corroborates Aquinas's declaration that "everyone loves the beautiful." We can appropriate this phrase as axiomatic and incorporate it into Lonergan's philosophy as an unrestricted desire for beauty.

Lonergan references and develops Aristotle's notion of wonder in *Insight* as the detached, pure, unrestricted desire to know. To be sure, the unrestricted desire to know pertains to the intellectual pattern of experience and is the source or operator as manifested in questions, at least insofar as those questions are unobstructed by obscurantism. We noted in the previous chapter that Lonergan made comments about a quasi-operator, or symbolic operator that corresponds more with the affective dimension of the human being. In terms of beauty, one might claim we all have a natural unrestricted desire for beauty. But it is a desire propelled and fostered by encounters with beauty rather than from questions arising in the pure desire to know – although the two are not unrelated.

How then can we say such a desire for beauty is unrestricted? In every encounter with beauty, be it a sunset, a work of art, or another human being, sustained attention gives rise to simultaneous feelings of impermanence and incompleteness. The pleasure in repeatedly listening to a beautiful melody will eventually exhaust itself. While the desire for ever-new beautiful music persists, the pleasure of the originating moment of the initial encounter cannot be sustained. In the most beautiful of sceneries there is the awareness that this beauty is fleeting and ephemeral. Edgar Allen Poe captures this experience brilliantly in "The Poetic Principle":

> An immortal instinct deep within the spirit of man is thus plainly a sense of the Beautiful. This it is which administers to his delight in the manifold forms, and sounds, and odors and sentiments amid which he exists ... We have still a thirst unquenchable, to allay which he has not shown us

the crystal springs. This thirst belongs to the immortality of Man. It is at once a consequence and an indication of his perennial existence. It is the desire of the moth for the star. It is no mere appreciation of the Beauty before us, but a wild effort to reach the Beauty above. Inspired by an ecstatic prescience of the glories beyond the grave, we struggle by multiform combinations among the things and thoughts of Time to attain a portion of that Loveliness whose very elements perhaps appertain to eternity alone. And thus when by Poetry, or when by Music, the most entrancing of the poetic moods, we find ourselves melted into tears, we weep then, not as the Abbate Gravina supposes, through excess of pleasure, but through a certain petulant, impatient sorrow at our inability to grasp now, wholly, here on earth, at once and for ever, those divine and rapturous joys of which through the poem, or through the music, we attain to but brief and indeterminate glimpses.[36]

And even if the aesthetic moment were to persist, as when we listen to our favourite music repeatedly, there is incompleteness to it. The pleasure wanes, and we pine for fresh melodic experiences. Our desire for beauty cannot be exhausted in a single encounter. A moment of beauty recedes, and we anticipate another. If we are fortunate, the moments are held together like pearls on the strand of our life experiences. Still, if this desire for beauty is insatiable, then can we anticipate some type of permanent fulfilment and satisfaction in the feeling of beauty? Does the ephemerality of beauty somehow enhance our appreciation of it? If we presume that there is an unrestricted desire for beauty, can we abstract to the notion of an unrestricted act of beauty, an *Urgrund* of beauty in which the entire created order is beautiful by virtue of its participation in this ground? The anticipation of such fulfilment of the desire of beauty is spoken of by the philosopher C.E.M. Joad:

In the appreciation of music and of pictures we get a momentary and fleeting glimpse of the nature of that reality to a full knowledge of which the movement of life is progressing. For that moment, and for so long as the glimpse persists, we realize in anticipation and almost, as it were, illicitly, the nature of the end. We are, if I may so put it, for the moment there, just as a traveler may obtain a fleeting glimpse of a distant country from an eminence passed on the way, and cease for a space from his journey to enjoy the view. And since we are for the moment there, we experience while the moment lasts that sense of liberation from the urge and drive of life, which has been noted as one of the special characteristics of aesthetic experience.[37]

Since this leads us to the topic of the surplus and ulterior significance and the potential transformative aspect of aesthetic experiences, we will refrain from further exposition for the time being. For now, suffice it to say there is room in Lonergan's philosophy for an aesthetic component to the unrestricted desire to know – a desire for beauty. It manifests in a twofold desire to contemplate and to create beauty, a topic to which we return in chapter 8.

Freedom from Instrumentality

In the language of Shusterman, "freedom from instrumentality" would allow us to demarcate or distinctively define the characteristic of aesthetic experience.

We get a clue of what characterizes aesthetic experience for Lonergan by his notion of the aesthetic pattern of experience in *Insight* (207–9) and in his definition of art as the "objectification of the purely experiential pattern" in *Topics in Education* (211).[38] For Lonergan, the "pure" of the "purely experiential pattern" means something very specific. When he uses the latter expression he does not mean that it is pure in the sense that the experience is free from all socially learned/constructed meanings, but in the sense that the subject's consciousness is free from other instrumentalized patterns of consciousness, such as the differentiations of common sense (ordinary living) and of theory. This emphasis is reminiscent of Arthur Schopenhauer's theory of aesthetic experience, which involves a suspension of the "the principle of sufficient reason" (viewing things in terms of their causes and relations) and a temporary suspension of the will, or "will-less knowing," in which one contemplates the beautiful. In terms of Kant's notion of "disinterested pleasure," as Roger Scruton puts it, "I am purely disinterested, abstracting from practical considerations and attending to the object before me with all desires, interests and goals suspended."[39] Lonergan would not accept Schopenhauer's epistemology and metaphysics (or Kant's for that matter), which posits a grasp of the Platonic Ideas in the aesthetic experience;[40] rather, he would acknowledge the grasp of intelligibility in the data given in the presentations to consciousness, grasped in understanding and affirmed in judgment.

While in *Insight* Lonergan speaks of the aesthetic pattern of experience, a closer scrutiny of Lonergan's text, as pointed out by Gerard Walmsley, reveals a distinction between the *aesthetic* pattern of experience and the *artistic* pattern of experience.[41] The former pertains to the experience as such, the latter to the communication of that experience in works of art.

As stated above, for Lonergan "art is the objectification of the purely experiential *pattern*" (*TE*, 211). The task of the artist is to "objectify" these "pure," non-instrumentalized experiences, where "objectify" simply means to make this meaning manifest symbolically in works of art. In contrast to the world of theory, where precision and technical language dominate, the world of the artist is one of images and symbols because these allow for a multivalent expression that is more fitting to express what Lonergan calls elemental meaning. Symbols can express contradictions, especially those invoking affective responses, in a way that the technical language of theory cannot. Again, artists live close to the world of symbols and images. Their consciousness is differentiated in such a way that they can apprehend the surplus and express it symbolically more readily than others. The multivalence of symbols is essential to express the ulterior significance of art.

This aesthetic pattern is characterized by spontaneity and liberation that is conducive to creative expression. Lonergan places both the aesthetic and artistic patterns between the biological pattern and the intellectual pattern. If one considers the caricature of the starving artist, this makes sense: the aesthetic pattern subsists through the basic meeting of the biological needs. Consequently, however, destitute societies struggling for basic, vital needs may not be able to experience this pattern because they are simply trying to stay alive. Of course, there are rare exceptions of creative geniuses who emerge from the margins of society, sometimes as prophets giving hope to their society and to the world.

In contrast, the intellectual pattern requires a further instrumentalization of consciousness in order to direct inquiry to some given data in a systematized way. Think of the bored student who finds release by doodling while listening to a tedious lecture that requires intellectual concentration. The freedom one experiences in the aesthetic pattern of experience is a release from the instrumentality that one experiences by living constantly in the worlds of theory and of practice. The sudden beauty of a sunset comforts the weary driver sitting in a traffic jam. The driver is momentarily lifted out of his or her predicament to be reminded that there is more to life than the hustle and bustle of everyday living. The liberation is twofold, and by stating this, I am suggesting a development in Lonergan's patterns. On the one hand there is a liberation simply by moving out of the intstrumentalized consciousness of which one may be growing existentially weary. It is this aspect of liberation that also pertains to play and entertainment. However, to the extent to which the play or entertainment becomes guided by interest, such as in games or sports, it becomes more instrumentalized and so distinct from the aesthetic experience per se. There is room in Lonergan's philosophy to develop and distinguish the entertainment and recreational patterned flows of consciousness. They would be analogous to the aesthetic pattern in that they involve a movement out of the practical, dramatic, and theoretical flows of consciousness, but they are distinct to the extent that they are guided by interest. In addition, in terms of the second aspect of liberation one can encounter a significance and surplus that enriches one more deeply in the aesthetic pattern, and this provides a further enrichment than just the release from instrumentality that one may experience in the more recreational or liberative patterns.

Elemental Meaning

Closely related to Shusterman's notion of the *phenomenological* characteristic of aesthetic experience, in that the experience is completely absorbing, is the distinct kind of meaning that is involved when the subject's consciousness is not instrumentalized into a specific pattern. Lonergan calls it *elemental meaning*. It is elemental in the sense that during the experience the subject-object distinction has not yet arisen (see *MT*, 61–3). One is swept up in the moment by a symphony, a dance, or a beautiful scene. Most of us experience this reality from time to time throughout the course of our ordinary living. At times these experiences can be momentous and life changing.

A transformation occurs as the subject slips into a world of non-instrumental consciousness: "The subject in act is the object in act at the level of elemental meaning" (*TE*, 217). It is meaning prior to inquiry, distinction, and conceptualization. For Lonergan, elemental meaning can be "set within a conceptual field" but conceptualization or objectification does not "reproduce" the original experience. It is the world Heidegger describes as "ontic," where one simply is present to the experience that one is having (*TE*, 217).

One could think of elemental meaning occurring within intersubjective relations as well. Two lovers consummating their relationship in fidelity and commitment become like one – at times, in ecstasy. Indeed, for Lonergan, being-in-love is closely connected with the aesthetic experience. There is a surplus in the encounter with the other in love that is better expressed in poetry and song than in theoretical constructs. This is the case not only for the love of another human being, but for those who fall in love unrestrictedly, that is, for those who fall in love with God. In the more dramatic instances, such as those experienced by the Spanish mystics, poetry and song speak to the ineffable reality one encounters in this loving relationship. In their experience of falling in love with God, the encounter is one of elemental meaning. It is elemental in the sense that the "object" that one encounters is not clearly apprehended.

Ulterior Significance and "Surplus of Meaning"

Shusterman speaks of the semantic dimension of aesthetic experience, which refers to its "effective power and meaning together" and explains "how aesthetic experience can be so transfigurative."[42] We have seen that for Lonergan an aesthetic experience from the side of the subject is one of elemental meaning in non-instrumentalized experience. However, from the side of the object, one encounters "ulterior significance" in the content of the experience itself. Gadamer refers to this as an *excess of meaning* when he states: "But the language of art means the excess of meaning that is present in the work itself. The inexhaustibility that distinguishes the language of art from all translation into concepts rests on this excess of meaning."[43]

Such experiences as a beautiful sunset are beautiful insofar as the integrity of the forms, the various plays of light, and our awareness of its ephemerality combine to give us pause to reflect and appreciate the beauty. The experience is enriching, and as such it is also a grasp of a surplus in the experience that accounts for the excess of meaning in these experiences.

In chapter 17 of *Insight*, Lonergan distinguishes between a *known* and the *known unknown* (*IN*, 555). In the intellectual pattern, these pertain to our knowledge and ignorance respectively. In the dramatic pattern, the known unknown can be charged with affectivity to give one a sense of mystery – of unplumbed depths. In turn, there is a correspondence between the two operators of the *unrestricted desire to know* and the *psychic-affective quasi-operator*. There is the possibility of two "spheres" of consciousness with their "variable content": the sphere of the "domesticated, familiar, common" and the sphere of the "ulterior unknown, of the unexplored and strange, of the undefined surplus of significance and momentousness." These two spheres can be quite distinct, "as separate as Sundays and weekdays," or they can "interpenetrate," as when life is viewed with "the glory and freshness of a dream" in the young Wordsworth (*IN*, 556). Later, Lonergan gives a more explicit indication of what he has in mind with respect to the two spheres. They can "interpenetrate, and that interpenetration is something like what is described by Wordsworth in his 'Intimations of Immortality'" where, as Lonergan puts it, "[e]verything is open to the divine, a manifestation of the divine."[44] The aesthetic experience can open us up to this surplus of significance, and as unrestricted, it directs us to the ever-horizonal expanse towards its ground.

In *Topics in Education*, Lonergan refers to this "undefined surplus of significance and momentousness" in terms of the goal of art to communicate this experience in symbolic works. Joseph Flanagan explains this aspect of Lonergan's thinking:

> Lonergan draws our attention to the defining essence of art. All art has an "ulterior significance," which means that art reveals something strange and startling about ourselves and our world. Art reveals that our ordinary world has a concealed dimension; hidden in our everyday world there is the splendor and mystery, the dark and demonic, waiting to be revealed and shown to us, and it is the artist who discloses this unsuspected majesty and mystery of our everyday world. There is in everything in our world a secluded surplus of meaning, a primordial, elemental meaning that will evoke within us transcendent feelings and values when they are given genuine symbolic expression by the artist. Not all expression has this extra dimension, this "ulterior significance," and when it is lacking, art tends to be clever, brilliant, even ingenious but in the final analysis it is not art but an expression of aesthetic enjoyment without "ulterior significance."[45]

Flanagan emphasizes the aspect of Lonergan's approach that is consonant with the emphases of Heidegger and Gadamer. And while each refers to this ulterior significance with respect to the role of art rather than aesthetic experience, equally for each the two are intimately related. Again, I will return to the philosophy of art in chapter 8, but for now there are two points worthy of mention.

First, Flanagan emphasizes "the splendor and mystery" concealed from ordinary (instrumentalized) experience. This experience is mediated by good art, but the experience itself is open to everyone. The artist simply has the ability to communicate it and draw people back into the experience. While he does not invoke the phrase in art, later Lonergan would call it a "mediated return to immediacy." Second, Flanagan invokes the language from Paul Ricoeur of "surplus of meaning" to describe this ulterior significance of art.[46] Even though Lonergan does not use the term explicitly, "surplus of meaning" describes this ulterior significance implicitly. Therefore, I will use that term when referring to the surplus, momentum, and ulterior significance of aesthetic experience or the attempt to communicate it through works of art.

Transformative and Distortive Aspects of Aesthetic Experience

The emphasis on aesthetic experience can be powerfully transformative and at the same time distortive. Concerning the powerful aspect of aesthetic experience, Gadamer speaks of it in relation to the experience of art: "The power of the work of art suddenly tears the person experiencing it out of the context of his life, and yet relates him back to the whole of his existence."[47] Lonergan often invoked a similar terminology from Arnold Toynbee, that of "withdrawal and return."[48] Although Lonergan did not use this phrase in reference to aesthetic experience and art, it does apply because for him the attempt to live simply in one pattern speaks of a lack of integration. Gadamer's explicit treatment of aesthetic experience as *Erlebnis* and *Erfahrung* helps to explicate this dimension of Lonergan's treatment of aesthetic experience in order to avoid the two distortions of aesthetic experience that Gadamer mentions.

There is a powerful and potentially transformative aspect in aesthetic experience that is suggested by Gadamer's words quoted in the previous paragraph. On this both Gadamer and Lonergan would agree, particularly when the ulterior significance in the aesthetic encounter comprises what Rudolf Otto would call the *ganz andere* or wholly other. For example, the Russian Orthodox theologian Sergei Bulgakov eventually converted from Communist atheism to theism while gazing on the beauty of the Caucasus Mountains, and he later converted to Christianity after gazing upon Raphael's *Madonna and Child* in Dresden. Similarly, F.D. Dostoevsky was so shaken by the *Ecce Homo* he encountered in a museum in Basel that he returned to Russia resolved never to gamble again. Still, just as the lived experiences of *Erlebnis* are potentially transformative, their transformation is effected through their further integration into *Erfahrung*.

There is a withdrawal and a return in Gadamer's notion of aesthetic experience – one that is consonant with Lonergan although Lonergan is not as deliberate in his expression of it. *Erlebnis* refers to this non-instrumentalized consciousness. Referencing its use in Heidegger, Ian Thompson describes it as follows: "A 'lived experience' is an experience that makes us feel 'more alive,' as Heidegger suggests by emphasizing the etymological connection between *Erleben* and *Lebens*, 'lived experience' and 'life.'"[49] In contrast, *Erfahrung* is the experience as mediated through instrumentalization of consciousness where one takes into account the embeddedness of art in a social-historical context. Further, there is a dialectical relation between *Erlebnis* and *Erfahrung* that can lead to two types of distortion.

An overemphasis on *Erlebnis* can lead to escapism. Gadamer speaks of this: "Aesthetic self-understanding is indulging in escapism if it regards the encounter with the work of art as nothing but enchantment in the sense of liberation from the pressures of reality, through the enjoyment of a spurious freedom."[50] This *aesthetic consciousness*,[51] as Gadamer calls it, obstructs the truth of the experience by indulging singly in the withdrawal with its failure to return. It is analogous to Kierkegaard's negative sense of the aesthetic sphere. This danger would be more likely to persist if there were not a further aspect of the aesthetic experience that is essential, and this is the grasp of what Lonergan calls *the surplus or ulterior significance*, provided of course that one attempts to return from the experience and to integrate it through the operations of intentional consciousness and in the common fund of collective knowledge. Related to this, a failure to account for the experiences in the social and historical contexts leads to a failure to adequately discriminate between real art and superficiality.

A second distortion is possible through an overemphasis on *Erfahrung* in terms of social and historical context that prevents one from transcending oneself and orientating oneself towards the Other in the lived experiences. The lived experience is reduced to theory and the surplus of meaning occluded. If I am reading Gadamer accurately, both of these distortions are important caveats to complement Lonergan's treatment of aesthetic experience.

Finally, in addition to Gadamer's warnings, there is a further caveat I derive from Lonergan's thought, concerning elemental meaning. In chapter 17 of *Insight*, "Metaphysics as Dialectic," he writes that an experience of elemental meaning can be one of myth or mystery. I have been presuming that elemental meaning is a positive experience, one that mediates mystery. However, the meaning that is encountered can also reflect a mythic consciousness (in the pejorative sense that Lonergan describes it), which can be co-opted into ideology. Such mythology, for example, swept the youth of Nazi Germany into ideological nationalism. Subsequent critical reflection by some young philosophy students, originally caught up in the ideological revelry, led them to form a resistance movement known as the White Rose, most of whose members were eventually executed by the Nazis.

Hence, not only is there a temptation to escapism and reductionism, but the exuberance of lived experience can lead one to be swept up by a fascination with myth or a preoccupation with darkness.

Lonergan and Shusterman

In this section I will return to the three axes regarding aesthetic experience that Shusterman identifies in order to suggest how Lonergan's philosophy of consciousness would respond to these axes. Recall the first axis: To what extent is the aesthetic experience "intrinsically honorific" (valuable) and to what extent is it "descriptively neutral"? By "intrinsically honorific," I presume Shusterman means the extent to which one apprehends value within aesthetic experience. "Descriptively neutral," I suspect, refers to the extent to which the object can be appreciated in a reflective way by aesthetic principles as detached from direct affective engagement. I suggest that for Lonergan the difference between the two poles of the axis can be clarified by distinguishing between the experience as such and the subsequent operations of intelligence, reflection, and expression.

The second axis asks: To what extent is aesthetic experience "robustly phenomenological or simply semantic"? "In other words," he asks, "are affect and subjective intentionality essential dimensions of this experience, or is it rather only a certain kind of meaning or style of symbolization that renders an experience aesthetic?" If I understand Shusterman correctly, he is asking: Is the aesthetic experience constituted primarily by the conscious intentionality of the subject's experience, or does the artistic symbolism or the aesthetic "object" as meaningful constitute the primacy of the experience? In this way, I think a clarification could be effected by recalling the distinction between the first level of Lonergan's theory of consciousness (presentations) and the second level (understanding) and applying that as a clarification to Shusterman's concern. This enables one to account for the absorption in the aesthetic encounter, and then subsequently to reflect on the question for intelligence, "Why was I absorbed in that encounter?" If there is a "certain meaning or style," as Shusterman puts it, in the experience, we have argued that it is to be accounted for by elemental meaning – a term to be applied after reflecting upon the experience.

In scholastic terminology, with respect to the question of beauty this is to ask, "What is the nature of beauty?" To address this question, in the next chapter I will draw on the three principal features of beauty as described by Aquinas: radiance or clarity (*claritas*), due proportion (*debita proportio*) or harmony (*consonantia*), and integrity (*integritas*) or wholeness (*ST*, 1.39.8).

Finally, the third axis Shusterman identifies is: To what extent is aesthetic experience understood as a distinct experience, and to what extent can it be expanded to include other human experiences? This inclination to preserve and expand the notion of aesthetic experience has its roots in the work of the American pragmatist John Dewey, from whom Shusterman takes some of his own inspiration. Dewey not only emphasizes aesthetic experience as a distinct and robust feature in the overall horizon of human experiences, but he also tries to expand the notion, seeking to free aesthetic experience from the narrow confines of museum art.[52] He states: "The task is to restore continuity between the refined and intensified forms of experience that are works of art and the everyday events, doings, and sufferings that are universally recognized to constitute experience."[53] While aesthetic experience takes centre stage in Dewey's philosophy of art, he is unable to account sufficiently for the relationship between aesthetic experience as such and its effects on other aspects of human living.

In the previous chapter, I discussed Lonergan's distinction between the aesthetic pattern and the dramatic pattern of experience, where, concerning the latter, he emphasizes that our first work of art is our own living. Hence, the clue to a resolution of the legacy of Dewey's dilemma can be clarified in terms of the polymorphic nature of human consciousness. In chapter 8 I will argue that the unrestricted desire for beauty certainly is manifested creatively in works of art, but it is manifest as well in the creative impulse of the human spirit in every aspect of life, whether that be bringing a creative harmony to ordinary living or in the sharing of love between two lovers.

The Sensible and Intellectual Perception and Apprehension of Beauty

In this chapter we have been discussing the notion of aesthetic experience and arguing that it occurs in a distinctive pattern, when consciousness is not instrumentalized in the biological, practical, or intellectual patterns of experience. Still, one needs to distinguish between beauty as an ontological notion and beauty as an aesthetic notion. It will principally be the articulation of the former that enables one to move beyond the belief that beauty is just in the eye of the beholder and claim that it is a fundamental property of being. However, there is obviously a sense in which aesthetic experiences of beauty vary. One also has to allow for personal preferences, cultural differences, and differences in talent, educational background, conation, and the extent of aesthetic differentiation to account for variances in taste and aesthetic pleasure.

In terms of differentiation, artists do not just move in and out of the aesthetic pattern of experience randomly; more deliberately, they live in the world of colour, patterns, and symbols in such a way that their sensitivity towards aesthetic perception is heightened. They can identify various colours in a leaf, for example, where the untrained eye sees only a single colour. This heightened sensitivity predisposes them to aesthetic apprehension.

Likewise, art critics are able to identify beautiful works of art insofar as their training in the history and methods of artistic expression guide their aesthetic judgments. As Jacques Maritain states, "the better informed the mind is ... the better it is prepared to receive."[54] It follows that the more individuals in a society are educated in the appreciation of the arts, the more the society will be able to identify and contemplate aesthetic value.

Second, there is the question concerning whether or not the perception creates the beautiful object. For Lonergan, following St Thomas, the apprehension of beauty in perception would not create the object as beautiful. Rather, the perception is an apprehension of "the shining forth of being, with its fullness, radiance and harmony" (AB, 31). However, for Lonergan there is a sense in which one must dispose oneself to receiving the beautiful, that is, insofar as one does not allow the instrumentalization of the other differentiations of consciousness that stem from one's prior choices to crowd out the possibility of aesthetic perception, one can perceive it.

Third, there is the question of whether beauty pertains specifically to sensitive apprehension or whether it can pertain to the intellect. On this account I would agree with Maurer that "[o]ur perception of the beautiful is also intellectual" (AB, 31). Our knowledge is gained through the senses, and in this way the intellect grasps the intelligible form in the data as mediated through the senses. Maurer's account of Aquinas's philosophy of mind is quite harmonious with Lonergan's: "The mind (or rather the person endowed with the mind) sees and understands, and by transcending the sensible, can come to know and delight in the purely intelligible, but only with great effort and always through the mediations of the senses" (*AB*, 31). "The external senses perceive this world and the internal senses, like the imagination and the *sensus communis*, bring together data furnished by them and offer objects to the penetrating gaze of the intellect" (*AB*, 32). The intellect grasps the splendour of the form so that there is a sense in which the intellect can delight in the clarity of ideas grasped in the act of understanding. The understanding itself is a grasp of clarity, but one subject to a fuller affirmation in judgment, and this judgment might make the difference between whether something is truly beautiful or simply kitsch.

Fourth, is it necessary to claim with Aquinas that the visual and auditory senses are more conducive to the apprehension of beauty? This question was never addressed by Lonergan, but I suggest, as I pointed out in chapter 2, that Aquinas's view is based on how knowledge occurs in the intellect: the senses of sight and hearing allow for the quickest supply of data into which insight can occur. I suspect that Lonergan would be sympathetic to Aquinas on this matter, which we can understand in Maurer's terms: "St. Thomas finds the reason for this in the fact that sight and hearing are the most knowledgeable of the senses; they are more closely associated with the mind than the other senses as avenues of knowledge. The other senses are better adapted to serve the biological needs" (*AB*, 33).

More recently however, such *ocularcentrism* (one could also say *auditory-centrism*) has been called into question by at least one leading Finnish architect, Juhani Pallasmaa, in her book *The Eyes of the Skin: Architecture and the Senses*.[55] She is on the frontier of her field in arguing that the tactile sense is an essential ingredient in the architectural experience.

For Lonergan, the intellect grasps through insight the unity or relations in the data, and the data can be supplied by all five senses. Therefore, there is no reason to preclude the other three senses (touch, taste, and smell) from aesthetic pleasure. It is often a combination of these five senses that to greater or lesser degrees, and depending on the context, participate in the aesthetic experience. However, Lonergan would, I think, agree with Aquinas that sight and hearing are more readily conducive to aesthetic apprehension, but not exclusively so.

Aesthetic Experience and the Sublime

A persistent and ongoing problem in contemporary aesthetics, one intimately related to the loss of beauty, is the question of the sublime: How are beauty and sublimity related? Are they two sides of the same coin? Are they dialectically opposed? More recently in philosophy there is a tendency to separate the experience of beauty from the experience of the sublime. The latter involves feelings of awe, horror, and even terror, and these experiences can be inextricably intertwined with aesthetic experiences in nature, making it at times difficult to distinguish between experiences of the beautiful and the sublime.

A Brief History of the Sublime

The sublime is a notion that is not easy to pin down. The experience of awe, speechlessness, overwhelming power in the face of nature, the awareness of our human diminutiveness in the face of magnanimity, incomparableness: these are just some of the phrases used to describe the experience of the sublime. Rhetoricians, philosophers, religious phenomenologists, poets, and others have approached the experience of the sublime from their individual perspectives. In the American abstract painter Barnett Baruch Newman (1905–1970), for example, there is an attempt to express the speechless experience of the sublime in art.

The idea of the sublime has its roots in ancient philosophy but does not appear in more modern philosophy until the eighteenth century. The author of *On the Sublime*, a work often attributed to Longinus around the first century CE, used the sublime in order to enrich and revive the art of rhetoric. Here it refers to a persuasive device, an orator's technique of evoking the affectivity of the audience by shocking them. Longinus departed from the formalistic techniques of his predecessors, which presumed that rhetorical skill can be mastered through the application of technique alone. While Longinus respected the use of skill in the rhetorical arena, he felt the most powerful persuasion occurs to the extent that one can evoke an emotive response – a response that cannot be put into words, leaving the audience speechless: "[F]or Longinus the electric shock of sublimity is all."[56] The use of the sublime is an attempt to move the audience in a way in which cool, reasonable delivery cannot.

In the eighteenth century, interest in the notion of the sublime was revived due in large part to the translation of Longinus' work. Three philosophers, independent of each other, traversed the Swiss Alps and had and recorded similar experiences of simultaneous beauty and terrible awe: John Dennis (1657–1734), Joseph Addison (1672–1719), and

Anthony Ashly Cooper, the Third Earl of Shaftsbury (1671–1713). The treacherous yet captivating landscape of the Alps provided them with an emotive basis that they found a language for in Longinus's treatise, allowing them to articulate their ambiguous experience of nature.

Cooper's contribution to the discussion is noteworthy. He laboured to preserve aesthetic value in an age characterized by increasing aesthetic relativism and scientific reductionism. He also began to articulate the experience of sublimity in the context of religious experience. Marjorie Hope Nicholson characterizes it in the following way: "To Shaftesbury the true 'Sublime' was not a rhetorical principle. Its source was not in style, but in God and in the manifestations of Deity in the superabundance and diversity of His cosmic and terrestrial works."[57]

His later influence, although perhaps indirectly, on German romantic philosophy is noteworthy, especially on German *Religionsgeschicte*. Rudolf Otto's *Das Heilige* (1917) offers a paradigmatic phenomenological description of the beautiful and sublime intertwined in the *mysterium tremendum et fascinans*.[58] The *tremendum* speaks to the terrifying nature of the Holy relative to the diminutiveness of the one who experiences it, and the *fascinans* speaks more to the enthrallingly beautiful aspect of the encounter. Although the sublime is "fascinating" as well, as we will see, this is usually from a safer distance and in retrospect, in reflecting upon the experience.

Such "religious" experiences of the sublime are reflected in English Romanticism as, for example, in the poetry of William Wordsworth. While crossing the Swiss Alps as well, Wordsworth records the following lines to capture the experience:

The immeasurable height
Of woods decaying, never to be decayed,
The stationary blasts of water-falls,
And everywhere along the hollow rent
Winds thwarting winds, bewildered and forlorn,
The torrents shooting from the clear blue sky,
The rocks that muttered close upon our ears,
Black drizzling crags that spake by the way-side
As if a voice were in them, the sick sight
And giddy prospect of the raving stream,
The unfettered clouds and regions of the heavens,
Tumult and peace, the darkness and the light
Were all workings of one mind, the features

Of the same face, blossoms upon one tree,
Characters of the great Apocalypse,
The types and symbols of Eternity,
Of first and last, and midst, and without end. (lines 556–72)[59]

Shaftsbury initiated a further development in the idea of the sublime in which the emphasis is less on the sublime in religious experience than on the opposition between the beautiful and the sublime. For Shaftsbury the experience of the beautiful and the sublime could coincide in a transformative encounter. By contrast, for Edmund Burke (1729–1797) the sublime and the beautiful are incompatible. His treatise A *Philosophical Enquiry into the Origin of Our Ideas of the Sublime and Beautiful* (1757) sought to differentiate between beauty and sublimity in terms of the subject's experience. Influenced by the philosophies of his day, he associated pleasure with the experience of beauty and pain with the experience of the sublime. Moreover, he associated the sublime with *the large* and the beautiful with *the small*:

The sublime, which is the cause of the former [admiration – respect], always dwells on great objects, and terrible; the latter [the beautiful] on small ones, and pleasing; we submit to what we admire, but we love what submits to us; in one case we are forced, in the other we are flattered, into compliance. In short, the ideas of the sublime and the beautiful stand on foundations so different, that it is hard, I had almost said impossible, to think of reconciling them in the same subject, without considerably lessening the effect of the one or the other upon the passions. So that, attending to their quantity, beautiful objects are comparatively small.[60]

The difference between the effects of the sublime and the beautiful are reflected in Burke's anthropology of the sexes, where he associates the characteristics of the sublime with authoritarian male behaviour and of the beautiful with that of female behaviour:

The authority of a father, so useful to our well-being, and so justly venerable upon all accounts, hinders us from having that entire love for him that we have for our mothers, where the parental authority is almost melted down into the mother's fondness and indulgence. But we generally have a great love for our grandfathers, in whom this authority is removed a degree from us, and where the weakness of age mellows it into something of a feminine partiality.[61]

Of course, feminist philosophers such as Bonnie Mann criticize this notion for its genderizing and stereotyping. According to her, Burke's attitude is indicative of the modernist tradition of the sublime that "dichotomizes ... the notions of the beautiful and the sublime." She states that for the modernists "[t]he two notions were deeply entangled with the norms of idealized European femininity and masculinity."[62] Still, the question remains whether a genderizing of aesthetics is solely the product of patriarchy, that is, whether such genderizing should be ruled out *tout court* on that basis. There is a similar genderizing of aesthetics that occurs in the traditional worldview of the Diné (Navajo) notion of beauty, although genderizing in that context does not necessarily relate to the beautiful and the sublime.[63]

For Immanuel Kant, the sublime is the "absolutely great," the "great beyond all comparison."[64] The experience of the sublime occurs in the encounter of our own limitation in the face of the immensity of nature, but at the same time in our awareness of a "nonsensual standard" of the rational faculty's superiority over nature.[65]

He distinguishes between two aspects of the sublime: the mathematical and the dynamic. The mathematically sublime comprises those experiences where imagination reaches its limit in the use of reason. Reason can grasp the magnitudes that imagination (as dependent on sensitivity) is incapable of apprehending. Kant states: "But because there is in our imagination a striving toward infinite progress and in our reason a claim for absolute totality, regarded as a real idea, therefore this very inadequateness for that idea in our faculty for estimating the magnitude of things of sense excites in us the feeling of a supersensible reality."[66] For example, reason affirms the existence of countless stars, but trying to imagine those numbers is overwhelming. The experience of the mathematically sublime is mixed with pleasure and displeasure. Pleasure arises out of respect for or awe of the experience of grasping reason's superiority over nature, while displeasure results from experiencing the limitations of the imagination.

The dynamic sublime refers to the experiences of "exciting fear" one encounters in the power of nature. This, however, occurs from a safe vantage point and simultaneously involves the realization of reason's superiority over even the magnitude of nature.[67] Kant describes it in the following way: "the irresistibility of its might, while making us recognize our own [physical] impotence, considered as beings of nature, discloses to us a faculty of judging independently of and a superiority over nature, on which is based a kind of self-preservation entirely different from that which can be attacked and brought into danger by external nature."[68]

The displeasure that occurs in the experience of the dynamically sublime arises from the awareness of one's impotence and limitation in the face of the magnitude of nature. However, the pleasure, albeit from a safe distance, arises from the awareness of one's superiority over nature through the power of reason.

In addition to distinguishing two types of sublime experiences, Kant grounds the sublime within the individual consciousness. He states: "Sublimity, therefore, does not reside in anything of nature, but only in the mind."[69] Again, the sublime is "the state of mind produced by a certain representation" and "not the object."[70]

With Arthur Schopenhauer, we regain the possibility of beauty and sublimity coinciding in the experiences of the subject if we assume, as Lonergan does, that consciousness can flow in various patterns and also interpenetrate. This would account for Schopenhauer's treatment of the sublime. He categorizes the different degrees or experiences of both the sublime and the beautiful in order to distinguish the two but also to show how they can coincide. He illustrates the difference by reference to the example of a landscape with changing weather conditions.[71]

The "lowest" or mildest degree of the sublime, he argues, is captured by the image of a lonely landscape with no human life or running water, desolate but still and with the presence of plants, trees, and some animal life. Stripping away the plants and animals and leaving the stark desert landscape with its "naked rocks" would manifest the sublime properly for Schopenhauer. Add to this a fierce storm and one has even a more powerful sense of the sublime. He states: "Our dependence, our strife with hostile nature, our will broken in the conflict, now appears visibly before our eyes."

As this storm grows even more intense, threatening the individual's life, the sublime is manifested in its strongest form: "This is the complete impression of the sublime," he states. "Hence, [one] obtains a glimpse of a power beyond all comparison, superior to the individual threatening it with annihilation." The important thing to notice in Schopenhauer's example is that the experience of the strength of the sublime is proportionate to the increasingly life-threatening conditions. This gives us a clue as to how this might be construed in terms of intentional consciousness – a matter I will return to below.

Since the resurgence in the eighteenth century there has been little reflection on the sublime until its recent adoption by postmodern thinkers. Postmodernism has appropriated the sublime in ways that avoid the rationalist tendencies of the Enlightenment. Philip Shaw states: "As far as sublimity is concerned, whilst postmodernism retains the Romantic feeling for the vast and the unlimited, it no longer seeks to temper this feeling through reference to a higher faculty. The postmodern condition therefore lays stress on the inability of art or reason to bring the vast and the unlimited to account."[72] The postmodernist appreciates the sublime as an alternative to all-powerful reason, therefore preserving an ineffable unlimited feature of existence.

Jean François Lyotard (1924–1998) takes Kant's mathematic sublime as a point of departure and emphasizes the unrepresentationality of the sublime. He sees this in the art world exemplified by the minimalist abstract work of Barnett Baruch Newman. Newman's work can seem simple at first, but it aims to draw the observer into the experience. Gazing at one of his works can result in frustration as the observer's mind demands forms from the canvas but instead has to be satisfied with a single "zip" running down the painting vertically or horizontally. No doubt this appeals to the postmodern sensibility because of its indeterminancy – an inability to answer the question "what" and forcing the observer to be content with "is." The sublime is "now" – the *is* happening rather than the *what is* happening. In this way "we maintain the specificity of the event and respond with openness to the challenge of its radical indeterminacy."[73] Lyotard states: "Newman's now which is no more than a now is a stranger to consciousness and cannot be constituted by it. Rather, it is what dismantles consciousness, it is what consciousness cannot formulate, and even what consciousness forgets in order to constitute itself."[74]

There is an anxiety or fear because the *is* happening cannot be formulated in terms of a *what is* happening. However, at the same time the experience is pleasurable because the moment, the now (i.e., the *is*), continues to happen. The dissonance between the *is* and the *what is* signals the "awareness of a possible ontological void."[75]

The theme of the sublime as an unrepresentational void occurs as well in the work of Jacques Lacan (1901–1981). He was influenced by Freudian analysis and appropriates the sublime into the psychological defence of sublimation. With respect to the latter, the sublime refers to the "Thing" that comprises the unrepresentional core of the subject. This wordless void is expressed through the psychological mechanism of sublimation, perhaps in creative works of art or other behaviours of creative expression.[76]

In this chapter, I do not plan to engage the postmodern appropriation of the sublime, which may have more to do with what Lonergan means by self-presence, but will instead focus on a clue Schopenhauer provides on the question. This can be done without adopting the latter's metaphysics of form and will.

The Sublime as Experienced

I argued in chapter 4 that the separation between Kierkegaard's aesthetic, ethical, and religious spheres can be addressed by their appropriation into various patterns, differentiations, and transformations of consciousness. Similarly, in trying to distinguish the aesthetic experience of beauty from that of the sublime, and relate the two, I turn again to the difference as understood within the intentional consciousness of the subject.

Schopenhauer's example of the varying degrees of treacherous landscape gives an important clue to my thesis. Leaving Schopenhauer's metaphysics of will and idea aside, one can glean from his examples the movement of two distinct patterns of consciousness that Lonergan identifies in *Insight* and of which we have spoken previously.

Recall that Lonergan identifies the biological pattern of experience, which he defines as "a set of intelligible relations that link together sequences of sensations, memories, images, conations, emotions, and bodily movements; and to name the pattern biological is simply to affirm that the sequences converge upon terminal activities of intussusception, or reproduction, or, when negative in scope, self-preservation" (*IN*, 206). The biological pattern is operative with respect to self-preservation, such as the human nervous system's instinctive fight-flight response when imminent danger is sensed.

In contrast, there is a further aesthetic pattern of experience that "slips beyond the confines of serious-minded biological purpose" and enables one to experience a twofold freedom from the "drag" of the biological pattern and the "weary constraints" of the intellectual pattern.[77] It is in this pattern, I argued above, that one is able to create and contemplate beauty.

Schopenhauer's degrees of the sublime in the example given above illustrate from the subject's point of view the blended flows of the patterns of consciousness in an experience of sublimity. I would argue that the difference between an experience of beauty and an experience of the sublime concerns the degree to which the aesthetic experience and biological patterns are blended. The aesthetic pattern is a response in the subject conducive to creativity, participation, and reflection upon beauty. The sublime pertains to the extent to which one's response is determined by the biological pattern of experience for self-preservation responding to an external threat. In the experience of the sublime, from the point of view of the subject's intentional conscious experience, there is a blend in greater or lesser degrees with the aesthetic and the biological patterns. For example, tornados are fascinating to observe, even aesthetically so in their own way, but not from a dangerously close range.

To elaborate further: in terms of the observer's consciousness, the sublime is experienced in what Lonergan would call a blend of the biological and aesthetic patterns of experience when, for example, the subject experiences the overwhelming power of nature and is conscious within those moments of a powerlessness in the face of it. The experience of beauty per se occurs more strictly in the aesthetic pattern of experience where one apprehends aesthetically pleasing forms but does not feel one's life is in jeopardy, or at least is not conscious of the power of the "object" in question to threaten one's life. For example, a person can enjoy a painting or professional photograph of a panther and appreciate the beauty of the animal, but that experience of beauty may be quite different in a zoo where the person is separated by a pane of glass as the panther paces back and forth, and even more so if he or she comes across a panther face-to-face in the jungle. When one meets a panther face-to-face, the biological pattern dominates as one's fight-flight mechanism takes hold. The differences in these experiences of the panther are based on the different degrees of blendedness of the biological patterns and aesthetic patterns. This view accounts for Wordworth's experiences as well as those of the three eighteenth-century philosophers in their traverse across the Swiss Alps, who were at times overwhelmed by the dangers they encountered.[78]

So what is the sublime? It depends on the context and the subject's patterned experiences during that context. Insofar as the biological pattern blends with the aesthetic pattern but does not dominate, the experience may be beautifully sublime. Insofar as the biological blends with the intellectual pattern, one may experience sublime curiosity, as Thales did, gazing at the wonder of the stars. Insofar as the biological pattern blends with the religious pattern, one experiences the *mysterium tremendum et fascinans* of the Holy, which, as it did of Moses, demands us to observe the holy ground. In each of these examples, insofar as the biological pattern does not dominate or, to use Kant's characterization, one is at a "safe distance," one can contemplate the sublimity of existence. However, insofar as the biological pattern dominates and one feels threatened, one may flee in horror, fearing oblivion.

Conclusion

We have been addressing the topic of aesthetic experience in Lonergan's philosophy in the context of the post-Kantian subjectivization of such experiences.

If beauty is pleasing when apprehended, then in aesthetic experience pleasure is accounted for in part through the liberation of the subject from the instrumentalization of consciousness. However, there is a further aspect of the pleasure, a significance and surplus of meaning perceived in the senses, apprehended by the intellect, and stirring one's affectivity.

In addition to pleasurable experiences, there are experiences of horror and terror. Hence aesthetic experience must also reckon with the question of the sublime. I have argued the latter is an experience arising to the extent that the aesthetic and biological patterns interpenetrate in response to a perceived threat to the individual.

Admittedly, our endeavours have been more suggestive than exhaustive, but hopefully provocative enough in their implications to illustrate Lonergan's potential contribution to the recovery of beauty. We proceed in the next chapter to clarify the conditions of beauty as grasped by the intellect.

6 The Intelligibility of Beauty

Beauty is self-transcendence expressed through the sensible.

– B. Lonergan

Beauty is grounded in form.

– Armand Maurer

In this chapter we will explore the nature of beauty, using the second level of Lonergan's theory of consciousness as a hermeneutic guide, not only in order to delimit our discussion, but also to prepare for a fuller discussion of aesthetic judgments in the next chapter. Specifically, I address how beauty would be conceived in Lonergan's philosophy at the second level of operations, understanding. Recall from. chapter 1 that this level pertains to intelligibility. In other words, what is grasped in the act of understanding is the intelligible unity in the data or the relations among the data. I will relate this to the intelligibility of beauty by borrowing from the work of Aquinas's conditions of beauty as *integritas-perfectio* (integrity-wholeness), *consonantia-debita proportio* (harmony–due proportion), and *claritas-splendor* (clarity, radiance-brightness).

Recall from chapter 2 that Aquinas has no systematic treatment of beauty. He did not treat beauty as a transcendental in *De Veritate*, his most systematic account of the transcendentals. However, Franz Kovach has argued that he incorporates it later, as evidenced by Thomas's commentary on Pseudo-Dionysus. Recall as well from chapter 2 the comment by Mark D. Jordan: "Such scattered remarks must be treated, not as fragments of an accidentally missing whole, but as specimens of a variegated language that might have been reworked by Thomas into a single account."[1]

These three aspects of beauty can be identified in an analogous manner in forms grasped by the intellect in the sensitive presentations. In keeping with Aquinas's claim that beauty pertains to formal causality, this correlates with Lonergan's second level of cognitional operations, understanding. The act of understanding grasps the intelligibility (*species*) immanent in the data, and this usually occurs in response to the question "What is it?" Insight grasps the intelligible unity in the data or the unity of relations among the data.

Aquinas is speaking broadly about beauty in a philosophical way that pertains to all beings that exist. As we have seen, beauty is also pleasing when it is apprehended, so at the level of understanding this means that we delight in the intelligible ordering of the data that the act of understanding brings when it grasps the intelligible unity in the sensitive data or the relations among the data, one that is delightful, as exemplified in the dramatic instance of Archimedes's cry "Eureka!" (see *IN*, 27–8).

However, for Lonergan at the level of understanding intelligibility is only formal and not actual – it is subject to the further criteria in the act of judgment. It should be noted, therefore, that the content that understanding grasps is not a being but a principle of being. Likewise, potency, form, and act are not beings but principles of being. If beauty is a transcendental then formal intelligibility can at best be a principle of beauty. To have a true and real being, act is required. Equally, it should follow, to have an instance of beauty, act is required. Again, I have reserved this issue for a later chapter on aesthetic judgments, and so we limit our application here to formal causality as a principle of beauty. I will attempt to illustrate this application by referencing Aquinas's three principles of beauty as analogously applied to a contemporary theory of architecture.

Finally, these signifiers of beauty – integrity, clarity, proportion/harmony, and pleasure – can be applied analogously to the notion of beauty in the generic sense. There is a more narrow aesthetic notion of beauty of which beautiful objects in nature and the created beauty of human beings are subdivisions. In the aesthetic encounter with natural and created beauty, I suspect beauty is grasped more frequently in a receptive way than as the fruit of inquiry.[2] In other words, usually people find themselves struck by beautiful scenes or objects, often being taken by surprise. Less often do people ask themselves, "Is this or that beautiful?"

In order to bring this into contemporary perspective, I will demonstrate how Aquinas's three characteristics of beauty are corroborated by a contemporary theory of architecture put forth by Christopher Alexander. He asks: What makes beautiful architecture beautiful? or, to put it in the words of Aquinas, what makes it pleasing? Alexander does not use these terms per se, but rather talks about the *life* that beautiful architecture radiates.

He proposes fifteen characteristics of beautiful architecture, which I will argue embody Aquinas's three properties in a more complex way. I will then attempt to articulate the intelligibility of beauty from Lonergan's perspective, drawing upon the second level of operations in his theory of consciousness in light of Aquinas's aesthetic principles.

Beauty and Architecture: The Example of Christopher Alexander

"I am interested in one question above all," says architect Christopher Alexander, "how to make beautiful buildings." He insists, "I am interested only in *real* beauty," unlike other architects who have "given up the making of real beauty" and by "implication, even given it up as an attainable ideal."[3] Alexander spent thirty-five years thinking through the confusion of the "modern mentality," which he says harks back to Descartes – the "mechanist-rationalist world-picture" (*PL*, 7). He admits his Cambridge education did not prepare him to identify and implement principles of beauty. He had to construct "a coherent view of order," one that dealt "honestly with the nature of beauty" (*PL*, 15).

Alexander derived fifteen principles of beautiful architecture that are often also identifiable in nature. What he means by "order" will be described in these fifteen principles, but he is clear that it includes harmony and wholeness. "The order itself – that order which exists in a leaf, in the Ise shrine, in the yellow tower or in a Mozart symphony, or in a beautiful tea bowl – a harmonious coherence which fills us and touches us .... it is *this* harmony, this aspect of order" (*PL*, 15). The principles he espouses will enable one to discriminate the various degrees of harmony and wholeness in architecture (*PL*, 17).

What is less clear, as we shall see, is the role of clarity, although I will argue that it is implicit within his fifteen principles. He does speak about the degree of life in nature and in architecture, which refers to the "plus" of meaning that one apprehends in beautiful phenomena (*PL*, 17). I suspect that "clarity," as Aquinas understands the term, would be an essential component in the life of a structure. And whereas Alexander here uses the term "life" metaphorically, I take to connote the presence of beauty mediated through the object, just as splendour does for the form in Aquinas.

Alexander's Fifteen principles

Alexander states: "For twenty years, I spent two or three hours a day looking at pairs of things – buildings, tiles, stones, windows, carpets, figures ... comparing them and asking myself: *Which one has more life? And then asking: What are the common features of the examples that have most life?*" (*PL*, 144; emphasis added). From this exercise he identified the following fifteen common elements: (1) strong centres, (2) levels of scale, (3) boundaries, (4) alternating repetition, (5) positive space, (6) good shape, (7) local symmetries, (8) deep interlock and ambiguity, (9) contrast, (10) gradients, (11) roughness, (12) echoes, (13) the void, (14) simplicity, (15) not-separateness.

I have listed them in the sequence that he originally catalogued them with one exception: I have put "strong centres" first, because Alexander came to discover that all fifteen properties bring objects to life precisely because they either pertained directly to or highlighted the centres. These centres are loci for the wholeness of objects and bring them to life. In other words, centres are integral, holding the various parts together. With respect to beautiful objects, strong centres are fundamental to beauty. This does not mean that the centre is located at the physical midpoint of the object; rather, strong centres provide a "center of attention or center of focus," be that in a symmetry with other centres or in geometric interplay and location of the centre (*PL*, 152). An object with a strong centre can also contain other smaller centres that when properly proportioned bring attention to the centre. Centers become important in the planning of public spaces such as urban complexes and university campuses.

The principle of *levels of scale* was Alexander's first discovery when he began his empirical collection of data. Objects can contain centres of various sizes. If the harmony between the centres is well proportioned, then these centres give the object its unity and harmony. Levels of scale are effective when "each center gives life to the next one"

(*PL*, 146). Commenting on a sketch of a woman's back by Henri Matisse, which Alexander feels demonstrates the principle par excellence, he states: "The range of scale forms a continuum which ties the drawing and makes it whole. This gives the drawing its life" (*PL*, 146).

On *boundaries* Alexander states, "Early in my studies I noticed that living centers are often – nearly always – formed and strengthened by boundaries" (*PL*, 158). Clear boundaries marking each of the levels of scale are important to delineate the centres. They "intensify the center which is bounded," thereby bringing attention to it. A strong boundary further "unites the center which is being bounded with the world beyond the boundary." The purpose of the boundary is to unite, separate, and intensify the bounded centre. The essential ingredient is the relation of the boundary to the bounded centre: "the boundary needs to be of the same order of magnitude as the center which is being bounded" (*PL*, 159). In general, large boundaries, such as those surrounding the door of a gothic cathedral, are most effective. In addition, the boundaries themselves are more effective when they are large enough to have centres as well. One can think of the decorative boundaries that highlight ancient manuscripts. Large boundaries with centres are "needed to establish the interlock and connection, coupled with separation" (*PL*, 161).

The boundary is a pervasive principle that applies even to the boundary itself: "every part, at every level, has a boundary which is a thing in its own right. This includes the boundaries themselves" (*PL*, 162). For example, think of columns that align arcades that have a large capital and base bounding the columns. While Alexander does not explicitly highlight this point, presumably the boundaries contribute to the decorative function of architecture as well and, with the contrast between strong boundaries and their bounded centres, produce plays of light that affect the clarity.

"Centers intensify other centers by repeating" (*PL*, 165). By this Alexander refers to *alternating repetition*. However, the repetition should not be simple or banal, but should alternate in a way similar to many phenomena of nature and produce harmonies that accentuate the whole. Alternating repetition as manifested in a glade of woodland ferns or in the patterns of a Japanese rake garden promotes life, whereas brute repetition is in most cases mechanical and banal. Alternating repetition speaks to the various flows of "all elements in that it is inexact, as in the waves in the sea. It is also best characterized by oscillation." This include the spaces between the centres (*PL*, 170). The repetition works best when subtly and gracefully implemented, as in a Matisse cut-paper of a nude woman (*PL*, 171–2).

Positive spaces between centres are used to highlight the centres in a harmonious way rather than being randomly created. Alexander states: "The definition of positive space is straightforward: every single part of space has positive shape as a center. There are no amorphous meaningless leftovers. Every shape is a strong center, and every space is made up in such a way that it only has strong centers in its space, nothing else besides" (*PL*, 176). In nature, the ripening kernels of corn-on-the-cob create positive spaces. Again, in a blue paper-cut nude by Matisse, the cut spaces harmoniously come to life. Positive space takes into consideration the whole space, whereas in poorer designs, "in order to give an entity good shape, the background space where it lies sometimes has leftover shape, or no shape at all. In the case of living design there is never any leftover space" (*PL*, 176).

A *good shape* "is a center which is made up of powerful intense centers, which have good shape themselves" (*PL*, 179–81). If this sounds like a circular definition it is because this obvious characteristic of beautiful objects has been one of the most difficult for Alexander to specify. Objects with good shapes are often constructed with smaller shapes based on simple geometric objects (triangles, rhombuses, squares, circles) rather than on "amorphous blobs." To further delineate good shape he identifies some common features: a good shape involves (1) a high degree of internal symmetries, (2) bilateral symmetry (almost always), and (3) a well-marked centre (not necessarily at the geometric middle); (4) the spaces it creates next to it are also positive (positive space); (5) it is very strongly distinct from what surrounds it; (6) it is relatively compact (not exceeding a 1:4 ratio); and (7) it has closure, a feeling of being closed and complete (*PL*, 183).

The arch of a wooden Japanese temple shrine, the exotic sail of an Egyptian boat, and the carved head of a Greek horse are hailed as examples of good shape. In contrast, the design of the Copenhagen police headquarters is judged as a "caricature" of good shape. In the strong examples, the integrity of the object is clearly identified and its centres harmoniously interplay.

Concerning the next principle, *local symmetries*, Alexander states, "perfect symmetry is often a mark of death in things." In fact, what makes things beautiful for Alexander is not so much the overall symmetry of an object but the presence of minor symmetries or numerous local centres that hold "within limited pieces of the design, leaving the whole to be organic, flexible, adapted to the site" (*PL*, 187). Local symmetries create coherence and proportion in ways that others do not. In fact, a series of experiments led Alexander to two basic conclusions: (1) there is a basic agreement on the effect of local symmetries on an object, and (2) the more local symmetries, the more life is present in the object. This is because the local symmetries act like an adhesive: "local symmetries provide a glue which binds the field of centers, thus making centers more coherent" (*PL*, 194). Alexander mentions the plan for the fourteenth-century Alhambra fortress/palace in Granada, Spain, as a strong example. He also refers to a row of canal houses in Amsterdam as demonstrating local symmetries (*PL*, 194).

The next principle Alexander identifies is *deep interlock and ambiguity*. He notes that "living structures contain some form of interlock: situations where centers are 'hooked' into their surroundings" (*PL*, 195). As a result, the centre is entangled or enmeshed with its surroundings, thus promoting a deeper unity within the work as a whole but also between the various centres. According to Alexander, the following exemplify this principle: the tile work of a sixteenth-century Tabriz Mosque, the deep interlock of a wooden dovetail beam, the stone interlocking of an ancient Incan wall, and the effective volume interlock of an arcade or square.

Next, the principle of *contrast* "creates differentiation, and allows differentiation" (*PL*, 203). Opposites enable the centres to be distinguished: "every center is made of discernable opposites, and intensified when the not-center, against which it is opposed, is clarified, and itself becomes a center" (*PL*, 200). The contrast can take a variety of forms using colours, patterns, or even contrasting materials. The role of contrast is not just aesthetic but functional, allowing one to distinguish between varying objects. The black-and-white-striped surface of a Persian bowl, the contrast in a Shaker school room, or the façade of Tuscan church are used as positive examples of contrast.

Gradients, variations of textual or ornate patterns in aesthetic objects, occur commonly in nature and in traditional folk art. However, in modern times, particularly in architecture, this principle has been lost due to the "naïve forms of standardization, mass production and regulation of sizes" (*PL*, 208). Alexander states the following about gradients:

> In something which has life, there are graded fields of variation throughout the whole, often moving from the center to the boundary, or from the boundary to the center. Indeed, gradients are essentially and necessarily

connected to the existence of a living center. Almost always the strengthened field-like character of the center is caused, in part, by the fact that an
organization of smaller centers creates gradients which "point to" some
new and larger virtual center. Sometimes the arrows and gradients set up
in the field give the center its primary strength. (*PL*, 207)

Gradients function as smaller centres contributing to larger centres either by highlighting them or by participating in them. Gradients assist the transition between centres as well, and they lend to the "inner
wholeness" of the object – the lack of which lends to a "mechanical"
structure (*PL*, 207). These gradients are created through the varying
sizes, spacing, intensity, and character that can be created through use
of changing light, windows, and structural heights (*PL*, 205). "A true
gradient requires that the morphology of elements – walls, columns,
roofs, windows, eaves, openings, doors, stairs – are able to exhibit sustained and gradual change of size and character, as one moves through
the environment, or through the building" (*PL*, 209). Among various
examples he mentions are the gradients forming the towers of the
Golden Gate Bridge, the façade of the Doge's Palace in Venice, the roof
of a Norwegian stave church, and the varying ridges in the glass surface of a Persian vase.

Concerning the next principle, *roughness*, Alexander states: "Things
which have real life always have a certain ease, a morphological roughness" (*PL*, 210). Alexander is not referring to roughness as a result
of shoddy craftsmanship but that which contributes to the harmony
and wholeness of an object. Nor should one attribute the charm of
the roughness to its being handmade: "Roughness can never be consciously or deliberately created. Then it is merely contrived" (*PL*, 211).
Roughness is created by "egolessness," a product of "no will." The creator of the beautifully hewn object achieves roughness by letting go,
by a free release of intention. Alexander references a Persian bowl with
hand-painted designs, the handcrafted tiles in a Kairouan mosque, and
carefully fitted stonework.

The principle of *echoes* is a difficult one to articulate. It concerns the
harmony of the object, how the different features coalesce in some kind
of family resemblance. This element is hard to pin down, but Alexander suggests that it often arises in relation to the angles in a particular
object. "Echoes, as far as I can tell, depend on the angles, and families
of angles, which are prevalent in the design" (*PL*, 218).

He chooses dramatic examples to illustrate the point. Perhaps sur-
prisingly, he contrasts an eclectic façade of a building by Michelangelo
with a Turkish prayer carpet. With due recognition of the former's great
paintings and sculptures, Alexander describes Michelangelo's architecture as a "hopeless hodgepodge," a "salad of motifs and elements"
producing "disharmony". This is because the array of "squares, circles,
broken circles, triangles" are placed in such a way that there is no cohe-
sive order. In contrast, the ornate Islamic prayer carpet with all its various motifs and multiple angles has "a single guiding feeling" (PL, 219).
In another example the Thyangboche monastery of Mount Everest illustrates the principle of echoes in the way its bilevel roof blends in
with the mountainous surroundings. The echoes in the structure itself
blend in with the scenery in a harmonious way.

The void, a space of emptiness, is an important feature in beautiful
objects. He states: "In the most profound centers which have perfect
wholeness, there is at the heart a void which is like water, infinite in
depth, surrounded by and contrasted with the clutter of the stuff and
the fabric all around it" (PL, 222). In another dramatic example, Alexander contrasts the empty space in a mosque to that of a floor plan
for a 1970s office building where there is "endless clutter and buzz.
Nothing is still." "The difference between the two cannot be fobbed
off as a difference between a religious building and an office building"
(PL, 224). In modern buildings, due to the dictates of fiscal efficiency,
this principle is often neglected. The result is the loss of a space conducive to psychological harmony. "There cannot be all fuss; there must
be a balance of calm and emptiness with the delirious detail" (PL, 225).
Vermeer's Woman in Blue Reading a Letter exemplifies this principle, as
the white spaces behind the figure reading the letter function as a void
to create a "quiet forcefulness to the woman" (PL, 225).

Next Alexander addresses the principles of simplicity and inner calm.
"The quality comes about when everything unnecessary is removed"
(PL, 226). He conjoins simplicity with inner calm because one can have
one without the other. For example, he references the design of a couple
of stylized Italian chairs from the 1920s, which he claims have simplicity but not inner calm. In contrast, he refers to a Shaker cabinet as an
example that manifests both simplicity and inner calm. "It has to do
with a certain slowness, majesty, quietness" (PL, 226).

Simplicity is achieved by removing those centres that are not "actively supporting other centers." This is not to say that complexity

cannot include simplicity and inner calm; he considers a carved Norwegian dragon to be "very complex but it still has inner calm" (228).
While simplicity and inner calm are essential to the wholeness of an
object, they pertain primarily to its harmony.

"The last of these properties – ultimately perhaps the most significant –
is *not-separateness*, connectedness" (*PL*, 230; emphasis added). One
might wonder why Alexander does not just use the word "unity."
But that term, he suggests, speaks to the actual object, whereas "not-
separateness" refers to the relationship, at least in the case of architecture, of the object with its environment, giving as examples a stone
path that blends in with the earth and a village that blends into the surrounding landscape. The principle also applies in painting, as he points
out by instancing Gauguin's *By the Sea*. "What not-separateness means,
quite simply, is that we experience a living whole as being at one with
the world, and not separate from it – according to its degree of wholeness" (*PL*, 230).

In contrast, objects, particularly architectural structures that deliberately stand out, manifest the egotism of the authors: he specifically
cites the "X" house in New York City, of which he says it's almost as
if it cries: "Look at me, look at me, look how beautiful I am" (*PL*, 231).

Not-separateness assists in capturing the harmony of an object but
also accentuates the integrity of the object, albeit in its harmonious relations with other objects. Alexander states that it "ties the whole together
inside itself, which never allows one part to be too proud, to stand out
too sharply against the next, but assures that each part melts into its
neighbors, just as the whole melts into its neighbors, too" (*PL*, 233).

Alexander's Principles and Aquinas

In this section I will consider Alexander's fifteen principles in light of
Aquinas's three conditions of beauty, arguing that Alexander's work
offers a corroboration of Aquinas's theory as well as identifying some
principles for the formal intelligibility of beauty.

Some clarifications are in order before proceeding. First, Alexander is concerned primarily with the beauty of human creations – with
aesthetic beauty. By contrast, Aquinas is concerned more generically
with transcendental beauty, of which human-created beauty is one
small part. While Alexander is not concerned with philosophical or
transcendental beauty, he does draw his principles from their analogy
with natural beauty. Second, it should be kept in mind that Alexander

Table 1.

Consonantia (harmony, proportion)	Integritas (integrity, wholeness)	Claritas (clarity, luminosity)
Levels of scale	Strong centres	Contrast
Alternating repetition	Boundaries	Positive space
Local symmetries	Good shape	
Deep interlock and ambiguity	The void	
Gradients	Not-separateness	
Roughness		
Echoes		
Simplicity/inner calm		

is carrying out a descriptive or phenomenological method in contrast to Aquinas's more generic and philosophical account.

It is possible to correlate Alexander's fifteen principles with Aquinas's three characteristics of beauty as represented in table 1:

Claritas. Alexander's thought does not make explicit use of clarity (light/radiance/luminosity/colour) as a category. Alexander's explicit focus lies more on integrity/wholeness and on harmony/proportion. This is to not say that matching Alexander's fifteen principles under Aquinas's three categories will not invite overlap, since within the fifteen principles themselves there is overlap. Gradients, for example, give texture to an object, which is analogous to Aquinas's principle of harmony, but the placing and spacing of the gradients can affect the complexion of an object in terms of the plays of light on its surface.

While clarity is a fundamental condition of beauty for Aquinas, it carries over analogously to aesthetic beauty. In terms of Alexander's principles, clarity is most explicit with respect to contrast. "Life cannot occur without differentiation ... The difference between opposites gives birth to *something*" (*PL*, 200). This is mainly due to the essential contrast between light and darkness such as is exemplified in the Creation story in Genesis when light and dark are separated. While Alexander's notion of contrast does not simply involve the opposites of light and darkness, still these are "practically necessary" for "cognitive clarity" (*PL*, 203). And effective use of contrast also affects the harmony and proportion of an object. Glare, for example, is not effective contrast because it is disproportionate (*PL*, 203). Effective contrast creates unity in an object through the complementarity of opposites and various centres in an object (*PL*, 202).

While the contrast between light and darkness is a foundational principle of aesthetic creativity, another principle, positive space, can emphasize or reveal clarity. Consider again to Alexander's reference to Matisse's cut-out of the *Blue Nude* as an example of positive space. This use of positive space obviously overlaps with the principle of contrast. With this Matisse work, as well as other types of occurrences, the gaps in the cut-out of the nude woman function as contrast and in this way invoke what for Aquinas would be the principle of clarity.

However, more often positive space supports the integrity and wholeness of an object. When effectively implemented, Alexander emphasizes, there is no "left over space" in an object. Positive space creates a "whole" (*PL*, 176). It also supports and highlights the shape of an object. It can function as a boundary, and by so doing, strengthen the integrity of objects.

Finally, while positive space reveals contrast and so contributes to the clarity of an object, conversely contrast can also add to the harmony of an object, as in the case of a musical score.

Integrity/Wholeness

Wholeness is an essential ingredient of beautiful architecture. Keep in mind, however, that Alexander's emphases on harmony and proportion overlap in many of the examples. I have correlated five of Alexander's principles with Aquinas's principle of integrity/wholeness: strong centres, boundaries, good shape, the void, and not-separateness. Alexander repeatedly emphasizes wholeness as an essential ingredient of life-giving architecture.

Recall that strong centres are one of the foundational principles as "key elements of all wholeness." They are "possibly the most important feature of a thing" (*PL*, 151). Strong centres are foundational to the unity of an object, bringing it together into a whole. Just as for Aquinas, the lack of integrity is an incompleteness or ugliness; similarly, the lack of strong centres can leave an object looking fragmented or amorphous.

A centre can singly be the main focus of an object or the object can consist of a number of smaller centres, which either complement other, larger centres or work together in their own synthesis. However, the purpose of strong centres is to help the object cohere, to integrate the various aspects of the object.

Boundaries are also important to the integrity of an object. Their purpose is twofold: to clearly bound the centres and to delineate where an object ends and where another objects begin. In Thomistic language we can say that the boundaries help to make the object visibly intelligible. For Alexander, the optimum is to have boundaries that highlight the centres at every level of scale and also demarcate the object from other objects: "Then the boundary both unites and separates" (*PL*, 159). Conversely, a lack of boundaries risks a lack of integrity to the object, making it amorphous or unsettling to the eye. However, it should be noted that the secondary function of boundaries, especially when they bound the various centres at every scale of the object, is to produce harmony. So this is another instance where Aquinas's principles of harmony and integrity would overlap.

It goes without saying that good shape is a feature of a well-proportioned object. Good shape occurs by virtue of the strong position and proportion of various centres and basic geometrical shapes. More fundamentally, however, good shape reflects the integrity or wholeness of an object. One of the qualities that good shape reveals is "a feeling of being closed, or complete" (*PL*, 183). Conversely, the lack of good shape reflects a lack of wholeness, as demonstrated for example, in Alexander's description of a futuristic chair as an "amorphous mass" (*PL*, 181).

While the void also contributes to the harmony of an object, it is essential to the integrity of an object, to its feeling of wholeness, although, as with positive space, under certain circumstances it can affect the clarity of an object when it functions as contrast. He states: "The fact that the void does not exist so often now, in the buildings and objects we have in our environment, is the result of a general disturbance in our capacity to make wholeness, which is not a necessary functional property of office buildings" (*PL*, 225). The void is a psychological requirement for the integrity of an object: "A living structure can't be all detail. The buzz diffuses itself, and destroys its own structure. The calm [created by the void] is needed to alleviate the buzz" (*PL*, 225).

Strictly speaking, not-separateness pertains to the relation of the object with its surrounding objects, and so one might be tempted to associate it with Aquinas's notion of harmony. In this way, the principle accentuates the relationship between the object and its surroundings, such as the pueblo-style adobe houses in New Mexico that blend in and harmonize with the landscape. However, as we stated above, it is also concerned with the wholeness or integrity of an object. Its harmony with the surrounding environment accentuates an object's integrity: "What not-separateness means, quite simply, is that we experience a living whole as being at one with the world, and not separate from it – according to its degree of wholeness" (*PL*, 230). It harmonizes with its environment "without giving up its character or its personality" (231). Hence, this principle pertains in a quasi way to Aquinas's principle of integrity: in order for an object to harmonize with its environment, it must maintain its integrity; otherwise it would dissolve into its surroundings or, conversely, set itself apart in an obnoxious manner.

Finally, we have been speaking of not-separateness in terms of an object *ad extra* in its relations with its surroundings. However, the principle applies equally to an object *ad intra*, in terms of the not-separateness of the various centres that make up an object. Here, the principle of integrity is more of a factor, because the weakness of the centres on the one hand, or their disproportion on the other, leads to a fragmentation rather than a unity within the object.

Harmony/Proportion

When we view Alexander's principles in terms of Aquinas's three characteristics of beauty, it might seem that harmony or good proportion can be invoked the most, but in reality, the matter is perhaps more complicated. Not-separateness, for example, refers to the overall unity of an object and would therefore pertain to wholeness. However, insofar as the object blends in with its surrounding environment, the not-separateness reflects the harmony of the overall scope of the object in relation to its surroundings. Nevertheless, levels of scale, alternating repetition, positive space, local symmetries, deep interlock and ambiguity, gradients, roughness, echoes, and simplicity/inner calm all contribute to the overall harmony of an object, although they overlap with the principles involving the integrity of the object, and in many instances they are dependent upon and make use of clarity to provide the harmony.

Effective levels of scale rest on the strength of the proportion between the different scales: "centers need a rather well-ordered range of sizes and scales in order to help each other most practically" (*PL*, 149). Lack of levels of scale or a disproportionate range of scales within an object places homogeneity, and thus harmony, at risk. Ideally, "the levels of scale create a field effect which *creates* centers: it is not only true that the small centers intensify the large ones, but the large centers also intensify the small ones. The property creates life [i.e., beauty] by helping centers to intensify each other" (*PL*, 149).

Alexander's principle of alternating repetition is closely related to levels of scale in the ability to reveal harmony. "Centers intensify other centers by repeating" (*PL*, 165). However, as noted above, the repeating is best when it alternates, like ocean waves. This is in contrast to the metronomic repetition of windows in many modern city buildings, for example, where the guiding principle is utilitarian – form following function. The alternating patterns of repetition, especially when slow and subtle, create a consonance among other centres. The repetition alternates in the spaces between the units rather than just the units themselves: "The life comes about only when alternating wholes are beautifully and subtly proportioned and differentiated" (*PL*, 171). Hence we have the clearest statement by Alexander that alternating repetition is best when it is harmonious and well proportioned.

Local symmetries act as a sort of "glue" that unifies the various centres in an object. Hence *prima facie* they have the function of cohering within the object and likewise assisting to reveal its wholeness, that is, its integrity. More fundamentally, local symmetries reveal the harmony within an object, giving it life: "Thus, the real binding force, which symmetry contributes to the formation of life, is not overall symmetry of a building, but in the binding together and local symmetry of smaller centers in the whole" (*PL*, 188). They are essential even though subtle in effect, for "they control the way in which a pattern is seen and the way it works" (*PL*, 192).

Deep interlock and ambiguity fundamentally serve to unify an object, but practically they reveal the harmony within an object. The various centres in an object are most effective when the centres "interpenetrate" with their surroundings either through overlap (interlock) or blending (ambiguity). This creates "a center enmeshed with its surroundings, and therefore achieves more life" (*PL*, 195). The interpenetration of the various centres reveals harmony of the object, such as in the interlocking of logs in a log cabin or in decorative tile work.

Gradients also reflect the harmony within an object. "Gradients must arise in the world when the world is in *harmony* [emphasis added] with itself, simply because conditions vary." To give life, gradients possess a "certain softness." They occur when "[q]ualities vary, slowly, subtly, gradually, across the extent of each thing" (*PL*, 205).

The extent to which the difference between the gradients is well proportioned, gradual, and slow insures that they help to assist in highlighting the various centres within an object, but they may also function as centres themselves. The overall effect of gradients is to reveal harmony, and this will be further effected by the availability and varying degrees of light.

In a similar way, roughness contributes to the harmony of an object. Perhaps the effectiveness of roughness is due to the way that it occurs in nature. Nevertheless, roughness cannot be "superimposed" or "arbitrary"; rather, it "lets the larger order be relaxed, modified according to the demands and constraints which happen locally in different parts of the design" (*PL*, 213–14).

The patterns on a Persian bowl are rough, not because its overall look is handmade, but because the look and placing of the decorations are imprecise and imperfect. Such roughness, according to Alexander, has a direct bearing on the harmony of an object. Of the spacing of the marks on the bowl, he says: "they vary in size, position, orientation, and according to the space formed by neighboring ornaments, and so make the space perfectly harmonious" (*PL*, 210).

Another reflection of harmony in an object is its use of echoes. As we have noted, echoes are difficult to define. They speak to the "family resemblance," a subtle unifying feature in the object among the various centres and patterns. They contribute to the unity of an object, but in such a way as to reflect the harmony and proportion among various centres and patterns. What makes this principle distinct from roughness and gradients is the emphasis on angles: "we see the family resemblance in different parts because they are simply similar in shape, again deriving from the angles" (*PL*, 219). For Alexander, the proportion and harmony between the various angles of an object ensure the life and beauty of an object.

Finally, simplicity and inner calm reflect the harmony and good proportion of an object. This does not mean that the object cannot possess complex patterns, but rather that "anything unnecessary is removed ... all centers that are not supporting other centers are removed" (*PL*, 226). Ornamentation must be proportionate and not overdone, lest the simplicity and inner calm be compromised.

The Intelligibility of Beauty in Lonergan's Theory of Consciousness

Having discussed Aquinas's three characteristics in terms of Alexander's principles of beauty, we are in a position to identify how beauty may be construed at the second level of operations in Lonergan's theory of consciousness, understanding.

For Lonergan, the intellect is propelled by a pure, detached, unrestricted desire to know. This desire to know manifests in a question for intelligence, "What is it?" (*quid sit*) and a question for reflection, "Is it so?" (*an sit*). This unrestricted desire is a transcendental intending for the intelligible, the true, and the real when the query leads to a judgment as a result of a question for reflection. At the level of understanding, the intellect grasps the intelligibility in the data. It is a formal intelligibility at this point subject to the further critical reflection of the question "Is it so?" in the level of judgment. I will address aesthetic judgments of beauty in the next chapter. At this point I limit my analysis to how the notion of beauty can be understood at the second level of operations in Lonergan's philosophy of consciousness, and specifically the grasp of intelligibility in the act of understanding or insight.

For Lonergan, the act of insight is a grasp by the intellect of the intelligible species or idea in the data or of relations among the data. In scholastic terminology, the possible intellect receives the *species impressa* and is actuated with respect to that *species impressa*. This grasp can be the fruit of inquiry, as many of Lonergan's examples in *Insight* demonstrate, and pertain to immanently generated knowing. However, there is also a notion of the grasp of intelligibility when the subject encounters the various communal meanings as learned particularly in the common-sense world.[4] Intelligibility, for Lonergan, is intrinsic rather than extrinsic to being; the intelligibility grasped and affirmed in judgment is "immanent in the reality of proportionate being" (*IN*, 523).

The level of understanding in Lonergan's thought pertains to formal causality, which he calls formal intelligibility. "There is the intelligibility that is known inasmuch as one is understanding; it is the formal intelligibility that is the content of the insight and the dominant element in the consequent set of concepts" (*IN*, 525).

There is a further aspect of intelligibility known as the actual intelligibility. This is the intelligibility that is affirmed in judgment. "It is what is known inasmuch as one grasps the virtually unconditioned; it is the intelligibility of the factual" (*IN*, 525). To have a true and real being, act is required – beyond that of formal intelligibility. Equally, it would seem to follow, to have an instance of beauty, act is required. This intelligibility pertains to transcendental truth, and again we have reserved this treatment for the next chapter.

At the level of understanding we can conceive of the potential grasp of beauty in the following way by applying Aquinas's three principles of beauty in an analogous manner. As formal intelligibility, the content of an insight is structured as such to embody the three principles of integrity, clarity, and proportion.

First, an act of insight grasps the unity in the data. This grasp can be of the unity in the data itself, or a grasp of relations among the data. But in either case the grasp is a unity of heretofore disparate clues or data, which quite likely prompted the query in the first place. Further, the act of insight occurs as the "release from the tension of inquiry." If beauty is pleasing when apprehended, as Aquinas declares, then analogously, at the level of understanding, part of the pleasure of the grasp of intelligibility comes through the release of the tension of inquiry – to encounter the hope of the possibility that one has grasped with the light of one's intellect the unity in the data or unifying relations, and that such intelligibility is potentially to be affirmed in a subsequent act of judgment.

The unifying aspect of the act of understanding is analogous to the principle of integrity – wholeness. Again, the content of the insight grasps a unity or the intelligible relations in the data. And the insight is subject to the subsequent question for reflection, "Is it so?" in the operation of judgment. However, at the level of understanding, the insight has a structuring and ordering effect on the data that unify it and order it for further critical reflection. Formal intelligibility grasps the unity in the data or the unifying relations in the data that is potency and form for actual intelligibility.

Next, the content grasped in the act of understanding insofar as it is an *answer to a question* is proportionate and harmonious with (*debita proportio-consonantia*) the question put to the data. However, two points should be noted. First, insight *rarely* grasps the intelligibility in data in anything like a full or complete way. There is always more to be understood in the data. Again, with understanding one does not arrive at the actual (where, I presume, beauty is to be affirmed) but only at the hypothetical. Second, with respect to a grasp of intelligibility, specifically in cases of immanent intelligibility, there is always an empirical residue in the data that is not pertinent to the specific query – although it may become pertinent in a subsequent query.

Hence, what I am claiming is that the content of the insight is proportionate-harmonious as an answer to the question asked. That is, the act of understanding does not grasp less than what the relevant data present, which would result if one were not attentive to all the pertinent data, nor does it claim too much for the data, as in a grand idea that is but a castle in the air. Rather, the intelligent grasp of the data and the content of that grasp as intelligible are proportionate and harmonious in the manner that the question as asked is harmonious and proportionate to the answer. This presumes, however, that the formal intelligibility is ripe to actual intelligibility. For it could be that in the subsequent act of judgment one discerns that one's idea is indeed a castle in the air. In other words, the analogy I am suggesting here only works if we presume that the formal intelligibility is soon to be determined as actual, and one is looking backwards on the process and asking how beauty can be understood at the level of understanding.

Third, the grasp of intelligibility involves the analogy of clarity or luminosity (*claritas*), both with respect to the power of apprehension and in the medium of apprehension. The power of apprehension is analogous to the light of the intellect. The agent intellect is likened to light, which participates in an eternal light, as capable of grasping intelligibility. The medium of apprehension pertains to the light that renders the content of the data intelligible, the content of the act of understanding, or the idea. It makes the difference between obscurity, as a failed grasp of intelligibility, and the clarity that results in the grasp of intelligibility.

In sum, as formal cause, the intelligibility grasped in an insight contains by way of analogy the three aspects of beauty. In this way we can say that the content of every act of understanding is analogous to beauty or that there is an analogous beauty proportionate to the content of that understanding.

Conclusion

We have endeavoured to articulate the notion of beauty in relation to the second level of Lonergan's theory of consciousness, understanding. The three principles of beauty in Aquinas's thought are present in the realm of aesthetics, at least implicitly, as demonstrated in Christopher Alexander's fifteen principles of beauty. Moreover, they are consonant with the content of the intelligibility grasped in the act of insight. So every proper act of the intellect as a grasp of intelligibility contains aspects that are analogous to beauty. But it is a grasp of intelligibility subject to further affirmation in the notion of judgment to which we now turn.

7 Judgments of Beauty

Is beauty in the eye of the beholder? Or, more precisely, is it *just* in the eye of the beholder? This common-sense adage permeates much of Western thinking about beauty. Philosophically, it reflects a relativism that has seeped into aesthetics and contributed to the loss of beauty. Indeed, it is not unusual these days to find a book on aesthetics that neglects the topic of beauty altogether, as aesthetics has been reduced to sense perception.

In this chapter we will bring Lonergan's theory of judgment to bear upon aesthetic judgments of beauty. This will entail asking the question: How can we understand transcendental beauty in terms of Lonergan's notion of judgment?

In what follows I will discuss beauty in terms of judgments of fact (the third level in his philosophy of consciousness) and judgments of value (the fourth level). More specifically, I will address the fourth level only partially in terms of judgments of value, leaving for the next chapter the fourth level as *decision* per se, as is lived out in creative expression and in contemplation. Lonergan would not separate the topics of value and decision. However, in the wake of Kant's *Critique of Judgment*, aesthetic judgments seem to have acquired a unique epistemological status that straddles both judgments of fact and judgments of value. Therefore, in the attempt to read aesthetic judgments of beauty into Lonergan's philosophy, it will be helpful to address the affirmation of truth and the grasp of value together. In this way, we can also avoid the legacy of Santayana's *The Sense of Beauty*, which presumes judgments of fact to be objective and judgments of value to be subjective.

Recall from an earlier chapter the statement that the transcendentals are convertible. If beauty is a transcendental, one can expect the true and the good to be reflected differently in the content of the two judgments. In Lonergan's judgments of fact, beauty is expressed as true and as existing; in judgments of value, beauty will be apprehended in feelings as value.

Aesthetic Judgments in Kant

We have been using the term "transcendental" to speak of the ontological status of beauty as a property that belongs to every being as existing and as notionally distinct from unity, truth, being, and goodness. This is not to be confused with the use of the term in the Kantian sense to refer to knowledge that is not derived from experience but is a priori within the subject – a move that contributes to the subjectivization of beauty.

Giovanni Sala has clearly identified the sharp differences between Lonergan and Kant all along the line of the latter's epistemology, including sense intuition, *Verstand*, *Vernunft*, and the a priori of the categories. Their respective epistemologies, although similar in some respects, are separated by a great divide between the impossibility of knowing that results from the Kantian epistemological legacy and the recovery of the possibility of knowing in light of Lonergan's endeavour. It is not necessary to repeat here Sala's meticulous and erudite efforts to identify the differences between the two thinkers.[1] It is enough to quote his conclusions: "The Kantian epistemology is highly obscure, fragmentary, and even contradictory. One must disagree with Kant in statement after statement of his analysis of knowledge. The significance of the KRV lies much more in its setting the problem than in its solving the problem."[2] In contrast, Sala concludes regarding Lonergan's *Insight* (which was an attempt to correct the problem that Kant established):

> The merit of *Insight* lies in its having advanced the transcendental analysis begun in the KRV, bringing to light the conditions for the possibility of objective knowledge. This has resulted in a threefold clarification: (1) of the a priori as the conscious-subjective dimension of knowledge, (2) of knowledge as an empirical, intelligent, and rational structure, and (3) of reality as intrinsically intelligible.[3]

To say that Lonergan "advanced transcendental analysis" does not mean that he simply developed Kant's previous initiative. Rather, it is to say that Lonergan corrects and advances it by allowing for the possibility of knowledge. For Lonergan all knowledge is derived from experience as grasped intelligently and reasonably affirmed in the sensible data. Kant may have been correct in the sense that he brings an emphasis to the a priori in human knowledge. However, rather than bringing categories to the object, Lonergan's a priori involves transcendental intending, an unrestricted inquiring with its threefold structure that is isomorphic with the content of those cognitional operations – experience, understanding, and judgment (*IN*, 470–2).

Moreover, according to Lonergan the intention or orientation of human striving for knowledge is transcendental in the sense that it is unrestricted. Each incremental increase in knowledge leads one continually to an ever-expanding horizon of questions in which human beings anticipate answers. Analogously, this sense of transcendental intending applies to goodness and beauty. Morally, we are not content with single acts of goodness, and aesthetically, our favourite music is not enough to quell our aesthetic appetite. Rather, it whets it for further appreciation, not only for further pieces of music, but also for more instances of beauty.

The legacy of the Kantian epistemology from the *Critique of Pure Reason* carries over to the *Critique of Judgment*. Recall Armand Maurer's statement: "The subjectivity of beauty and ugliness is a legacy to modern philosophy from Immanuel Kant" (*AB*, 25). Kant's opening statements in the third critique support Maurer's statement: "The judgment of taste is therefore not a judgment of cognition, and is consequently not logical but aesthetical, by which we understand that whose determining ground can be *no other than subjective*."[4]

How, more precisely, does this thinking occur with Kant? We will narrow our focus to the eclipse of beauty as it emerges in its modern form in the philosophy of this towering philosophical figure rather than tracing the subsequent legacy to postmodernity. Kant's aesthetic judgments cannot be clearly interpreted within the framework of what Lonergan calls judgments of fact (cognitive) and judgments of value (the good). From Lonergan's perspective, Kant situates aesthetic judgments insufficiently between the two types of judgments. The undetermined ontological status of aesthetic judgments in Kant's legacy facilitates the subjectivization of judgments of beauty.

Four Moments of Aesthetic Judgments

Kant's philosophy of judgment ripens in the third critique. He distinguishes between two functions of judgments: (1) determining judgments that involve the sorting of the particular under a universal of an already established concept; and (2) reflective judgments that involve seeking a universal for a particular. The former pertains to the pursuit of scientific inquiry through hypothesizing, testing, analysing, and the like. In contrast, reflective judging pertains to aesthetic judgments, and in particular the beauty of nature.

Kant outlines three categories of aesthetic judgments: judgments of agreeability/disagreeability, judgments of beauty (or taste), and judgments of the sublime. I will focus on the so-called pure judgments of the beautiful, which principally pertain to beauty in nature.

There are four moments comprising an aesthetic judgment of the beautiful in Kant's "Analytic of Aesthetic Judgments." First, judgments of beauty are based in a disinterested feeling of pleasure. The "disinterested" aspect is distinguished by the fact that it neither arises out of nor arouses a desire for the object: "that of taste in the beautiful is alone a disinterested and free satisfaction; for no interest, either of sense or of reason, here forces our assent" (§5). Moreover, aesthetic judgments are unique in important respects from other judgments. They are distinct from simple judgments of agreeability and disagreeability, which do effect a desire for an object. They differ from cognitive or factual judgments based on sensitivity, or what Lonergan would call judgments of fact, because they involve the subject's affectivity in the grasp of intelligibility. They are different from moral judgments, or what Lonergan would call judgments of value, because they do not arise out of a desire either for the moral good or for some practical end.

The second moment in judgments of taste involves a claim to universality. The presumption in a judgment that a certain object is beautiful holds objectively for other individuals, or at least others would or should consider it beautiful. "For the fact of which everyone is conscious that the satisfaction is for him quite disinterested, implies in his judgment a ground of satisfaction for all" (§6). This universality is not based on rules or prescribed principles because Kant does not consider them to be cognitive judgments. However, unlike judgments of fact or other value judgments such as those of pleasure/distaste and moral judgments, which are based on concepts, the judgments of beauty do not fall under concepts, or if they do, it is unclear exactly how they do so. And because they are not under a concept, the cognitive powers for Kant are in free play. "The beautiful is that which pleases universally without [requiring] a concept" (§9). Later, Kant concedes that they fall under "indeterminate concepts," but the meaning of these is itself indeterminate (§57).

The third moment reiterates the difference between aesthetic judgments of beauty and value judgments of the good. Unlike the latter, the former do not involve a desire for an end. However, aesthetic judgments do involve a sense of purpose or importance, which makes them at least analogous to judgments of value. Kant's describes the sense as "the subjective purposiveness in the representation of an object without any purpose" (§11). This sense of "purposiveness" is perceived in the object and in the imagination as it engages the aesthetic object, but it serves no other purpose than aesthetic delight. In sum, "*[b]eauty* is the form of the *purposiveness* of an object, so far as this is perceived in it *without* any *representation of a purpose*" (§17; his emphasis).

The fourth moment refers to the "necessity" involved in aesthetic judgments. "The beautiful is that which without any concept is cognized as the object of a *necessary* satisfaction" (§22). There is a necessary relation between myself as perceiver and the beautiful "object" that I perceive as pleasing. This necessity is closely related to the claim to universality wherein I presume that, given the same circumstances, people *would* think the object is beautiful. More precisely, the judgment is exemplary in that it is a judgment that others should corroborate or agree with. "[T]his necessity which is thought in an aesthetical judgment can be called exemplary, i.e. a necessity of the assent of all to a judgment which is regarded as the example of a universal rule that we cannot state" (§18).

In her summary of Kant's aesthetic judgments, Hannah Ginsborg identifies six criticisms raised against Kant's theory regarding judgments of beauty.[5] First, there is a discrepancy concerning the role of feelings of pleasure in an aesthetic judgment. Does the feeling of pleasure precede a judgment or does it follow the judgment? Ginsborg argues that the judgment and the feeling are simultaneous. Second, there is a lack of clarity about the role of the imagination and the role of concepts in understanding. Third, there is uncertainty as to whether the feeling of pleasure has an intentional content. Fourth, what is the precise epistemological status of the claim to agreement in an aesthetic judgment? Is it a judgment of fact or a judgment of value? Fifth, and closely related to the fourth criticism, are aesthetic judgments objective? Finally, what about negative judgments or judgments of ugliness and feelings of revulsion?

These questions raised by Ginsborg and others signal the problems left in the wake of Kant's legacy and his contribution to the philosophical loss of beauty. While I will not be able to address all of these issues,

I hope that many will be addressed in my appropriation of beauty from Lonergan's perspective.

Lonergan and Judgment

Judgments of fact and judgments of value are the same kind of operations in intentional consciousness for Lonergan, insofar as they are both judgments, but they differ in terms of their objects. The object or content of a judgment of fact is the true, while the object or content of judgments of value is the good.[6] The former concern knowledge of facts, and the latter the affirmation and carrying out of the good. The good is always concrete for Lonergan. As concrete, our values are inextricably connected with our decisions, so that our values guide our decisions and our decisions reflect our values.

Here I treat these two types of judgments together because, first, there is an ambiguity in Kant over whether aesthetic judgments are judgments of fact or of value; second, treating them together is necessary, following the tendency of some aesthetic theories such as George Santayana's, to acknowledge the objectivity in judgments of fact but *not* in judgments of value; and third, such treatment is necessary for fleshing out the ontological status of aesthetic judgments from Lonergan's viewpoint.

Judgments of fact. A judgment of fact follows from asking and answering the question for reflection, "Is it so?" A correct judgment demands a grasp of the virtually unconditioned. The question for critical reflection follows naturally from the prior question for intelligence, "What is it?" which pertains to the second level of operations, *understanding*. However, the answers to questions for intelligence give rise to further questions for reflection (*IN*, 106). Whereas the former are concerned with intelligibility, the latter are concerned with *existence* or reality. Likewise, answers to questions about existence or reality comprise part of the third level of consciousness, which Lonergan terms *rational* consciousness or *judgment*. Again, the question pertinent to making a judgment asks singularly, "Is it so?" As such, it is answered in the affirmative or the negative, and to answer in the affirmative means that what is affirmed exists independently of the subject. Napoleon's defeat at Waterloo is a historical fact that exists independently of whether or not I believe it to be true.

Within the pattern of operations in intentional consciousness, a judgment occurs in the following way: (1) from the further unfolding of the desire to know, the question "Is it so?" emerges from the content of the preceding cognitional operations; (2) reflection ensues wherein one marshals and weighs the evidence, asking whether the conditions for making a judgment have been fulfilled; (3) reflection culminates in an additional insight in which one grasps that the conditions to render a judgment have been fulfilled (a grasp of the virtually unconditioned); (4) the judgment follows (*IN*, 305–6).[7]

The objective veracity of the judgment rests upon what Lonergan calls a grasp of the *virtually unconditioned*. If the conditions for judgment have been fulfilled, then a judgment ought to follow. The conditions have been fulfilled if there are no further relevant questions concerning the query. On the other hand, the subject should refrain from making a judgment if the necessary conditions have *not* been fulfilled – if there are further relevant questions to ask.

Nevertheless, the influence of bias on human thoughts and actions can result in biased or unreasonable judgments, as when one makes a rash judgment before acquiring sufficient evidence, or when the conditions for judgment are fulfilled yet one refrains from judging. The precept Lonergan prescribes for making proper judgments of fact is "Be reasonable," which means faithfully asking all the relevant questions regarding a given query (*MT*, 231).

The level of judgment is the foundation for Lonergan's epistemology in that he claims that when one reaches a grasp of the virtually unconditioned, one *knows*. Likewise, he distinguishes three types of objectivity, each corresponding to a the level of experience, understanding, or judgment:

> There is an experiential objectivity in the givenness of the data of sense and of the data of consciousness. But such experiential objectivity is not the one and only ingredient in human knowing. The process of inquiry, investigation, reflection, coming to judge is governed throughout by exigences of human intelligence and human reasonableness; it is these exigences that, in part, are formulated in logics and methodologies; and they are in their own way no less decisive than experiential objectivity in the genesis and progress of human knowing. Finally, there is a third, terminal, or absolute type of objectivity, that comes to the fore when we judge, when we distinguish sharply between what we feel, what we imagine, what we think, what seems to be so and, on the other hand, what is so.[8]

In short, knowing in the strict sense occurs when a judgment is arrived at that *expresses* a virtually unconditioned. This is based on one's prior attentiveness to the data and the intelligent grasp of unity or relations in the data. Then one attains absolute objectivity. In other words, one attains absolute objectivity when one has acknowledged with respect to a specific inquiry that all the conditions have been fulfilled, and all questions regarding that inquiry have been sufficiently answered. When this occurs one attains a grasp of the virtually unconditioned through what Lonergan calls a *reflective insight*. The virtually unconditioned rests upon the ground of a formally unconditioned (i.e., God), which has no conditions whatever and is the ground of truth, reality, necessity, and objectivity.[9]

A judgment within the human subject that reaches absolute objectivity has a twofold significance. On the one hand, subjectivity is transcended and the judgment refers to existence independent of the subject. On the other hand, because the content of a judgment is an objective fact, the subject is personally committed to the judgment. That is, a person is accountable for his or her judgments: "Good judgment is a personal commitment."[10]

The level of judgment is also the foundation for metaphysics in that, in a strict sense, what one knows when one reaches a grasp of the virtually unconditioned in judgment is *being* and being(s) *exists* (IN, 381). More specifically, Lonergan refers to what is known through the compound of experiencing, understanding, and judgment as *proportionate being* (IN, 416). Moreover, whereas in Lonergan's epistemology the ground of the virtually unconditioned is the formally unconditioned, in his metaphysics he refers to the ground of all other beings as the primary being (IN, 681–2).

Although Lonergan does not address the topic of judgments of beauty, we can ask whether a judgment of beauty would be a judgment of fact or of value. Since the transcendentals are convertible, we might suppose that a judgment that something is beautiful, although a judgment of value, is also true – that a particular thing *is* beautiful. Alternatively, because the apprehension of beauty involves the affectivity of the subject, as we will see below, and since for Lonergan values are often apprehended in feelings, an aesthetic judgment of beauty would be a value judgment in his philosophy. I will say more about this below, for now confining my attention to how one understands truth in judgments of beauty.

If I judge truly that something is beautiful, it is indeed a fact that it is beautiful, but not because, as Kant would suggest, everyone ought to think it is beautiful. While it may be true that these judgments to a certain extent depend on an individual's sociocultural background, education, conation, talent, habits, and the like, so that some are more qualified than others to grasp certain types of beauty, it remains the case that the content of the aesthetic judgment of beauty is a *fact* by virtue of its convertibility with the true.

But what is someone grasping in terms of the virtually uncondi-tioned when he or she judges an "object" to be beautiful? In short, the intelligibility grasped in insight is affirmed in the judgment. One is grasping intellectually the content of harmony, wholeness, and clarity in the aesthetic content to greater or lesser degrees. I argued this in the previous chapter, that the intelligible, as grasped by the intellect, involves the light of the intellect to grasp it. The content of the insight is proportionate to the grasp of intelligibility to be affirmed in judgment, as well as a unity in the data that reflects the integrity or the wholeness in the intelligible content grasped and affirmed. This interpretation is consonant with Lonergan's own statement that "[a]esthetic value is the realization of the intelligible in the sensible" (*TE*, 37). With this latter acknowledgment of aesthetic value, let us turn to judgments of value in Lonergan's thought.

Judgments of value. Once one arrives at knowledge, which culminates in the act of judgment, further questions arise concerning deliberation, value, and decision. That is, one asks questions such as "Is it valuable?" or "What is to be done about it?" This constitutes the fourth level of in-tentional consciousness, which Lonergan calls *rational self-consciousness* or the level of *decision*. At this level one intends the truly good as op-posed to the apparently good. One decides and acts in accordance with what one knows and affirms to be valuable.

In many instances of affirmations or judgments of value, there is, first, an *apprehension* of possible value that occurs in one's affectivity. Specifi-cally, such apprehension and affirmation of value reflects the feelings associated with a drive towards moral self-transcendence rather than those associated with the satisfaction of the sensible appetites (*MT*, 37–8). Values are inextricably linked to one's decisions and actions, so that deliberation involves the clarification and affirmation of values, which in turn leads to responsible decisions. Accordingly, the precept for the fourth level is to *be responsible*. That is, one must make decisions based upon a careful weighing of the evidence while adhering to the short- and long-term effects of those decisions.

In *Topics in Education*, Lonergan distinguished between *aesthetic* value, *ethical* value, and *religious* value in his discussion of the context of the good. Value comprises the third component in his discussion of the structure of the good (particular goods, good of order, and value), where he states: "Aesthetic value is the realization of the intelligible in the sensible". It reflects the clarity that shines through when the good of order is functioning efficiently and effectively. The apprehension of aesthetic value "enables people to apprehend the human good on its profoundest level or, on the contrary, to sense something wrong, in a very immediate fashion [e.g., ugliness]" (*TE*, 37).

Second, there is ethical value. This pertains to the moral development within the subject as an "autonomous, responsible, free" individual (*TE*, 37). The subject chooses the responsible course of action, which, as Lonergan explains in *Method in Theology*, means that one considers both long- and short-term implications of one's decisions. Third, there is religious value, where reason and will are subordinate to a transcendent Other.

Given my argument in chapter 4 about transposing Kierkegaard's existential spheres, it seems quite probable that Lonergan appropriated those spheres as the three values, aesthetic, ethical, and religious, in his discussion of the structure of the good in *Topics*. However, after *Topics*, Lonergan does not treat these values in the same way. In *Method in Theology* he develops the preferential scale of values, consisting in vital, social, cultural, personal, and religious, which does not directly address aesthetic value.

Further, Lonergan retains the threefold structure of the human good as particular goods, the good of order, and values (*MT*, 48), although he now refers to the final contents in that structure as "terminal values," which are "the values that are chosen; true instances of the particular good, a true good of order, a true scale of preferences regarding values and satisfactions" (*MT*, 51). He ascribes the good of order under social values insofar as it "conditions the vital values for the whole community" (*MT*, 31). However, the question remains: in *Method and Theology* what happens to the distinction he made in *Topics in Education* between the aesthetic, ethical, and the religious? Does he abandon it?

I would argue that *religious value* is retained intact in his discussion of religious value, and he also includes a chapter on religion in the same book that expands upon the topic (*MT*, 32). The notion of ethical value per se, as it is referred to in *Topics in Education*, is expanded to include the entire scale of values insofar as a person chooses values over satisfactions. "The judgment of value, then, is itself a reality in the moral order. By it the subject moves beyond pure and simple knowing. By it the subject is constituting himself as proximately capable of moral self-transcendence, of benevolence and beneficence, of true loving" (*MT*, 37). Ethical values are also now understood in the broader context of originating values. The values are expressed in "authentic persons achieving self-transcendence by their good choices" (*MT*, 51). In sum, in *Method*, ethical value is broadened and expanded in chapter 2 on the human good, and it is to be understood more broadly in terms of the transcendental notion of value. Religious value is expanded on in the chapter on religion and is construed as *the dynamic state of being-in-love in an unrestricted manner*.

What, then, after *Topics*, did Lonergan do with aesthetic values? As far as I know, he does not again refer to the category. This does not of course mean that he disregards it. Robert Doran suggests that it later becomes part of cultural values in the preferential scale in *Method in Theology*.[11] There is a precedent for this if one considers Lonergan's earlier reflections on cultural value. Recall that in *Method in Theology* he refers to cultural values by declaring that human beings "do not live on bread alone" (*MT*, 32). By this he means that vital and social values alone are not enough to fulfil the human being's transcendental intending towards the good. Food, for example, is a vital value, but the culinary arts are something more than that – an aesthetic plus, so to speak, rather than simply the consuming of vital values. This impulse to create speaks to the human desire to express creativity and to beautify the ordinary aspects of life, a topic we return to in chapter 8.

Lonergan's supplement to his *De Verbo Incarnato*, titled *De Redemptione*, although written before *Method in Theology*, contains an early formulation and expansion upon what he will eventually describe as cultural values.[12] Lonergan includes the example of literature among other types of knowledge, but he does not explicitly treat art or aesthetic meaning in the section.[13]

While it is true that aesthetic value would pertain to the fine arts and the role of art in a society at the level of the cultural good, and while there may be a sense in which aesthetic value is subsumed into cultural values, still Lonergan seems to have something a little different in mind when speaking of it in *Topics in Education*. Let us turn again to his quote at length:

> Aesthetic value is the realization of the intelligible in the sensible: when the good of order of a society is transparent, when it shines through the products of that society, the actions of its members, its structure of interdependence, the status and personality of the persons participating in

the order. You can recognize a happy home or a happy community. The
good of order can be transparent in all the things made, all the actions
performed, in the habits and the institutions. It strikes the eye ... It is aesthetic value, then, that enables people to apprehend the human good on
its profoundest level or, on the contrary, to sense something wrong, in a
very immediate fashion, an immediate apprehension that we may later be
able to analyze a bit; for the moment it is enough to recognize its existence.
(*TE*, 37)

The *claritas* of transparency shines through attentive, intelligent, reasonable, and responsible functioning individuals and the institutions
they constitute. This notion of aesthetic value is very close to that of
Bonaventure, who declared that beauty is, in the words of Maritain,
"the splendour of all the transcendental together."[14]

While *Topics in Education* is an early attempt by Lonergan to address
the notion of value, it seems, interestingly, that he is directly transposing the three existential spheres of Kierkegaard into the three classes of
value, aesthetic, moral, and religious. However, when one looks at Lonergan's treatment of value in *Method in Theology*, especially chapter 2
on the human good, there is no mention of aesthetic value. Rather than
saying that Lonergan abandoned the three values after *Topics in Education* (1957), it is probably more accurate to say that he fleshes out and
broadens them in the three foreground chapters in *Method in Theology*:
chapters 2 ("The Human Good"), 3 ("Meaning" – where he treats artistic meaning), and 4 ("Religion"). I suspect that in Lonergan's mind he
is addressing aesthetic value in terms of artistic meaning in the third
chapter on meaning. In his lectures in Dublin (1971) on method in theology, he indicates that aesthetic value, that is, beauty, is treated in the
third chapter on meaning.[15]

If this is the case, then an important hermeneutic comes to light. Lonergan's encounter with Kierkegaard's three existential spheres takes
three steps: (1) his initial encounter with Kierkegaard as evidenced in
Insight (*IN*, 647); (2) his transposition of Kierkegaard's three existential
spheres into the threefold structure of the good in *Topics in Education*:
aesthetic, ethical, and religious value; and (3) his further broadening of
those spheres into the three foreground chapters in *Method in Theology*.

Nevertheless, Lonergan's lack of treatment of aesthetic judgments remains a lacuna in his philosophy. In order to see how he might address
the topic, let us look more closely at the notion of value and its relation
to affectivity as argued in chapter 2 of *Method*.

Value in Method in Theology

The notion of value is a transcendental one, so that just as "the transcendental notions of the intelligible, the true, the real head for a complete intelligibility, all truth, the real in its every part and aspect, so the transcendental notion of the good heads for a goodness that is beyond criticism" (*MT*, 36). I will make six preliminary points before summarizing judgments of value per se.

First, there are two types of value judgments for Lonergan: "simple" and "comparative." Simple value judgments "affirm or deny that some *x* is truly or only apparently good." Comparative judgments "compare distinct instances of the truly good to affirm or deny that one is better or more important or more urgent than the other" (*MT*, 36).

Unlike Kant, Lonergan does not include in this notion of judgment the personal preferences such as "intentional responses to such objects as the agreeable or disagreeable, the pleasant or painful, the satisfying or dissatisfying" (*MT*, 38). I suspect there is a sense in which these are judgments in a very limited sense insofar as they are reflections of individual preferences. However, Lonergan is clear that they do not involve a direct grasp of value; in fact, they can interfere with such a grasp, although in some cases personal likes/dislikes can be reflections of personal value.

Hence, a fundamental difference between Kant and Lonergan on judgment comes to the fore. For Kant, there are judgments of the agreeable/disagreeable; for Lonergan, there may be a judgment of fact that someone likes *x* or that one prefers *x* to *y*, but that is not necessarily based on a grasp of value, and so for Lonergan it is not a value judgment per se. Therefore, if we are to transpose this in terms of aesthetic judgments from Lonergan's perspective, we can presume that aesthetic judgments will be simple or comparative but will not involve what Kant refers to as judgments of the agreeable/disagreeable.

Second, Lonergan's notion of *moral conversion* involves the choice of value over satisfactions in cases where an individual is locked into the habituated pattern of choosing satisfactions over value. For example, someone in the habit of eating fast food chooses the immediate satisfaction of its consumption over a more healthy diet. Moral conversion restores one to the ability to choose value over satisfaction (*MT*, 240).

Third, the criterion for a judgment of value is the self-transcending subject in her/his authenticity or inauthenticity. The meaning of the judgment of value is objective: "To say that an affirmative judgment of value is true is to say what objectively is or would be good or better. To say that an affirmative judgment of value is false is to say what objectively is not or would not be good or better" (*MT*, 37).

Fourth, "[j]udgments of value differ in content but not in structure from judgments of fact" (*MT*, 37). In terms of content, judgments of fact declare what is or is not the case, while the content of judgments of value is the good: "one can approve of what does not exist or disapprove of what does" (*MT*, 37). The two do not differ in structure in that both entail a similar criterion and meaning, where by "criterion" Lonergan means they both rely on the transcending subject. This criterion is "cognitive in judgments of fact but is heading towards moral self-transcendence in judgments of value" (*MT*, 37). In terms of meaning, in both types of judgments the content is independent of the subject who judges; although judgments of fact state what is or is not the case – the content is the *true* – and in judgments of value, the content affirms what is truly good or better – the content is the *good*.

Fifth, a judgment of value does not mean that one necessarily follows through with a decision or action: "True judgments of value go beyond merely intentional self-transcendence without reaching the fullness of moral self-transcendence. That fullness is not merely knowing but also doing" (*MT*, 37).

Sixth, "[i]ntermediate between judgments of fact and judgments of value lie apprehensions of value. Such apprehensions are given in feelings" (*MT*, 37). The feelings Lonergan is referring to are not *the unintentional states and trends* or *the intentional responses to objects as agreeable or disagreeable*. Rather, he is talking about the feelings one has that are specific responses to value. One of the values he mentions is beauty: "the ontic value of a person, the qualitative value of beauty, of understanding, truth, of noble deeds, of virtuous acts, of great achievements" (*MT*, 38). This statement indicates that Lonergan considered beauty to be a value and that beauty is apprehended in feelings. He has in mind the more dramatic experiences of affectivity when "we respond with the stirring of our very being when we glimpse the possibility or the actuality of moral self-transcendence" (*MT*, 38).

I suspect the more dramatic instances of the apprehension of value occur in what Lonergan describes as *explicit acts of vertical liberty*: "Then one is responding to the transcendental notion of value, by determining what it would be worth while for one to make of oneself, and what it would be worth while for one to do for one's fellow [human beings]" (*MT*, 40). Lonergan gets this distinction between vertical and horizontal liberty from Joseph de Finance (*MT*, 40),[16] an instance of his habit of gleaning his own insights from the various authors he read. The important issue, however, is his interpretation of de Finance's work: "Horizontal liberty is the exercise of liberty within a determinant horizon and from the basis of a corresponding existential stance. Vertical liberty is the exercise of liberty that selects that stance and the corresponding horizon." He goes on to clarify:

> Such vertical liberty may be implicit: it occurs in responding to the motives that lead one to ever fuller authenticity, or in ignoring such motives and drifting into an ever less authentic selfhood. But it can also be explicit. Then one is responding to the transcendental notion of value ... In such vertical liberty, whether implicit or explicit, are to be found the foundations of the judgments of value that occur. Such judgments are felt to be true or false in so far as they generate a peaceful or uneasy conscience. (*MT*, 40)

This distinction in de Finance, at least as appropriated by Lonergan, is important for understanding the fourth level of operations, decision. When Lonergan treats value he is emphasizing vertical liberty, those decisions that constitute who we are – a gracious person or a thief, for example. In contrast, while not denigrating its importance, he gives less explicit attention to horizontal liberty, those decisions, often reflexive and automatic, that are not self-constituting in the same way although they may be reinforcing a habit. Such habits have their origins in the exercises of vertical liberty, such as when one decides to quit smoking.

Indeed, the exercise of horizontal liberty is constituted and motivated by value as well. If I choose to work eighty hours a week, one can glean from that fact what I value or disvalue. It is also with respect to horizontal liberty that decisions within the practical pattern of experience of getting things done occur. But Lonergan has little to say about horizontal decisions. This is probably due to the fact that he assumes them, and that *Method in Theology* was written later in his career and following a series of health problems, so he wrote the book more rapidly than *Insight* and did not have time to work out the fourth level as systematically as he did the second and third levels in *Insight*. As well, and more practically for pedagogical purposes, the dramatic examples of vertical finality can more easily serve as examples for decisions. Therefore, in the chapter on value Lonergan emphasizes the vertical liberty primarily pertaining to moral beings: "It is by the transcendental notion of value and its expression in a good and an uneasy conscience that [human beings] can develop morally" (*MT*, 41). I will return to this in the next chapter when I deal more deliberately with decision and constitutive meaning with respect to beauty.

Making judgments of value. "Three components unite" in a judgment of value: "knowledge of reality, especially human reality," the "intentional responses to value," and "the initial thrust towards moral self-transcendence constituted by the judgment of value itself" (*MT*, 38).

The interaction between knowledge and values is intimate; a deficiency in the former leads to "moral idealism, i.e. lovely proposals that don't work out and often do more harm than good". Yet knowledge alone is not enough: "moral feelings have to be cultivated, enlightened, strengthened, refined, criticized and pruned of oddities" (*MT*, 38).

Knowledge and moral feeling "head to existential recovery," the realization that one's choices make oneself (*MT*, 38). For Lonergan, this involves personal value because one must face one's personal responsibility. More remotely, the awareness of one's own weaknesses and failings eventually gives rise to the question of God, or religious value.

Finally, Lonergan states that judgments of value occur in different contexts. There is the context of personal and collective choices for values (in the preferential scale) over the merely agreeable/disagreeable. And there is the context of the individual's personal appropriation of his or her social, cultural, and religious belief.[17] The transcendental notion of value orients one towards the proper choice for value by one's reflecting upon one's choices and assessing the data of an easy or uneasy conscience (*MT*, 41).

As we stated above, Lonergan did speak of beauty in reference to value. Since beauty is pleasing to the person when it is apprehended, affectivity plays a role in the grasp of beauty, just as it does, at least most of the time, in judgments of value. However, a judgment of value also presumes that one has a grasp of reality. Let us attempt to articulate how Lonergan might have conceived of aesthetic judgments had he had the time to do so.

Judging Beauty for Lonergan

In this section I will attempt to conceive how aesthetic judgments can be appropriated into Lonergan's philosophy and to outline some of the general forms they would take. First, I will respond to Kant's four moments in aesthetic judgments from the perspective of Lonergan's philosophy. Again, this is not to say that Lonergan is a Kantian, but rather to provide an alternative to the subjectification of beauty that is a legacy of Kant. The alternative is made possible by appropriating a more adequate epistemology that affirms the possibility of human knowing. Second, I will address the question of how beauty manifests differently within the preferential scale of values. Finally, I will suggest three different grasps of aesthetic value based on a recent fresh interpretation of Lonergan's three basic ways of making judgments of value.

A Lonergan Appropriation of Kant's Four Moments

Recall for Kant that *the first moment* of an aesthetic judgment is the experience of the *disinterested feeling of pleasure*. The disinterestedness sets it apart from other feelings that are attached to desire and have a goal. Roger Scruton describes this feature in Kant's thought in the following manner: "I am purely disinterested, abstracting from considerations and attending to the object before me with all desires, interests and goals suspended."[18] Cynthia Freeman further explicates Kant's disinterested feeling: "Beautiful objects do not serve ordinary human purposes, as plates and spoons do. A beautiful rose pleases us, but not because we necessarily want to eat it or even pick it for a flower arrangement. Kant's way of recognizing this was to say that something beautiful has 'purposiveness without a purpose.'"[19] For Lonergan, this "purposiveness" connotes the presence of value, but "purposiveness without a purpose" indicates something beyond moral and practical value and deliberation. In this way the Thomistic insistence on beauty as a formal cause rather than a final cause would perhaps provide a way of understanding the special place of beauty as evidenced when Kant distinguishes aesthetic judgments from moral and practical judgments.

For Lonergan, the grasp of beauty would not arise as a response to a non-intentional state or trend, but would instead be an intentional response in feelings to an apprehension of value in the object. (Recall "the qualitative value of beauty," *MT*, 31.) In other words, it is similar to the distinction C.S. Lewis draws between "Need-pleasures" and "Pleasures of Appreciation." The latter he describes in terms of experiences of beauty that take us by surprise: "They make us feel that something has not merely gratified our senses in fact but claimed our appreciation by right."[20] With beauty, there is nothing "to be done," so to speak, as there is in moral or practical deliberation, save to contemplate the beautiful object for its aesthetic or veracious beauty (as when one contemplates a profound truth). This grasp of qualitative beauty occurs in one's feelings (for the most part), specifically feelings related to self-transcendence that bring to light what we referred to in chapter 5 as *the surplus of meaning* to existence. Recall Lonergan's assertion with respect to aesthetic value that we do not live on bread alone. In other words, we need the surplus of meaning and mystery to enrich life and give us purpose.[21]

Finally, there is another way of viewing the disinterested pleasure in terms of Lonergan's philosophy that is closely related to what we have already stated. The disinterested pleasure is similar to Lonergan's claim regarding freedom from the instrumentality of consciousness that we mentioned in chapter 5. The aesthetic pattern of experience occurs outside of the practical, dramatic, and theoretical patterns of consciousness. In the aesthetic pattern one is not concerned with the "objects" one encounters in terms of their practicality or theoretical or other considerations. In other words, with respect to Lonergan's fourth level of operations, decision, in the aesthetic pattern there is nothing *to be done*. However, as I will address in the next chapter, there is a call from beauty to contemplate it. So there is a sense in which there is a fourth-level operation inextricably linked to the apprehension of aesthetic value, but I believe that a major aspect of the fourth-level operation as such is contemplation.

The other aspect of Kant's first moment we should consider is that he distinguishes judgments of beauty from cognitive judgments (judgments of fact) because they involve one's affectivity. He also distinguishes them from moral judgments (judgments of value) because they do not intend to a certain end as in final causality.

However, as we noted above, for Lonergan judgments of value do involve the subject's affectivity. Therefore, how are we to account for this seemingly special status of aesthetic judgments of beauty? How do we account for these judgments as distinct from judgments of agreeableness/disagreeableness, on the one hand, and from cognitive judgments, on the other? Moreover, how do we account for them as distinct from moral judgments (in the absence of a desired end) although still involving the subject's affectivity?

If we presume that beauty is a transcendental, then for Lonergan a judgment of beauty would be true in the cognitive sense, but at the same time it would be a value judgment: "it exists and it is good that it exists." However, the judgment of value would lead one to a contemplation of the content rather than the need to "do" something, as

Lonergan's fourth-level operations might otherwise imply. So it would appear that the content of an aesthetic judgment is a value ("*X* is beautiful" Or "*X* is more beautiful than *Y*"). However, on the assumption that beauty is a transcendental property of being, beauty reveals the wonder of being. In a word, it is the occasion for contemplative delight, and this delight includes a surplus of meaning that, as we will see in the next chapter, cannot be reduced simply to sensitive delight, although it does not exclude it.

The *second moment* in a judgment of beauty for Kant pertains to the universality of the judgment. Recall Kant's claim: "For the fact of which everyone is conscious that the satisfaction is for him quite disinterested, implies in his judgment a ground of satisfaction for all" human beings (§6). In other words, when one experiences disinterested pleasure, which does not arouse a desire for the object, one can presume that it would be satisfying for all.

The problem with this statement is that it presupposes an epistemological leap that is derived just from one's experience of disinterested pleasure. By contrast, for a Lonerganian interpretation, the content of a judgment of beauty, while notionally distinct, would be convertible with the true and the good. As convertible with the true, it means that one has reached a grasp of the unconditioned; as convertible with the good, it means that the legitimate grasp of value in the judgment is true. For example, I may comment that the *Mona Lisa* is a "plain Jane" while an art critic explains with knowledgeable criteria why it is a masterpiece. After the explanation I am still free to hold the opinion that the painting itself is mediocre, but that opinion says more about my ignorance than about the value of the painting. Again, for Lonergan, a judgment of fact is rooted in a grasp of the virtually unconditioned, while a legitimate grasp of value is convertible with the content of that judgment, so that the judgment that something is beautiful would simultaneously mean it is a true and valuable judgment. One of the main differences between judgments of fact and judgments of value is that values are often grasped in one's affectivity. I can claim that the sunset is beautiful, and it is true that it is beautiful regardless of whether the dozens of people sitting in traffic along side of me are aware of it or not.

Another issue pertaining to the second moment concerns Kant's claim that beauty, particularly in nature, is not grasped by a concept and therefore concerns the free play of imagination. Recall that "[t]he beautiful is that which pleases universally without [requiring] a concept" (§9). Judgments of personal preference, cognitive and moral judgments all invoke concepts, but not so in a judgment of beauty.

As we pointed out above, Giovanni Sala delineates the sharp epistemological differences between Kant and Lonergan. For the latter, knowledge is not a matter of bringing concepts to the data. In an insight, one grasps the intelligibility in the data. The intelligibility is expressed in concepts, but is further subject to the operation of judgment as to whether it is true or not. Then the further question of value arises.

Lonergan would probably agree with Kant that there is a free play of the imagination in the aesthetic encounter, but that free play is the fruit of one's movement *out of* the instrumentation of consciousness from the biological, dramatic-practical, theoretical, and other patterns of consciousness (*IN*, 208)[22] and into an aesthetic pattern where (1) one grasps a surplus of meaning in the data, which may not be easily articulated, and (2) the distinction between the subject and the object is not clearly differentiated – where one fully attends to the beautiful object or scene.

The free play is *not* a result of the fact that the beautiful scene that one adverts to does not fall under a concept; rather, it results from the fact that one has moved out of the "normal" instrumentation of consciousness. This condition liberates the psyche and gives rise to play, spontaneity, creativity that is unencumbered by being patterned by the dramatic-practical, theoretical, and other patterns.[23]

Therefore, I suggest, Kant's claim that a judgment of beauty occurs without coming under a concept so as to give rise to free play of the imagination can be better understood in terms of the spontaneity of one consciousness. This occurs when one moves out of the "normal" patterns of consciousness and into the aesthetic; for example, when one moves out of the "habitual, half-tide of things," to invoke a phrase by Thomas Merton, free of the instrumentation of consciousness.[24] We will see in the next chapter that this requires an advertence to, and even a commitment to, creating and contemplating beauty.

The third moment in Kant's judgment of the beautiful is a clarification of "purposiveness" in an aesthetic judgment, as distinct from a judgment of value. Recall that *"Beauty is the form of the purposiveness of an object, so far as this is perceived in it without any representation of a purpose"* (§17).

This "purposeless purposiveness" is perhaps reminiscent of Aquinas's claim that beauty pertains to formal causality rather than final causality, so that to delight in a beautiful object is to delight in the form of the object, not in the end of the object as such (*ST*, 1.5.4 ad 1). That is, there is no practical or theoretical purpose per se to the aesthetic encounter; there is nothing to do or to be done with the object of the aesthetic encounter – save advert to it, appreciate it, or contemplate it.

It is worth noting that the prominence of utilitarian philosophy in the West contributes to the inability to view beauty in this way. Roger Scruton explains:

> Maybe people have lost their faith in beauty because they have lost their ideals. All there is, they are tempted to think, is the world of appetite. There are no values other than utilitarian ones. Something has a value, if it has a use. And what's the use of beauty? "All art is absolutely useless," wrote Oscar Wilde … For Wilde, beauty was a value higher than usefulness. People need "useless" things even more than they need things for their use. Just think of it, what is the "use" of love? Of friendship? Of worship? None whatsoever. And the same goes for beauty. Our consumer society puts usefulness first, and beauty no more than a side effect. Since art is useless, it doesn't matter what you read, what you look at, or what you listen to.[25]

When one encounters the beautiful, one is aware of a sense that the apprehended object is valuable in and of itself. If one does not advert to the beautiful sunset, for example, there is the sense of a missed opportunity; one should have adverted to it, or at least, it would have been good to advert to it.

As a more contemporary Thomist, Lonergan understands the formal cause to pertain to the intelligible unity in the data while recognizing that the intelligibility is further subject to the level of judgment as existing. The beauty of an object(s) pertains to the intelligible form(s) wherein one apprehends a "purposiveness." In this way a judgment of beauty is like a judgment of value, for one is grasping value in one's affectivity. However, in another way, a judgment of beauty is *not* like a judgment of value, at least strictly speaking: the delight in beauty is not by way of a final cause, as final causes pertain to the good, which for Lonergan is affirmed in judgments of value. Rather, the delight is linked to the formal cause.

It is perhaps this lack of clarity surrounding the judgment of beauty that has led some, such as Étienne Gilson, to conclude that the beautiful is a subdivision of the good. Moreover, such ambiguity gives a clue to how we can conceive of beauty as a transcendental. The special status of beauty as a transcendental to being requires that beauty emphasize a particular aspect of being. What beauty invokes is pleasure or delight, and this pleasure/delight is not to be limited to perception by the senses but also includes intellectual delight, contemplative value, and the general orientation of a person to create and contemplate beauty – in short, to love the beautiful. It is the plus reflected in the subject's whole striving for self-transcendence insofar as that living reflects the intelligible, the true, and the good.

The fourth moment concerns the content of aesthetic apprehension and its feeling of necessity. "The beautiful is that which without any concept is cognized as the object of a necessary satisfaction" (§22). For Kant, the inclusion of pleasure/delight in the aesthetic moment means that the judgment functions as exemplary, that is, that others ought to agree with the judgment. The necessity is not the result of the aesthetic object coming under a concept, or if it is, the concept is indeterminate and therefore not apprehended in a clear way. The claim to universality is felt as necessity but the universal rule for such a claim cannot be articulated (§18).

In contrast, for Lonergan, what Kant means by a grasp of necessity could be understood as a grasp of a realized possibility in a virtually unconditioned affirming the intelligibility grasped in the presentation as true. In the case of a grasp of value, the value as grasped is true. It is possible, however, that one could be in error, in which case the grasp is incomplete or premature and is based on a failure of intelligence rather than the proper use of it in that instance.

The thorny issue is: How does one articulate the conditions, or universal rules, for a grasp of beauty? Some may try to clarify the conditions of beauty in terms of such rules. However, I do not think it is the job of a philosopher to list the specific criteria for aesthetic judgments, especially since there are a multitude of artistic expressions and media. That task belongs to the art critics, who are well acquainted with the particular methodologies of the various media they critique.

In keeping with Lonergan's generalized empirical method (experience, understanding, judgment, decision), which establishes the upper hermeneutic blade in terms of a philosophy of consciousness and leaves it to the specific disciplines to develop their own more precise methodologies, I suggest something analogous is at issue here. The goal of the philosopher of beauty, then, is to identify the general features of the philosophical presence of beauty. I have been doing that in general by dividing the topics of beauty into a philosophy of beauty that would accord with Lonergan's philosophy in terms of aesthetic experience, understanding, judgment, and aesthetic creativity and contemplation (the next chapter). In addition, I have attempted to show how some of the problems in aesthetics, such as those set up by Kierkegaard, or in the treatment of the sublime can be resolved by understanding them in the context of differentiations of consciousness as Lonergan understands them.

For more specific hermeneutics with respect to beauty I adhere to the following principles in Aquinas: (1) beauty is pleasing when apprehended (i.e., to the senses, the intellect, and the affectivity – the whole person); (2) there is a general desire for beauty – "Everyone loves the beautiful"; and (3) the three conditions of beauty lie in the intelligible form(s) insofar as they are integral, clear, and proportionate. The lack of any one of these conditions is a lack of beauty, while the robust presence of each of these is beauty. All told, these can form the general criteria for identifying aesthetic judgments.

Moreover, it is important to keep in mind the distinction between philosophical or ontological beauty, on the one hand, and aesthetic beauty that speaks more specifically to a deliberate beautification or artistic expression, on the other.

Beauty and the Preferential Scale of Values

To the extent that beauty is a value, one can expect that beauty will be expressed differently within the various aspects pertaining to the preferential scale of values. Vital values are those values that relate to our physical health and well-being. However, we are not satisfied with the basic necessities of life. When socioeconomic conditions allow for it, human beings create cuisine, they beautify their homes and gardens, and they enjoy being physically fit. At the level of social values, when a society is functioning in line with the precepts of attentiveness, intelligence, reasonableness, and responsibility, the aesthetic value shines through. As we stated above, this is what Lonergan suggests in his earlier formulation when he speaks of aesthetic value in *Topics in Education*. Joy, spontaneity, and freedom are the signs of aesthetic value.

At the level of cultural value, society reflects upon itself, often through the arts, its universities, and other cultural institutions. It asks, how can the integral preferential scale of values be better implemented, improved, or maintained? What are the fundamental values in our community and how do we promote them? Social critiques may involve advocating the equitable distribution of particular goods and economic structures, improved laws, representative polity, and the like. The visual, performing, and musical arts remind communities, as Lonergan was fond of saying, that they "do not live by bread alone." In this way, the arts may direct or stir up deeper longings for self-transcendence and basic fulfilment.

As for "personal value," scholars still need to specify the kinds of things and relationships Lonergan meant by this term. However, one obvious personal value is that of friendship. Armand Maurer applies one of Aquinas's principles of beauty, *consonantia*, or harmony, to friendship, considering it to involve two people who share the same outlook or values (*AB*, 75). Out of such harmony, he suggests, friendships thrive.

Religious value concerns the ultimate ground of beauty; all beauty exists by virtue of participation in this ultimate ground. It is the beauty that impels St Augustine to declare, "O Beauty so ancient and so new," or Aquinas to state, "Nothing exists that does not participate in beauty" (*De Divinis Nominibus*, 4.5).[26] This religious value can also be grasped through beautiful objects or scenes in nature, as we remarked in an earlier chapter of Sergei Bulgakov, a Russian Orthodox theologian, who after gazing upon the Caucasus Mountains embraced theism over communism. Indeed, as I will suggest in the following chapter, religious art can to some extent be distinguished from "secular" art in its attempt to express religious mysteries rather than aiming to objectify the purely experiential pattern, and thereby to draw the observer deeper into those mysteries as a participant.

Three Moments of Beauty

In addition to the different ways in which beauty is expressed in the preferential scale, one of Lonergan's successors, Robert Doran, has clarified the three exercises of vertical liberty based on the three types of election in the *Spiritual Exercises* of St Ignatius.[27] Doran correlates the three types of election with three basic exercises of vertical finality in Lonergan's fourth-level operations.

The first moment occurs when the grasp of value is immediate and the direction is clear. The second moment is when the feelings with respect to a deliberation are confused. This is because the feelings respond both to satisfactions and to value, so one must discern the true value by distinguishing between it and apparent value or satisfaction. The third time of election occurs when the affectivity is not a strong factor in the discernment; one's rationality is invoked to simply weigh the pros and cons and decide according to the greater weighted option.

It is possible to apply these three types of election in an analogous manner and distinguish three grasps of beauty, that is, when aesthetic judgments grasp the qualitative value of beauty and affirm that either something is beautiful or that one thing is more beautiful than another.

In the first case, the grasp of beauty in affectivity can be immediate, dramatic, and transformative – unmistakable.[28] This corresponds to the first time of election.

In a second case, the appreciation of beauty is not as apparent, and it needs to be discerned, especially in the case of human creations. The problem inherent to the contemplation of beauty is the difficulty of distinguishing art from artifact, art from play, art from entertainment, or in other words to distinguish pleasure as satisfaction from the pleasure in a legitimate grasp of aesthetic value. This is where we can draw on an expert to inform us in our attempts to grasp beauty. We may rely on the expertise of a critic, historian, or teacher, in order to educate ourselves on the context and magnificence of a work of art or architecture. At a cultural level, the education system can support the appreciation of beauty by educating students on these matters.

In the third case, when our affectivity is not immediately engaged or apparent, we have to actively remind ourselves of the presence of beauty – to be attentive to the beautiful. Another feature of Ignatian spirituality emphasizes *repetition*, a continual return of one's attention to the same data in order to achieve a deeper appreciation in insight. This is in keeping with the philosophy of beauty of the Diné–Navajo, who rise before dawn, offer corn pollen, and remind themselves: "Beauty above me, beauty below me, beauty before me, beauty behind me, may I walk in beauty."[29] In order to live in beauty, the Diné believe that beauty needs to be recreated, and so they have a complex ceremonial system to restore, foster, sustain, and protect beauty. The third moment of aesthetic appreciation flows from a prior decision to see beauty and acknowledge its presence even when it is not immediately apparent.

The three moments of beauty go hand in hand and are interrelated. One comes to be open to and contemplate the momentous and dramatic encounters with beauty (first moment). One promotes the education of aesthetic sensibilities and the further differentiating of aesthetic consciousness in order to grasp beauty and to distinguish more beautiful from less beautiful objects (second moment). One makes a deliberate and sustained commitment to be attentive to beauty and to orientate oneself to aesthetic appreciation and disposition in order to foster more frequent encounters with beauty (third moment). These three moments, in turn, condition the possibility of further immediate and momentous grasps of beauty.

Is Beauty Distinct from Goodness?

In the bulk of this chapter I have been trying to show how beauty can be understood as a value in terms of Lonergan's philosophy. But a further question arises: If beauty is a value, is it transcendentally distinct from the good?

Some thinkers argue that beauty is a subdivision of the good. In his discussion of the transcendentals in Aquinas, Gilson interprets Aquinas's distinction between beauty and goodness to mean that "[t]he beautiful is a variety of the good. It is a particular kind of good to be experienced, by a knowing power, in a very act of knowing an object eminently fit to be known."[30]

While it is true that Lonergan did not speak much about beauty, he did in fact explicitly speak of a transcendental notion of value. In a move similar to Gilson's, Joseph Flanagan, SJ, one of Lonergan's successors, favoured incorporating the transcendental notion of value into his own attempt to develop a philosophy of art from Lonergan's theory, but he admitted that he did not think that the term "beauty" was necessary.[31] It is easy to see how one could come to a similar conclusion once beauty is restricted to transcendental goodness – it diminishes the distinctiveness of beauty. But the question remains, how is beauty distinct from goodness?

Armand Maurer acknowledges the similarities between the good and the beautiful in that they both exist and are both desirable in their perfection. A ripe, "perfect" apple, for example, is to be preferred to one that is less ripe or rotten (AB, 17). However, the difference between the two ways of understanding the apple lies in the differing types of causality pertaining to it:

> The good attracts our attention, makes us restless, and sets us in motion to possess it; and once it is possessed we are satisfied and in peace. The ripe apple catches our eye, and, if we are hungry, we reach out for it and eat it. The beautiful also catches our eye, arouses our attention, not to take possession of it, but to enjoy it. (AB, 17)

As a formal cause, beauty is pleasing when seen, that is, when it is apprehended or acknowledged:

> Beauty and goodness in a thing are identical fundamentally; for they are based upon the same thing, namely, the form; and consequently goodness is praised as beauty. But they differ logically, for goodness properly relates to the appetite (goodness being what all things desire); and therefore it has the aspect of an end (the appetite being a kind of movement towards a thing). On the other hand, beauty relates to the cognitive faculty; for beautiful things are those which please when seen. Hence beauty consists in due proportion; for the senses delight in things duly proportioned, as in what is after their own kind – because even sense is a sort of reason, just as is every cognitive faculty. Now since knowledge is by assimilation, and similarity relates to form, beauty properly belongs to the nature of a formal cause. (*ST*, 1.5.4 ad 1)

Maurer recalls that the Greek word for beauty, *kalos,* is closely connected to the word for "the good" (*to kalon*), which are in turn related to the word for "to call" (*kaleo*). "Both beauty and goodness call us but in different ways" (*AB*, 17). The apprehension or knowledge of beauty delights us. We do not seek to possess it but rather to contemplate or appreciate it. Yet even in contemplation of it, there is awareness of its impermanence and incompleteness (*AB*, 19).

Yes, beauty is a value; but while this much is clear, in order to claim that it is a transcendental and not simply a subdivision of the good we must presume that there is more to beauty than the fact that it is good. There is something more that makes it a distinct transcendental.

Beauty includes a surplus of meaning in the object one encounters in aesthetic moments that provoke a response from the individual. One is surprised by and taken by beauty. In this way, it is analogous to what Lonergan describes as "being in love," what would later be called a fifth level. Whereas the fourth level concerns decision, the fifth level concerns commitment, the reorientation of vertical liberty that establishes a horizon in which subsequent decisions are made. Beauty is loved not for its usefulness, but because it provides some basic fulfilment in human intentionality – we appreciate it for its own sake.

Again, I find myself in agreement with St Bonaventure, who sees beauty as the splendour of the transcendentals. As I stated in chapter 2, Lonergan says something very similar:

Beauty as a transcendental, yes. But it is in terms of developing consciousness, and consciousness at a level in which the higher reaches, the higher concerns, such as truth, reality, value are apprehended through the sensible and are, as it were, a sort of plus to the harmony, the unity, the balance, and so on, that is found in the sensible or the denial of them … To know value you have to know reality; and to know reality you have to know truth; to know truth you have to grasp intelligibility; and to grasp intelligibility you have to attend to the data; and so it is all one thrust. Beauty is self-transcendence expressed through the sensible.

The plus to the harmony, unity, clarity of the true and the valuable, the pleasure that arises in contemplation of the surplus or ulterior significance of the object, and how it captivates the whole person in the encounter, these are the marks of transcendental beauty. However, it makes beauty, as it were, a different type of transcendental.

What more precisely is meant by the *pleasing* nature of beauty, and how do we understand this in terms of Lonergan's philosophy? Hugo Meynell invokes the term "aesthetic satisfaction" based on an artwork's ability (depending, of course, on the skill of the artist) to effect an "enlargement of the capacities constitutive of human consciousness."[32] While I am sympathetic to Meynell's argument, I find his choice of the term "aesthetic satisfaction" unfortunate, as we are trying to articulate the nature of aesthetic values, and as a student of Lonergan, Meynell is well aware that Lonergan's use of "satisfaction" is often in contradistinction to value.

There is a sensitive delight when one apprehends a harmonious, integral, and clear artistic or natural beauty. But entertainment can be satisfying yet far from aesthetically beautiful.[33] Similarly, a warm bath is pleasing to the senses, but we do not typically describe it as beautiful.

There can also be a cognitive delight in reason's grasp of the intelligibility in the unity or relations in the data. The mathematician, for example, is pleased by the harmony, proportion, and clarity of reason that enables her to derive the proper result in a mathematical formulation.

There is an affective delight in the encounter with beauty when value is apprehended. Artistic and natural beauty can mediate to us not just sensitive beauty, but a deeper encounter with meaning that invokes feelings conducive to self-transcendence.

The beauty of truth and value can shine through a particular artistic medium, bringing one to contemplation. I was once moved to tears watching a performance of *Les Misérables*, particularly the scene when the bishop grants Jean Valjean a reprieve. At that point, the beauty of love as an act of kindness and mercy shone through. If Aquinas is correct in saying that everyone loves the beautiful, then it would also seem that love itself is beautiful. Loving acts of kindness, mercy, fidelity, have a beauty reflective of those acts and are reflective of the person who performs them.

Finally, in the aesthetic encounter with beauty the "pleasure" itself does not have to be delightful. Instead it can be deeply moving and even disturbing, as when Dostoevsky contemplated the dramatic image of Hans Holbein's *Christ in the Tomb* in a museum in Basel, Switzerland (1867). He was so physically shaken that his wife had to sit him down. The experience, although horrifying, was transformative.[34]

Conclusion

We have been labouring to conceive of aesthetic judgments of beauty from the perspective of Lonergan's theory of judgment as they pertain to judgments of fact and judgments of value. In doing so, we acknowledged the expression of beauty in its philosophical sense to the extent that a judgment of fact affirms that the content of an insight *exists*. Consequently, there is a beauty reflective of the content that is grasped in its clarity, integrity, and proportion. With respect to judgments of value, we have affirmed beauty as an aesthetic value that is grasped in affectivity and is pleasing to the senses, intellect, and affectivity. We have tried to demonstrate how an aesthetic judgment of the beautiful fits within Lonergan's philosophy in terms of the scale of values and three aesthetic moments. Finally, we have acknowledged that if beauty is a transcendental, it is not reducible to the good as such. It is a different type of transcendental in that it opens up to a surplus that gives rise to contemplative pleasure. Beauty is the splendour of the transcendental intending for the intelligible, the true, and the good together, and the fruits of that transcendental intending are beautiful insofar as they are unobstructed by bias that interferes with the pursuit of it.

Moreover, the advantages of our endeavour enable us to respond to the problems in the Kantian legacy of aesthetic judgments. Recall Ginsborg's summary of those problems. The first issue is the lack of clarity as to whether the feeling of pleasure precedes or follows the judgment. Lonergan's notion of judgment enables us to declare that for the most part the feelings of pleasure would accompany the judgment, insofar as the affectivity grasps true aesthetic value, but in some cases, once the grasp of value occurs the judgment follows naturally – immediately.

Second, Ginsborg identifies lack of clarity concerning the role of the free play of the imagination and the role of concepts in understanding. In Lonergan's approach, the free play is the result of freedom from instrumentality and not, as Kant would have it, freedom from concepts. Lonergan's view enables the preservation of this notion of free play, but retains the intellectual grasp of beauty as intelligible.

Third, Ginsborg flags the uncertainty in Kant over whether the feeling of pleasure has an intentional content. For Lonergan, if the feeling of pleasure grasps true aesthetic value, then it is because the subject's intending of the good has grasped value. The good is concrete for Lonergan, and the apprehension of aesthetic value means concretely that the value is grasped by intentional consciousness.

Fourth, Ginsborg raises the question of the precise epistemological status of the claim to agreement in an aesthetic judgment. Is it a judgment of fact or of value? If it is a judgment of fact, insofar as the intelligibility that is grasped and affirmed by judgment is proportionate, integral, and clear, then there is a beauty proportionate to the intelligibility as grasped and affirmed as existing. If a judgment of value, insofar as the content of the judgment is a grasp of true rather than apparent value, the content of the judgment not only exists, but exists as valuable. There is the further unique status of beauty: it is not exhausted in the judgment of value but instead is loved for its intrinsic worth rather than for its usefulness.

Fifth, and closely related to the fourth, is the question of whether or not aesthetic judgments are objective. Here, one's claim that a certain object is beautiful is not based on the presumption that others should think it is so, but rather on the supposition that one has grasped true value.

Finally, Ginsborg raises the question of negative judgments or judgments of ugliness and feelings of revulsion. From the perspective of Lonergan's more contemporary Thomistic orientation, in terms of intelligibility, ugliness would suggest a lack of one of the three principles of clarity, integrity, and proportion/harmony. However, this does not mean that negative feelings *de facto* negate the presence of beauty. Truth can be painful but yet necessary, as when some matters become "painfully clear." In these cases, the disturbing feelings are revealing a truth, and the truth has an intelligibility that is clear, integral, and proportionate to the situation. For example, the Holocaust Museum in

Washington, DC, has a display of a pile of shoes taken from Jews before they were sent to concentration camps. The smell of the shoes, the various sizes, and other such details provide a disturbing image for onlookers. However, there is also a kind of residual consolation in the fact that the truth is now being told and is no longer obscured by the victimizers. Beauty is present in the consolation.

Finally, in this chapter we have prescinded from articulating the so-called fourth-level operations for beauty, and we restricted our inquiry to beauty as a grasp of the virtually unconditioned and of value. The fourth-level operations of beauty would be contemplation and creation, to which topics we now turn.

8 Creating, Contemplating, and Loving Beauty

There is an artistic element in all consciousness, in all living.

– Bernard Lonergan

Every utterance and every gesture that each one of us makes is a work of art.

– R.G. Collingwood

It appears to be a particular mark of the beautiful, that it is contemplated with quiet satisfaction, that it pleases, even though it be not in our possession, and even though we be never so far removed from the desire to put it to our use.

– M. Mendelssohn

Human beings need the surplus of meaning provided by beautiful nature, art, and *le joie de vivre* in order to expose them to more than just the ordinary business of everyday living. Hence, human beings create and contemplate beauty.

In this chapter I will identify the various ways in which beauty pertains to the fourth-level operation, decision – the creation of and contemplation of aesthetic meaning. First I will identify an aesthetic/dramatic impulse in the human spirit that seeks to create and contemplate beauty. I will then flesh out how that desire for beauty in its creative aspect manifests in works of art and in dramatic and ethical living. Finally, I will suggest how this desire manifests in contemplation, which in turn leads us to the topics of beauty, love, and the question of an ultimate ground of beauty.

The Aesthetic/Dramatic Operator

Recall that Lonergan speaks of four basic desires of human living: the desire to know, the desire for the good, the desire for happiness, and the desire for immortality. These are fundamental orientations of the human spirit. Most of Lonergan's endeavours sought to develop the first, *the unrestricted desire to know*. However, as we suggested in chapter 4, there is an implicit reference in Lonergan's thought to an additional operator or desire that is closely related to the unrestricted desire to know. At times he refers to it as a quasi-operator, symbolic operator, or *élan vital*.[1] Robert Doran develops this implicit idea in Lonergan and speaks of a psychic operator or, later, of aesthetic-dramatic operators. He writes that "the meaning they express is elemental. It is a meaning that never will be exhausted in the categories of human thought, even as we do reach for and attain some imperfect and analogical understanding of the mystery."[2]

There is then an *aesthetic-dramatic operator* that intends the beautiful – a desire to create and contemplate beauty. It expresses itself in a twofold manner and is dynamically present throughout the subject's intentional operations. The first manner of operation is the creative or constructive aspect of the operator; the second manner is the receptive or responsive aspect of the operator. Let us first look at the constructive or creative aspect of the transcendental intention for beauty before turning to the contemplative aspect of this operator.

Philosophy of Art

In this section I will focus on summarizing the context or strand of philosophy of art that Lonergan's thinking about art draws upon. While a full-scale philosophy of art is beyond the scope of this book, I will consider how such a philosophy bears on Lonergan's thought and will emphasize how art is an expression of the human spirit's drive to create and contemplate beauty.[3] In addition, I will address the questions: to what extent can we say that art *is* art (as opposed to artefact); and to what extent, if any, is it beautiful? My account will be generic.

Aesthetic and Artistic Patterns of Experience

Our discussion of Kierkegaard's aesthetics emphasized the polymorphic nature of human consciousness and how consciousness flows in various patterns and can interpenetrate. The aesthetic existential sphere in Kierkegaard is analogous to what Lonergan identifies as an aesthetic pattern of experience.

We noted in chapter 5 the distinction between the *aesthetic pattern of experience* and the *artistic pattern of experience*.[4] The commonality between the two lies in the spontaneity and freedom of the psyche conducive to the flow of consciousness as pre-predicative or pre-intellectual.

The aesthetic pattern refers to the flow of consciousness that directs our attention to the liberation and joy of experiencing for the sake of experiencing. It is conducive to play, entertainment, recreation, and aesthetic contemplation.[5] Following Gadamer, we also note this pattern can lead to escapist tendencies, which was also Kierkegaard's oversight with respect to the aesthetic sphere. The aesthetic/artistic patterns of experience recognize that our existence is more than just biological: "one is led to acknowledge that experience can occur for the sake of experiencing, that it can slip beyond the confines of serious-minded biological purpose, and that this very liberation is a spontaneous, self-justifying joy" (*IN*, 208). It is the world of elemental meaning, where the subject/object distinction blurs or is not yet differentiated, a world where one encounters a meaning that is not readily thematized in language. It is also the soil from which creativity emerges.

In many ways the aesthetic pattern characterizes the world of the artist, but the pattern of the artist is more deliberate: "just as the scientist seeks intelligible systems that cover the data of his field, so too the artist exercises his intelligence in discovering ever novel forms that unify and relate the contents and acts of aesthetic experience" (*IN*, 208). The deliberate expression of contents of the aesthetic pattern in objects of symbolic meaning occurs in the artistic pattern of consciousness. The artistic pattern is not as immediate as the aesthetic pattern in that it requires a contemplative distance: "artistic composition recollects emotion in tranquility" (*MT*, 63).

For Lonergan, art is "an expression of the human subject outside the limits of adequate intellectual formulation and appraisal" (*IN*, 208).[6] He continues: "Prescientific and prephilosophic, it may strain for truth and value without defining them. Post-biological, it may reflect the psychological depths, yet by that very fact it will go beyond them" (*IN*, 208). Walmsley summarizes this meaning as follows: "The symbol, the work of art, expresses elemental meaning in a way that does not bring the movement of free exploration to an end, but rather invites it to go further."[7] In other words, the work of art invites the observer into participation.

This is consonant with Heidegger, especially his fascination with van Gogh's *Farmer's Shoes*. It also resonates with Gadamer when he states that "the inexhaustibility that distinguishes the language of art from all translation into concepts rests on an excess of meaning." It is a meaning that does not rely solely on the *mens auctoris*.[8] Although for Lonergan art reflects the creative and original insights of the artist, those insights point to the kind of excess of meaning Gadamer refers to; Lonergan's approach would not attempt to reduce the interpretations of an art-work to the artist's intention.

Finally, there is something profoundly personal about a work of art, which Gadamer points out. The art may speak to a historian of art in a particular way, but it will speak to each participant in a personal way: "it says something to each person as if it were said especially to him, as something present and contemporaneous."[9] Gadamer emphasizes the ability of art to speak in the present moment across historical contexts while also retaining the meaning of those contexts: "The work of art always has its own present. Only in a limited way does it retain its historical origin within itself."[10] In Lonergan's words, this means that the original insights of the artist, as expressions of elemental meaning, can appeal to the observer-participants in a way that speaks to them personally. In other words, the work of art can lead observer-participants to insights into themselves as well as into the world around them.

Art as Meaning

As stated previously, a comprehensive philosophy of art, while valuable, is beyond the scope of our inquiry; the goal of this work is a philosophy of beauty rather than a philosophy of art. In this section I seek to highlight the general form of a philosophy of art in terms of Lonergan's philosophy by identifying the general horizon of thinkers that influence him, that is, *art as expression*; I also explore how transcendental beauty can pertain to art in an age where art is no longer about beauty.

In *Insight*, Lonergan's treatment of the aesthetic/artistic patterns of experience was most likely confirmed by his discovery of Susanne Langer's work after his initial draft of *Insight*.[11] Later, he acknowledged that R.G. Collingwood's work also shaped his thoughts on the subject, and the latter's influence was gaining increasing ascendance over Langer's in his thinking.[12] However, it is clear that Langer influenced his early thoughts on the topic, and that influence survives in some of Lonergan's principal texts. There is no material that develops the Collingwood influence in any substantial way. Moreover, since both Collingwood and Langer are disciples of Benedetto Croce, the influence of Collingwood on the later Lonergan probably does not significantly change Lonergan's earlier formulations of art drawn from Langer. Still, a brief excursus into the philosophy of art is helpful in order to put Lonergan's philosophical approach to art in context.

The legacy of Langer's theory extends to her from G.W. Hegel and Croce through Collingwood. Despite the fact that Heidegger criticizes this tradition, it is possible to proceed by taking his criticisms into account.

In the late nineteenth century and through the turn to the twentieth, with the invention of photography and the rise of manufacturing, art ceased to emphasize *imitation* and *beauty* and became about the expression of meaning. This tradition traces its origins to Hegel, although even he still emphasized that such expressions can be beautiful. Summarizing Hegel's emphasis on art as expressive, Stephen Houlgate writes:

> The principal aim of art is not, therefore, to imitate nature, to decorate our surroundings, to prompt us to engage in moral or political action, or to shock us out of our complacency. It is to allow us to contemplate and enjoy created images of our own spiritual freedom – images that are beautiful precisely *because* they give expression to our freedom. Art's purpose, in other words, is to enable us to bring to mind the truth about ourselves, and so to become aware of who we truly are. Art is there not just for art's sake, but for beauty's sake, that is, for the sake of a distinctively sensuous form of human self-expression and self-understanding.[13]

For Hegel, art is the sensuous expression of free spirit. Beauty remains in his view of art but it pertains to the Idea, the human form – since humans are capable of self-consciousness and use of their rationality as free spirits.[14] For Hegel, the exemplar is the works of classical Greek art, which reflect a noble anthropology. Such beauty is surpassed only by Romantic art because the latter captures the interior disposition and reflective attitude that is conducive to rational reflection. By contrast, modern art fails to represent these principles of free spirit and intuitive reflection, and so falls short of beauty.

Following Hegel, the notion of art as expression comes to the fore with Benedetto Croce (1866–1952). But in his views, unlike Hegel's, beauty begins to fall to the wayside. Croce "thus sets the outlook of most twentieth-century philosophies of art which replace the concept of beauty with that of expression, or identify beauty, as Croce does, with expression."[15] Through his subsequent disciples, R.C. Collingwood (1889–1943) and Susanne Langer (1895–1985), the view of art as an expression of meaning moves further away from being strictly about the expression of beauty. Croce emphasizes the intuition-expression, the idea in the mind of the artist, which is communicated in the work of art. He also incorporates the role of feeling, an emphasis that will factor heavily into Langer's work.

In general, Croce's emphasis on the mind of the artist in the creative act is consonant with Lonergan's emphasis on art as the expression of the artist's insights as the artist reflects upon the purely experiential pattern of consciousness.The emphasis on feeling and affectivity pertaining to the creative act is also consonant with Lonergan. However, Lonergan would not accept the notion of an "intuition." He favours his own notion of *insight* as an act of understanding, where the agent intellect grasps the intelligible unity or relations in the data and then communicates that understanding, albeit in a work of art such communication is multivalent and open to personal interpretation.

Collingwood attempts to circumscribe what art is by delineating it from four things it is not. Art is not craft, representation, magic, or amusement. Craft, the aesthetic embellishing of created objects for a useful end, is to be distinguished from the unique expressive meaning of art, which does not have a useful end as such. Representation requires that the artist not rely on his/her own creative ideas but instead be guided primarily by the meaning he or she is communicating in the work of art. By magic, Collingwood means the performative rituals in human cultures that bring about a specific outcome or instill hope in a community. Finally, art may be amusing, but its primary purpose is not to entertain but to express emotions. It is of course possible for art to interpenetrate with these four aspects to greater and lesser degrees.

In the words of Lonergan, Collingwood locates the origin of a work of art in the mind of the artist, who has an insight into the expression of emotion. The expression of the emotion involves a release, not in the cathartic sense, but in the release of the tension of expressing/articulating the emotion. According to Collingwood, "[t]he characteristic mark of expression proper is lucidity or intelligibility."[16] Collingwood likens it to an actress who portrays weeping in a performance. "In that case, it is not her ability to weep real tears that would mark out a good actress; it is her ability to make it clear to herself and her audience what the tears are about. This applies to every kind of art."[17] One can see why Collingwood's thought would appeal to Lonergan, especially in its emphasis on art as an expression of the intelligibility of emotion. This resonates with Lonergan's notion of insight as an act of understanding that grasps intelligibility. For Lonergan, the creation of a work of art is analogous to the movement from an insight to the construction of a definition (*TE*, 218). Of course, Collingwood's emphasis is primarily on the mind of the artist, and as such tends towards idealism. For Lonergan this would need to be complemented by an emphasis on the work of art. After all, an art critic's critique of a work of art is at once a critique of the artist's work and the extent to which the expression is successfully and effectively communicated.

For Lonergan the distinctions Collingwood draws between art and craft, representation, magic, and amusement can be understood more broadly in terms of the aesthetic-dramatic impulse to create and contemplate beauty. In terms of *craft*, the chef who dices onions skilfully does so in an artistic manner despite the primarily practical end, the cuisine. The manner in which the onions were diced has no ultimate bearing on the final product. In terms of *representation*, the artist can put his/her own creative stamp on a portrait, as in Picasso's portrait of El Greco. In terms of *magic*, Tibetan Buddhist and the Diné-Navajo sand paintings are exquisite and beautiful art in and of themselves, apart from their ritual purposes. Concerning amusement, the distinction between the aesthetic and artistic patterns enables us in Lonergan's philosophy to distinguish a pattern of experience that is conducive to play, amusement, entertainment (I have suggested a liberative pattern), but is not aesthetic in the artistic-creative sense. Finally, Lonergan's treatment of bias as a flight from understanding enables one to understand how art can be distorted, but in such cases the distortion is a reflection of bias rather than a reflection of an authentic expression of meaning.

Susanne Langer (1895–1985) was one of the most influential aesthetic theorists of the twentieth century. She continues the tradition of Croce and Collingwood by emphasizing art as expression. However, influenced as she was by Ernst Cassirer's *Philosophy of Symbolic Forms*, she focuses on the relationship between art and symbol.

Each of the arts expresses a particular form of feeling in a symbolic manner. This notion clearly comes out in her description of music, which she focuses on for the most in her *Feeling and Form*. The goal of music is not to stimulate the senses per se but to express feeling in a symbolic way: "the function of music is not the stimulation of feeling, but expression of it; and furthermore, not the symptomatic expression of feelings that beset the composer but a symbolic expression of the forms of sentience as he understands them."[18] Again, Langer's work influenced Lonergan's early thinking on art – although he abstracts his own definition from it. As we noted earlier, art is the symbolic expression of the purely experiential pattern of experience.

This expressionist school of thought has its critiques, chief among them Heidegger. Given the more recent influence of the later Heidegger on aesthetics, it is important to mention his critique, especially those aspects that view the artist's work as an expression of his or her subjectivity and life experience. Heidegger is skeptical of the ability of aesthetic categories to express "lived experience." For him, something is lost when we try to thematize "aesthetic" experience. The subject/object distinction, which is inextricably part of instrumentalized consciousness, cannot preserve lived experience. Modern aesthetics as Heidegger conceives it cannot maintain the richness of lived experience when it treats art as objects to be observed.

This lived experience of primal encounter is at once a concealing/unconcealing of *aletheia*. For Heidegger, van Gogh's painting of a farmer's shoes exemplifies this principle. "The art work lets us know what shoes are in truth ... This entity emerges in its unconcealedness of its being ... aletheia."[19] The painting at once reveals and conceals the *nothingness* of primordial existence – that which cannot be totally apprehended and thematized.

Iain Thompson describes the encounter with art for Heidegger as follows: "What we encounter in art is something more deeply rooted in existence which the modern subject/object dichotomy skates right over. Our encounter with the work teaches us that the meaning does not happen solely in the art object or the viewing subject but instead takes place, we could say, *between* us and the work."[20] Thompson continues: "Art teaches us to embrace the initially tragic insight that being will never be completely revealed in time as the very thing that makes it possible for human beings to continue to understand what-is in new and potentially more meaningful ways."[21]

Lonergan's approach to aesthetics and art in many ways agrees with Heidegger's.[22] However, the two are complementary in the sense that Heidegger seeks to preserve "lived experience," a notion I think correlates with what Lonergan means by "elemental meaning" and "ulterior significance." Lonergan would agree with Heidegger's claim that *aletheia* is simultaneously an uncovering and a covering over of truth, but for Lonergan this is because the desire to know is unrestricted, and so each grasp of intelligibility is a potential increment in the horizon of knowing. The finite mind can only know in increments. But *pace* Heidegger, knowledge is also cumulative. There are as well leaps of intelligibility that can expand intelligibility considerably, as when one moves from algebra to calculus.

Second, Lonergan's more intellectualist approach is more confident in the subject's ability to grasp insights in the data of lived experience. In fact, for Lonergan intellectual abstraction is an enriching process where one gains understanding. Nevertheless, Heidegger's emphasis on the surplus of meaning in the purely experiential pattern can serve to complement Lonergan's more intellectualist approach. Lonergan's emphasis is on the artist's *insights* rather than the artist's subjectivity as the expression of meaning. Those insights that are expressed in works of art as elemental in meaning would be conducive to preserving the surplus of meaning of concealment/unconcealment of *aletheia*, but simultaneously the surplus would also invite the observer into the painting by way of participation.

This approach to art is also consonant with that of Heidegger's student, Gadamer, who states that a work of art "consists in its being open in a limitless way to ever new integrations of meaning."[23] On this matter, Wamsley states of Lonergan: "There is a fundamental exigence in elemental wonder for being-more-alive, for creative becoming. Human experience in its most original form is not neutral because the human spirit is engaged."[24] Gadamer would agree with this involvement of the subject: "For of all the things that confront us in nature and history, it is the work of art that speaks to us most directly. It possesses a mysterious intimacy that grips our entire being, as if there were no distance at all and every encounter with it were an encounter with ourselves."[25]

Developing Lonergan's View on Art

In chapter 5 we referred to Lonergan's definition of art in *Topics in Education*, appropriated from Langer, as the "objectification of the purely experiential pattern" (*TE*, 211).[26] Later, in *Method in Theology* (see *MT*, 61–4) and also influenced by Langer, he expounds upon the same definition. In Lonergan's philosophy the significance of the difference between the aesthetic pattern and the artistic pattern of experience becomes clearer. The aesthetic pattern is non-instrumentalized experience; it is conducive to play and entertainment as well as aesthetic contemplation. By contrast, in the artistic pattern, the artist attempts to embody the insights of the purely experiential pattern from a "psychic distance." As we stated above, "artistic composition recollects emotion in tranquility" (*MT*, 63). Art attempts to express the elemental meaning of the aesthetic pattern, and to the extent it is successful, it invites the observer to participate in the work of art (*MT*, 64). Hence, there is a sense in which the artist withdraws or steps back from the aesthetic pattern in order to express the insights obtained while in it. Subsequently, the observer is drawn into the elemental meaning by way of participation.[27]

The advantage of the distinction between the aesthetic and artistic patterns is that it enables one to distinguish, from the point of view of the subject's intentional consciousness, the realm of play, entertainment, aesthetic delight, on the one hand, and the more constructive, active expression of the content experienced in that pattern through the creative production of artistic works on the other.

There is an additional feature to a work of art that is important to note, which Lonergan did not identify as such but which can be drawn out from his thinking. An artwork is an *original* creative expression as an act of meaning. This uniqueness, along with the skill it takes to communicate it successfully, contributes to its value. However, some immediate qualifications of this claim come to mind.

First, the loss of beauty in Western society translates into the loss of both the meaning of art and the ability to distinguish true art from other forms, such as artefacts, kitsch, and at least to some extent ready-mades or found art. It is perhaps not a coincidence that Balthasar's claim of the loss of beauty coincides with Hegel's and Heidegger's criticisms of the loss of true art in modernity.

To illustrate this, consider the artist Tracy Emin's 1998 *My Bed*, where she presents her actual unmade bed as an expression of artistic meaning. I would argue that this is *not* a work of art, but rather an artefact. It may someday be worthy of study by archeologists for its cultural and social value, but not for its aesthetic value. In contrast, Imogen Cunningham's (1883–1976) photograph "Unmade Bed" (1957) *is* art because she captures an ulterior significance and surplus that is larger than the image captured by the photograph itself. The photographer is able to use the camera as a tool to shape the end result. Presumably Cunningham took the photo of the unmade bed because she saw something more in that scene mediated through the bed as unkempt. There is a softness, a harmonious play of light in the folds, and a simplicity that invite contemplation in a way that Emin's bed does not.

The artist presents not only the facts but an interpretive creative interpretation shaped by his or her specific media. Take the example of the photography of Edward Burtynsky in his documentary *Manufactured Landscapes*. His photography depicts typically industrial, alienating, ugly scenes and landscapes but in an aesthetically beautiful manner. Indeed, because the author reveals these scenes beautifully, one is tempted to call the objectivity of beauty into question. Rather than supporting the relativity of beauty, however, his work is a demonstration of the creative intelligence and specially differentiated consciousness of the artist. The artist is able to see and construct beauty, at least to a certain extent, where people might not readily see it. In Burtynsky's case, he uses the camera. His photos beautify scenes we might consider ugly. However, the observer of the photograph is not privy to the environment of the originating photograph, for instance the smells, sounds, and tactile sensations. Hence, while Burtynksy demonstrates the artist's ability to beautify a certain scene, it does not follow that the actual scene of the photograph *as experienced* would be beautiful. His artistic method is similar to that of the Impressionist painters, whose landscapes captured a surplus of meaning in the ordinary.

In addition to being an original expression, art is a creative expression of elemental meaning. If the extent to which the meaning communicated by the work of art is intelligible and effective depends on the skill and insight of the artist, then beauty is proportionate to the truth of the meaning communicated in the art. In this way, a work of art may not be aesthetically beautiful per se, but if the meaning it communicates has a personal, social, or political meaning that is controversial, repulsive, or profound and worthy of contemplation, then the work is nevertheless beautiful in that the truth communicated is proportionate to the successful communication of the meaning. Art can provoke a response that is not necessarily pleasant and can even be shocking (although it goes without saying that some contemporary artists deliberately attempt to shock observers in order to be noticed).

The work of art as a creative, interpretive expression of the artist constitutes its *originality*. Contrary to some current trends in aesthetics, art is *not* copy, at least in the sense of manufactured reproductions. Artists may be influenced by other artists and they can inspire each other, as did the famous Group of Seven in Canada, thus making it possible for art historians to describe movements and schools. However, to be genuine, the art must be an original creative interpretive expression of the artist. But are there no exceptions to this? Indeed, the whole premise of religious iconography in the Orthodox faith is about the masterly copying of original icons. While this may be true, the humility of the iconographer who *writes* the icon does not presume, for example, that his or her work is greater than say, Rublev's.[28]

Let us take a very different example. Francisco Goya's (1746–1828) most famous painting, *Saturn Eating His Son*, was discovered on the wall of his home after he died. It was carefully transcribed from the wall to a canvas; the original did not survive, but insofar as the transcribers were careful to preserve the genius of Goya's image, the image remains an original expression of his creative intelligence. There is a surplus of meaning to Goya's ghastly image that is timeless and worthy of contemplation. Is this ghastly image beautiful? Insofar as the image holds a surplus of meaning and reflects the psychological depths of a tortured psyche, there are profound truths revealed in the painting – concerning among others the domination of sons by their fathers in a violent, soul-crushing manner.

But what about ready-mades or found art? Are they original? What do they indicate about art? Is there any sense in which they can be considered beautiful? Two examples that come to mind are Marcel Duchamp's *Fountain* (1917) and Andy Warhol's *Brillo Boxes* (1964).

Duchamp shocked the art world when he displayed a urinal fountain and signed it "R. Mutt." Hoping to show the absurdity of what the art world had become, Duchamp forced the art world to ask "What is art?" This question had a residual effect that he could not have anticipated: it prompted artists to conclude that *anything* can be art.

As meaning, Duchamp's urinal was effective in causing the art world to reflect on itself. The meaning was thus political; that is, the locus of meaning had nothing to do with the aesthetic value, or lack thereof, of the urinal itself. Perhaps any plumber would have thought it a fine urinal, insofar as form follows function, but that is not what Duchamp was trying to say. The urinal was a symbol of something more. In this way Duchamp was a visionary, so that to speak of any beauty in the message he wanted to communicate would be to speak of the beauty that is proportionate to the political-social-cultural meaning symbolized by the urinal. The effect was magnificent, although it was followed by numerous absurd ready-mades, such as the Italian artist Piero Manzoni's *Can of Shit* (1961).

Art is about meaning, but if the meaning is intelligibly communicated, then the beauty is proportionate to the truth of the meaning, even if it lacks aesthetic meaning per se. It may not be aesthetically beautiful, but the meaning it communicates can nonetheless have a personal, social, or political meaning that is controversial, repulsive, or profound and therefore worthy of contemplation.

However, having said that, it is important to keep in mind that the loss of beauty leads to the loss of ability to make aesthetic judgments. A significant result of this is that aesthetic value becomes driven by the market economy. The market in the art world drives the value of the work of art. This feature, in turn, forces artists to be more outlandish in their creative ideas in order to be noticed – much like a pop music star. The competition for notoriety can interfere with the authentic creative impulse.

The other effect of this is that art and beauty become a luxury only the wealthy can afford. More recently, critical theorists such as Adorno, Benjamin, and Foucault have shed light on this aspect of aesthetics and the art world.

In light of my argument concerning originality in art as an expression of the creative intellect and skill of the artist in communicating elemental meaning, how would one apply this to the beauty of nature? Kant favoured the beauty of nature over created art, but I am sympathetic to Gadamer, who disagrees with Kant on this point.[29] The principle of originality that constitutes a work of art does not in the same way apply to the beauty of nature.

I would argue that Aquinas's three conditions apply no less to the beautiful landscape, sunset, flower, and so on. However, what intensifies the beauty is the ephemeral or transitory nature of the beautiful scene. The ephemerality of beauty in nature, I suggest, stands as an analogue to originality in human creations of beauty. We value the original in a work of art in a similar way as we value the ephemeral in nature. The sunset is transitory, so we are beckoned to enjoy it while it lasts. The quiet snow will melt come spring, the cherry blossoms wilt after a few days, the summers end, and the autumn leaves change colour and drop to the ground. The ephemerality of these things reminds us that each aspect of natural beauty is changing. It is here that the Japanese aesthetics of *wabi-sabi* can help us gain a deeper understanding of this aspect of natural beauty.[30]

Finally, we can ask how religious art is different from other types of fine art or so-called secular forms of art. In general, the meaning of religious and secular works of art can interpenetrate. The difference between the two is one of the intention of the artist. In religious art, the artist is intentionally trying to communicate the mystery of the sacrality of existence and to invite people into it by way of participation and contemplation of the work. Secular art, by contrast, does not intend to communicate an ineffable mystery; it may have that effect, but it does not endeavour to do so.

Summing Up: Lonergan on Art

Our goal in this section has not been to offer a detailed philosophy of art, but rather to outline the general features of such a philosophy. It is possible to suggest some general features for a philosophy of art based on Lonergan's thought and that retains the notion of beauty.

First, there is an aesthetic pattern of experience that is uninstrumentalized, liberating the human spirit in a pattern that is reflective of play, entertainment, pleasure, and aesthetic enjoyment. It is a pattern where one is involved with one's whole attention, where the subject/object distinction is dissolved while in that pattern. And it is one where there is a surplus of meaning, pre-predicative, as with Heidegger, where to express part of the experience is simultaneously to lose part of the experience.

Second, there is an artistic pattern of experience, where the liberation is not as spontaneous as in the aesthetic pattern because the artist is deliberately bringing her/his reflection and intelligence to bear in an act of creative expression, a task that requires at least some instrumentalization of consciousness in order to achieve the created work. Here the skill, creative intelligence, and experience of the artist bear upon his or her ability to express the meaning effectively.

Third, the work of art is an *original* act of creative expression. That artists are influenced and inspired by other works and may incorporate the insights of other artists within their own work is not to say, as some aesthetic theorists do, that art is copy. Rather, it is to affirm that artists bring their own creative interpretation and insights to bear upon their works of art, after reflection on the experience. The artwork is a creative expression in an artistic media of the artist's own original interpretation. Finally, the creative originality in a work of art is analogous to the ephemerality of beauty in nature.

Fourth, the meaning expressed in an artwork is elemental. This means that (1) it pertains to non-instrumentalized patterned experience; (2) it expresses a surplus of meaning, which resists precise thematization;

and (3) the subject-object distinction is not clearly differentiated in the experience of it. The work of art, in turn, invites observers into elemental meaning.

However, *pace* Heidegger's desire to preserve *lived experience*, which he believes can be lost in the intellectual abstraction, the fact of elemental meaning does not make such meaning more ontological than the intelligibility affirmed in the judgment of an act of understanding. Both the creation of art and the act of understanding are abstractions from sensible presentations. However, the intelligibility in the act of understanding is more narrowly confined to the content of the act, whereas the art work, as an abstraction from the purely experiential pattern, may hold multiple insights and is open to multivalent expressions. In both cases, however, abstraction is enriching and, in the case of art, is bolstered by observers' ability to participate in the art work itself and be brought out of their own instrumentalized consciousness into the surplus of meaning communicated in that work.

Life and Beauty

For Lonergan consciousness flows in various patterns: biological, aesthetic/artistic, dramatic, intellectual, interior, mystical, and so on. The dramatic pattern of experience is analogous to the aesthetic/artistic pattern, but it pertains to two aspects of human living: the practical world of getting things done and human relations. The aesthetic-dramatic operator works as an undertow in human consciousness: "behind palpable activities, there are motives and purposes; and in them it is not difficult to discern an artistic, or more precisely, a dramatic component" (*IN*, 210).

In the tasks of ordinary living, of getting things done and dealing with people, the emphasis is more on the roles one plays in society. "But aesthetic liberation, artistic creativity, and the constant shifting of the dramatic setting open up vast potentialities. All the world's a stage, and not only does each in his time play many parts but also the many parts vary with changes of locality, period, and social milieu" (*IN*, 214). According to Lonergan, ordinary living is "charged emotionally and conatively" in such a way that human beings are "capable of aesthetic liberation and artistic creativity" in every aspect of their lives:

Not only, then, is man capable of aesthetic liberation and artistic creativity, but his first work of art is his own living. The fair, the beautiful, the admirable is embodied by man in his own body and actions before it is given a still freer realization in painting and sculpture, in music and poetry. Style is the man before it appears in the artistic product. (*IN*, 211)

In other words, people who are operating within the dramatic pattern of experience seek to accomplish the tasks of daily living with a creative style (*IN*, 212). This potential flair for style and creativity that humans possess differs from that of the artist. Whereas the latter seeks to express meaning creatively in works of art, those operating in the dramatic pattern make creative expressions out of their own lives, although perhaps not as self-consciously as the artist does when creating a work of art. Hence, human beings shape and create the drama of life with their own individual contributions, and they in turn are shaped by the drama of life.

Not only does the aesthetic-dramatic operator move human beings to create a work of art with their own lives, there is also the desire to beautify the ordinary aspects of one's life. Here we have a difference between art as the expression of elemental meaning and the beautification of ordinary living that pertains to dramatic living. Nor is the line between the two always clear. Great architecture is functional in a way that great music is not. The former may stimulate the imagination, but it also provides shelter; the latter may soothe the soul, but it cannot shelter one from the elements. In the realm of art, artists seek to express the surplus of meaning in original expressions, but in the world of practical living, human beings seek to beautify their homes, cuisine, lives, and other aspects of their lives. The dramatic pattern flows in a world where the subject is engaged, *zuhanden* in the words of Heidegger, rather than *vorhanden*. Of course, this was perhaps more apparent prior to the age of manufacturing when craftspeople were more apt to imprint their products with artistic flair.

Finally, there is the human drama of intersubjective relations. The world of practical living and the good of order require the cooperation of individuals, communities, and nations. The drama of human living also includes the relations of friendship, love, family, and progeny. People not only strive to create works of art with their own lives, they create lives together. However, conflict is inevitable, and so one has to confront the flight from understanding within oneself and in others. There remains the most significant drama in the lives of human beings, and that is the choice for authenticity and the withdrawal from inauthenticity.

Ethical Living

The aesthetic-dramatic operator carries over into ethical living. As we noted in chapter 4 on Kierkegaard, for Aquinas virtue (*honestum*) reflects spiritual beauty (*ST*, 2-2.145.3). Moreover, Aquinas's three conditions of beauty reflect authentic ethical living. People of integrity practice what they preach, and their knowing is consistent with the true values they affirm. Their relations with others are spontaneous, reflecting a creativity that is proportionate and harmonious with what they affirm to be truly valuable. And there is a clarity in the moral person who is committed to the truth and an honesty that does not obstruct it. There is also the radiance of the truly ethical person, especially as exemplified by outstanding individuals such as Gandhi, Martin Luther King, Jr, and Nelson Mandela.

Again, the drama of human living is one between authenticity and self-transcendence on the one hand, and on the other the withdrawal from authenticity that gives rise to the ugliness of violence and evil. Robert Doran explains:

> The ultimate drama of my life, in fact, is this drama of authenticity and inauthenticity. The authentic person is the person who pursues understanding, who seeks truth, who responds to what is really worth while [value], and who searches for God and God's will. The inauthentic person is the person who flees understanding, who runs from the truth, who resists further questions about his or her decisions, and who tries to escape God. And those feelings never go away. They are present in the entire drama. They are precisely what make it so dramatic.[31]

In chapter 18 of Lonergan's *Insight*, he argues that human beings are incapable of sustained development and overcoming the problem of evil by their own natural capacities. In chapter 3 of this work we saw how Nietzsche's aesthetics reflects a deviated transcendence that not only perpetuates the loss of beauty, but feeds the cycle of violence. And so the restoration of philosophical beauty will raise again the question of a ground of beauty, and with it the possibility of a theology of beauty that addresses the divine restoration of beauty in the created order. The latter lies outside the scope of this book, but we will return to the question of a ground of beauty after addressing the topic of contemplation.

Finally, the creation of a work of art with one's life is inextricably linked with the beauty of existence. The beauty of life is linked to the fact that it is transitory, ephemeral, fleeting. Part of the value of life flows from the fact that it is impermanent. Each of us has only so much time on the planet, and so the challenge is to live life fully, in the words of Lonergan, to create a work of art with our own lives and in the twilight of our years to reflect on and contemplate it.

Contemplating Beauty

In addition to the human impulse to create beauty, there is the inclination of the human spirit to contemplate beauty. Indeed, we have discussed what Lonergan calls the fourth-level operation, and this entails the level of decision and action. A ground-breaking work by one of Lonergan's successors, F.E. Crowe, interprets Aquinas on this point in an attempt to flesh out the latter's notion of will in its active and passive dimensions. Traditionally the role of the passive aspect in his thought was not as emphasized, in part because it is not fully explicated in Aquinas's thought. Crowe seeks to interpret the two as *complacency* and *concern*[32] (although he admits that "complacency" is not the optimal term given its connotation in English with inertness). I will not summarize Crowe's lengthy exegesis of the relevant passages in Aquinas here. For our purposes it is important only to emphasize that Crowe argues for two ways in which the fourth-level operations function: the *via receptionis* and the *via motionis*.[33] The former pertains to the will as an end to the rational act and the latter to the will as the beginning. Crowe spends the bulk of his essay arguing for the *via receptionis* but by way of contrast with the *via motionis*, since the former has been neglected in Aquinas's thought.

Crowe's Thomistic hermeneutics seeks to bring back the emphasis on the *via receptionis*, or passive aspect of the will. He does this with "the conviction that it is the Cinderella of studies in psychology and spirituality, chronically pushed off the stage by the more palpably evident activity of the will in active pursuit of the good."[34] While this "pushing aside" of the passive aspect of the will is perhaps not as devastating as the eclipse of beauty, still the two are intimately related in that the recovery of one entails the recovery of the other.

For our purposes, we might simply emphasize the two ways of the will (fourth-level operations) in terms of contemplation and action, or the reflection upon and the creation of beauty. This is to say that the appropriate fourth-level response to beauty in terms of the *via receptionis* is to "receive" intelligibility in its due proportion, integrity, and clarity and to contemplate or simply delight in the beautiful forms of beauty.

The proper response to beauty is repose, though the matter hardly ends here. In fact, the effects of repose on the will are to enrich, inspire, reassure, and promote further acts of the human spirit that are conducive to and reflective of the encounter with beauty. For example, as we suggested earlier, these further effects are embodied in the ideal of the Diné, or Navajo, notion of beauty. Their encounter with beauty is inextricably tied to the creation of beauty in every aspect of their lives. The entire healing/chantway system of ceremonies is structured with the aim of restoring and creating beauty. To walk in beauty is at once to contemplate and create beauty.

Loving Beauty

We have noted Aquinas's axiomatic statement that everyone loves the beautiful. Conversely we can ask, What role does beauty have in being in love? To "love" the beautiful means different things pertaining to the different levels of consciousness. First, it is to be open to the desire for beauty in its radical unrestrictedness. At the level of experience or presentations it is to delight in the sensitive colours, sounds, and patterns presented to the senses and the imagination. At the level of understanding, it is to delight in the unity or relations grasped in the forms that are integral, proportionate, and radiant. It is to delight in the order. At the level of judgment, it is to delight in the truth and existence of the beautiful and to further apprehend a surplus of meaning pointing one beyond what is affirmed as beautiful. At the level of decision one seeks to create beauty in every aspect of one's life and to contemplate the value of beauty as apprehended.

Further, as we pointed out in chapter 1, there has been suggested a "fifth level" of consciousness in Lonergan's thought concerns being in love with one's family and community and with God. This is to say that there are proportionate and disproportionate ways of being in love. To put the matter succinctly, to fall in love with people is natural, to fall in love with God is supernatural.

In *Insight*, Lonergan distinguishes between central and conjugate potency, form, and act. The central form pertains to the unity-identity-whole of a specific being, and the central act pertains to the existence of the being as a concrete unity-identity-whole (*IN*, 460–3). Central form is basically what Aristotle means by substantial form. Conjugate forms concern the specific characteristics of central form/act that are subject to change. For human beings, the central form/act would also relate to their unique identity as a human being, intimately related to their soul. Conjugate forms/acts would pertain to the individual characteristics that are subject to change, such as hair colour, physique, and habits.

In terms of being in love, the locus of the appreciation of beauty is centred not in the conjugate forms/acts per se but on the central forms/ acts of the two people who are in love. The specific conjugate forms/ acts of a beloved's particular appearance and demeanour may bring to the lover's mind the central form of the beloved, as for example when a lover says, "No one has her smile." In the mystery of falling in love and being in love, the lovers are given privileged and private access to their beloved's central form/act in its integrity, proportion, and clarity in an unconditional way that is analogous to God's love for the individual. Part of being in love is the repose of the beloved to the lover. When we behold our beloved, our repose is non-instrumentalized, to invoke Lonergan's term, and disinterested in the Kantian sense. In other words, we do not want anything from the person but just to be in their presence – this makes us happy.

Moreover, it is because of this privileged access to the beloved's central form/act that one might be sympathetic to the adage that beauty is in the eye of the beholder, or as Albert Einstein declared, "Gravitation cannot be blamed for people falling in love." However, this fact speaks more to the mystery of love than to the relativity of beauty, the question of why the lovers have been given privileged access to appreciate each other's central form and act in the first place. Exactly why two specific people fall in love and stay in love can only be explained by a confluence of factors, including opportunity, availability, and means; however, it is this privileged access that is the ground of the relationship. Whether they will stay together, all things being equal, is a question of their level of commitment to each other despite the obstacles they encounter in life.

Finally, there is a further notion of being-in-love that is disproportionate to our natural desires, but at the same time the only one that can satisfy the ultimate thirst for beauty. It is to this notion that we now turn.

Beauty and God

To posit the transcendental notion of beauty as a fundamental property of being is ultimately to raise the question of a primary act of beauty, or

God, in which all beings participate, and by virtue of which participation all beings are beautiful.

In discussing such matters we are reaching the limit of a philosophy of beauty that takes us beyond the natural knowledge of God and to the threshold of a theological aesthetics. Therefore I will limit this inquiry to the possibility of an aesthetic argument for God's existence.[35] It is an argument that is often related to the transformative encounter with beauty.

From Aesthetic Experience to the Beauty of God

We mentioned in chapter 5 that Lonergan appropriates Aristotle's notion of *wonder* into what he elaborates in *Insight* as the detached, pure, unrestricted desire to know. We used this as analogue when we argued for an unrestricted desire for beauty that is indicated by the ephemeral nature of beauty and the inability of a single encounter with beauty to satisfy the appetite for it,[36] illustrating the point using Edgar Allen Poe's "The Poetic Principle": "It is no mere appreciation of the Beauty before us, but a wild effort to reach the Beauty above."[37] In other words, the contemplation and appreciation of beauty opens us up to something beyond ourselves. Ultimately this will raise the question of a ground of beauty, as C.E.M. Joad suggests when he states: "In the appreciation of music and of pictures we get a momentary and fleeting glimpse of the nature of that reality to a full knowledge of which the movement of life is progressing."[38]

We have indicated that there is a natural disposition within everyone to appreciate beauty and that beauty is experienced as ephemeral, temporal, and transitory. Further, the surplus of meaning eventually raises the question within us of some ultimate meaning or perhaps some ultimate ground of beauty. In other words, aesthetic experiences such as Joad refers to provide a context for the question of God's existence to arise. These moments, as fulfilling, lend support to a subjective confirmation of some ultimate significance. We can extrapolate from the experience to affirm the existence of an ultimate ground of beauty.

The conversion of the famous Russian Orthodox theologian Sergei Bulgakov exemplifies the movement from aesthetic experience to the question of God. His conversion from Marxist atheism to Christianity was affected by two pivotal experiences he underwent, while contemplating the beauty of the Caucusus Mountains and later while contemplating a piece of religious art.[39] The first experience occurs in 1896:

I was twenty-four years old. For a decade I had lived without faith and, after stormy doubts, a religious emptiness reigned in my soul. One evening, we were driving across the southern steppes of Russia. The strong scented spring grass was gilded by the rays of a glorious sunset. Far in the distance, I saw the blue outlines of the Caucasus. This was my first sight of the mountains. I gazed with ecstatic delight at their rising slopes. I drank in the light and air of the steppes. I listened to the revelation of nature. My soul was used to the dull pain of seeing nature as a lifeless desert and of treating its surface beauty as a deceptive mask. Yet, contrary to my intellectual convictions, I could not be reconciled to nature without God.

Suddenly and joyfully in that evening hour my soul was stirred. I started to wonder what would happen if the cosmos were not a desert and its beauty not a mask or deception – if nature were not death, but life. What if the merciful and loving Father existed, if nature was a vestige of his love and glory, and if the pious feelings of my childhood, when I used to live in his presence, when I loved him and trembled because I was weak – what if all this were true …

O mountains of the Caucasus! I saw your ice sparkling from sea to sea, your snows reddening under the morning dawn, the peaks which pierced the sky, and my soul melted in ecstasy … The first day of creation shone before my eyes. Everything was clear, everything was at peace and full of ringing joy. My heart was ready to break with bliss. There is no life and no death, only one eternal and unmovable now. *Nunc dimittis* rang out in my heart and in nature. And an unexpected feeling rose up and grew within me – the sense of victory over death. At that moment I wanted to die, my soul felt a sweet longing for death in order to melt away joyfully, ecstatically, into that which towered up, sparkled and shone with the beauty of first creation … And that moment of meeting did not die in my soul, that apocalypse, that wedding feast: the first encounter with Sophia. That of which the mountains spoke to me in their solemn brilliance, I soon recognized again in the shy, gentle girlish look on different shores and under different mountains.[40]

The "shy girlish look" he refers to speaks to his second major aesthetic-religious experience, which occurred in Dresden in 1900. His encounter with Raphael's *Sistine Madonna* drew him further away from his atheism and closer to Christianity.

I went to the art gallery to do my duty as a tourist. My knowledge of European painting was negligible. I did not know what to expect. The eyes of the Heavenly Queen, the Mother who holds in her arms the Eternal Infant, pierced my soul. There was in them an immense power of purity and of prophetic self-sacrifice – the knowledge of suffering and the same prophetic readiness for sacrifice that was to be seen in the unchildishly wise eyes of the Child … I cried joyful, yet bitter tears, and with them the ice melted from my soul, and some of my psychological knots were loosened. This was an aesthetic emotion, but it was also a new knowledge; it was a miracle. I was still a Marxist, but I was obliged to call my contemplation of the Madonna by the name of "prayer."[41]

By 1908 Bulgakov's conversion to Christianity is definitively effected and by 1918 he becomes an Orthodox priest. From these accounts we can trace how Bulgakov became increasingly convinced of the existence of God, thereby leaving his Marxist atheism behind. One does not have to be convinced that there is a God based on other people's experiences of God. Bulgakov's writings demonstrate that aesthetic experience can transform and lead one to the belief in transcendent religious value.

Conclusion

In this chapter I have suggested how the notion of transcendental beauty can be articulated in terms of Lonergan's fourth level of decision and the so-called fifth level. Taking the hermeneutics of Crowe's interpretation of Aquinas on complacency and concern as a lead, I have argued for a twofold aspect of beauty – an active and a passive component.

The active dimension gives rise to a philosophy of art wherein the artist creates works of art that express the surplus of meaning that is elemental. The desire to create beauty also flows over into the dramatic and practical patterns of living in the desire to create a work of art with one's life, one that is worthy of contemplation. It also entails an ethics that is measured by aesthetic categories of integrity, clarity, and proportion.

In terms of a passive dimension, at the fourth level we contemplate beauty – in nature, art, life, and existence. In love, we contemplate the beauty of the other person. This also leads us to the question of an ultimate ground of beauty; we noted that in some instances aesthetic beauty has brought people to belief in God.

In the next and final chapter I will summarize this philosophy for a theology of beauty and point out some further avenues one might explore in developing a theology of beauty or theological aesthetics.

9 Philosophy for a Theology of Beauty

If beauty is to save our world, as Dostoevsky suggests, we must recover it. In the previous chapters we have been trying to work out a philosophical framework for recovering beauty in a context described by H.G. Gadamer as dominated by a post-Kantian subjectivization of aesthetics. We have been arguing for Lonergan's contribution because he reckons with the turn to the subject by completing and correcting it, as summarized in his tag "objectivity is the fruit of authentic subjectivity." It remains for us to summarize briefly what we have been up to and then to conclude with some suggestions of a philosophy for a theology of beauty – one that may provide an opportunity to revisit Balthasar's enormous theological aesthetics with transposed Thomistic philosophical foundations.

A Summary and Overview

The context in which we have been operating is the loss of beauty in the West as diagnosed by Balthasar. For him, Aquinas's philosophy was the last Western approach that was conducive to holding together the transcendentals unity, truth, goodness, and beauty. There are two limitations to this view. First, it presumes that Aquinas had a systematic treatment of beauty as he did with truth, unity, and goodness as evidenced by his *De Veritate*. Second, Balthasar refuses to engage those more modern interpreters of Aquinas who have attempted to address the post-Kantian turn to the subject.

The loss of transcendental beauty leads not only to its subjectification but to the loss of the other transcendentals as well. Since this analysis is suggestive in Balthasar, it was necessary to flesh out the further implication of the loss of beauty, specifically the relation between its loss and the perpetuation of violence. Nietzsche's aesthetics via its reading by Girard becomes a potential conduit and perpetrator of the cycle of violence and the scapegoat mechanism. In contrast, we attempted to read his binary aesthetics through the lens of Lonergan's philosophy in a way that would preserve the brilliance of the binary distinction and at the same time clarify it in order to prevent potential distortions. Therein the Dionysian pertains to the world of immediacy and the Apollonian to the world mediated by meaning and motivated by value.

Still equally problematic is the pejorative legacy of aesthetics left in the wake of Kierkegaard's negative view of the aesthete as a hedonist, dominator, and drifter. The fact that Kierkegaard pits this view of the aesthetic against the ethical and religious spheres was for Balthasar a further sign of the subjectification and loss of beauty. In our reading, however, we proposed that the existential spheres be interpreted as functioning like patterns, differentiations, and transformations of consciousness. On this reading, since the flows of consciousness can interprenetrate, blend, and transform, there need not be a bifurcation between the aesthetic, ethical, and religious spheres. However, *pace* Balthasar's identification of the negative aesthetic, which we agree, but the blending and integration of the three spheres, we argued, can be more fully understood through Lonergan's philosophy of consciousness.

In addition, we have argued that the lack of a systematic treatment of beauty in Aquinas, rather than discounting beauty as a transcendental, points more directly to the fact that beauty is a different kind of transcendental. From the side of the object, beauty is the splendour of the transcendentals together, as suggested by Bonaventure. From the side of the subject, beauty is the fruit of authentic subjectivity, the fruit of attentiveness, intelligence, reasonableness, responsibility, and love.

Beauty is pleasing when seen or apprehended. The experience of beauty occurs in those moments when our consciousness is freed from the instrumentation in the biological, practical, and intellectual patterns of consciousness. We encounter a surplus of meaning that is pleasing, or rather, affectively moving to greater or lesser degrees and in the more dramatic experiences can even be transformative. Beauty can appeal directly to the senses, or to the intellect, or to the subject's affectivity where the apprehension of beauty can also include the apprehension of value fostering contemplative appreciation. In romantic love, one delights in the central form/act of the beloved's being.

Beauty pertains to formal causality and the three conditions. Beauty pertains to formal rather than final causality. This lends to the appreciation of the form as such rather than an object's purpose or usefulness. Moreover, the extent to which the form is whole (integral), harmonious/ proportionate, and luminous/radiant is the extent to which it is beautiful. When the intellect apprehends beauty, it apprehends the luminosity of the integral forms that possess due proportion and/or harmony.

Everyone loves the beautiful. There is a desire to contemplate and create beauty in one's life in the ordinary work of everyday living and the ethical life, and the desire to create beautiful art worthy of reflection and contemplation. While the aesthetic pattern is readily accessible to all, the artist seeks to express his or her insights symbolically in works of art, in order to bring observers back into the significance and surplus · of elemental meaning.

Falling in love with another human being grants one the privileged access to appreciate another's central form/act. It is one of the mysteries of human existence. On the other hand, to fall in love with God is to fall in love with the ground of all beauty. Such a dynamic state can be facilitated or perpetuated by the beauty in nature or a work of art, and likewise by a beauty that can be expressed, or at least attempted, in works of art such as religious iconography.

This brings us to the threshold of a theology of beauty. While we have hoped to provide a philosophical basis for beauty as a transcendental property of being, we have also been aware of the need to revisit Balthasar's theological aesthetics in light of these renewed and transposed Thomistic foundations. In the following section[1] I will outline some additional aspects that will need to be accounted for, but that Balthasar did not consider, in order to arrive at a fuller theology of beauty.

Towards a Theology of Beauty

Having argued for the foundations for a philosophical approach to beauty from Lonergan's philosophy of consciousness, what can we anticipate in terms of a theology of beauty and a fuller appropriation of Balthasar's lifelong endeavour to recover beauty in theology? I will address only a few of the principal avenues for development: the engagement with non-Western notions of beauty, incorporation of ecological concerns, a theological aesthetics that takes into account liberation praxis and with it *the preferential option for the poor*, a fuller appropriation of the incarnational aspect of beauty that responds to the dualist anthropologies, the incorporation of insights from other Christian ecumenical traditions, and a renewal of Mariology.

In incorporating the insights from non-Western notions of beauty it is important to say something about the possibility of differing notions of beauty from other religious traditions that may in turn enrich a theological aesthetics.

For Lonergan, "theology mediates between a cultural matrix and the significance and role of a religion in that matrix" (*MT*, ix). What is implicit in this axiom is that there is bound to be an interplay between what Lonergan called special theological categories (categories from a specific religion, e.g., sanctifying grace) and the more general categories (those derived from cultures or other disciplines, e.g., consciousness). Robert Doran has argued that Balthasar's emphasis "by and large, uncovers the grounds of those categories that are specific to theology," and that Lonergan's emphasis "uncovers the grounds of the categories shared by theology with other sciences and disciplines."[2] Further, Doran has argued for a complementarity between their respective theological and philosophical endeavours on the basis of the potential interplay between special and general categories.[3] If it is legitimate to say that theology makes use of general categories as well as special theological categories, then it is legitimate for theology to make use of the special categories from other religious traditions insofar as those categories assist us in providing a deeper understanding of the mysteries of the faith.

In his foreword to *Herrlichkeit*, Balthasar admits that his present work "remains all too Mediterranean." He suggests that there is a need to include insights from other cultures and religions, "especially ... Asia" (*GL*, I, iii). In other words, Balthasar admits the need to take into account non-Western approaches to beauty in order to enrich a theological aesthetics but admits the task is beyond his expertise.

Thus far, in reflecting on the future of a theological aesthetics, I have been arguing that there is a need to flesh out the philosophical foundations for beauty that can ground such an aesthetics, one that would take the form of a transposed Thomistic philosophy for which Lonergan has provided the framework. However, as Balthasar suggests, there is a need to consider how non-Western approaches may enrich a theological aesthetics. These should be considered in a larger project and in dialogue with the respective experts, but let me at least hint at the provocative nature of two examples.

First, one can consider how the Diné (Navajo) notion of beauty might contribute to such an endeavour.[4] The word for beauty in the Diné language is *hózhó*, which means beauty, goodness, harmony, prosperity, health, and general well-being. The notion is provocative because it is at once psychological, philosophical, ethical, and religious, as well as encompassing community and the environment. One could say that it includes the transcendental properties of being: truth, goodness, unity, and beauty, with beauty having a privileged aspect. However, the Diné notion of beauty is probably an undifferentiated one, containing all of these elements in a compact way.

The anthropologist Gary Witherspoon emphasizes that the prefix *ho-* of *hózhó* connotes reference to the larger environment, as opposed to a more specific reference, which would use the prefix *ni-*.

> Thus when one says *nizhóní* [one] means "it (something specific) is nice, pretty, good," whereas *hózhóní* means that everything in the environment is nice, beautiful, and good. As verbal prefix, *ho* refers to (1) the general as opposed to the specific; (2) the whole as opposed to the part; (3) the abstract as opposed to the concrete; (4) the indefinite as opposed to the definite; and (5) the infinite as opposed to the finite.[5]

In this way, Witherspoon emphasizes that "*hózhó* refers to the positive or ideal environment. It is beauty, harmony, goodness, happiness, and everything that is positive, and it refers to an environment which is all-inclusive."[6] One begins to get a sense of the provocative nature of this notion for an environmental ethics.

For the Diné, beauty is not something to be simply gazed upon but rather something to be integrated within one's life, and something that permeates all of one's life. Witherspoon states: "The Navajo do not look for beauty; they normally find themselves engulfed in it. When it is disrupted, they restore it; when it is lost or diminished, they renew it; when it is present, they celebrate it."[7] The ideal of such integration can be summed up in this excerpt from a Navajo prayer:

> With beauty (*hózhó*) before me, I walk.
> With beauty behind me, I walk.
> With beauty above me, I walk.
> With beauty below me, I walk.[8]

For Christians, this view will include a systematic theology that adequately accounts for ecological concerns, and the Diné notion of *hózhó* (beauty) could provide an integral component for an ecological ethics and theology of beauty. Therein the emphasis lies with human beings' recognition that the beauty of God is mediated through all creation, and therefore they have a sacred responsibility to be stewards of it. Admittedly, my reflections are far from exhaustive. Nor is it my intention to paint a nostalgic picture of the Diné worldview. Rather, I believe by listening to the wisdom of their tradition they can assist in a recovery of transcendental beauty so that we can begin, among other things, to heal the Earth from the use and abuse of humanity.

Wabi-Sabi. From Japanese Zen there is the provocative notion of beauty known as wabi-sabi. D.T. Suzuki refers to wabi-sabi as "the Eternal Loneliness," which is an aesthetics distinctively Japanese in spirit. It is reflective of the beauty of autumn and winter rather than of spring and summer: "The trees become bare, the mountains begin to assume an austere appearance, the streams are more transparent." These features of autumn can mediate moments of a transcendent reality: "There is a great Beyond in the lonely raven perching on the dead branch of a tree."[9] Crispin Sartwell summarizes that "wabi-sabi is an aesthetic of poverty and loneliness, imperfection and austerity, affirmation and melancholy. Wabi-sabi is the beauty of the withered, weathered, tarnished, scarred, intimate, coarse, earthly, evanescent, tentative, ephemeral."[10]

In such phrases, one gets a glimpse of the provocative nature of wabi-sabi that, in Christian theological aesthetics, may provide categories probing the mysteries of the Incarnation and the Passion of Jesus Christ. Wabi-sabi is a sophisticated and complex notion of beauty, but its complexity is just the kind that might get at what Balthasar was attempting to articulate about the beauty of the kenosis of the Incarnation and the Passion of the Cross: kenosis as the self-emptying of God, and in the Passion of the Cross, the loneliness and emptiness of Jesus Christ in his last hours before death. These moments culminate in a feeling of utter abandonment – the possibility of the hopelessness of death. One would not normally consider these features of the Paschal Mystery to be beautiful, and this is further complicated by the lack of categories to express such a paradoxical notion of beauty. Consider that, according to Leonard Koren, one of the principles of wabi-sabi is that "Beauty can be coaxed out of ugliness."[11] Hence, as a special "theological" category derived from Japanese Zen, it may enable us to express the beauty of certain moments in the Christian story for which there is no readily available vocabulary from Western aesthetics.

Next, the exigencies of our times demand a philosophy of beauty and theological aesthetics that promotes a stewardship of creation. That is, we need one that can promote and perhaps ground an ecological ethics. The Protestant theologian Stanley Grenz suggests that the traditional Christian theology of sin contributes to ecological irresponsibility:

> The destruction of community occurs on the level of our relationship to creation. As we noted earlier, sin means that we no longer live in harmony with the "garden" in which the Creator placed us. Designed to enjoy fellowship with the rest of God's good creation, we now live in alienation from the natural world around us. Rather than seeing ourselves as creative beings under God, we seek to be the creator, to control nature and enslave it to serve us. We no longer see the earth as an organic whole which we serve on God's behalf. Rather, in our insatiable but misguided quest for a "home," we view the earth as the raw material for our transforming activity.[12]

Grenz speaks to the negative aspect of dominion that has contributed to a degradation of creation. A restoration of transcendental *beauty* into theological reflection could readily include an ecological component embracing the beauty in all creation. For Thomas Berry, who refers to himself as a *geo-logian* (rather than a theologian), the healing of the Earth is inextricably connected with embracing the beauty of God that is mediated through the Earth and all of creation. He states: "Intimacy with the planet in its wonder and beauty and the full depth of its meaning is what enables an integral human relationship with the planet to function."[13]

The mainstream Protestant voice behind this critique of the traditional view of dominion in creation theology is Jürgen Moltmann. In his work *God in Creation* he sets out an ecologically friendly doctrine of creation that sees God's being as inextricably present in the created order, while the created order is inextricably within God. The relationship is analogous to Trinitarian *perichoresis*, "the reciprocal indwelling" and "mutual interpenetration" of the divine persons.[14] Such a presupposition affects not only a theology of dominion but will affect the realm of aesthetics: given the intimate and mystical relationship between the Creator and the creation, beauty must permeate the entire created order. Again, for Moltmann the being of existence and the ground of all being are intimately intertwined; thus the beauty of being and the beauty of God are intimately linked, not in some pantheistic way but in a *pan-en-theistic* (literally, "all in God") way where the beauty of God permeates creation and the beauty of creation resides in God. The implications of this can be further developed, but for now suffice it to say that a notion of beauty to ground a theological aesthetics should take into account the serious ecological exigencies of our times, and in this way should also influence an ecological ethics.

Next, Robert Doran has said of Balthasar's work that it needs "a good jolt of liberation theology."[15] Consider that for Balthasar one of the effects of the eclipse of beauty is that theology can overemphasize "praxis," perhaps echoing his ambivalence, along with that of John Paul II for whom he was an advisor, towards liberation theologians. One of the unfortunate effects of Balthasar's analysis is that there has been little attempt to account for the poor and marginalized of society within a theological aesthetics. What is more, aesthetic beauty is commonly perceived as the province of the educated and wealthy, who have access to the world of art collectors and dealers. There has been little reflection on the notion of the poor and beauty or an attempt to account for the *preferential option for the poor* within a theological aesthetics. Dorothy Day once said, "The poor need beauty." Recent scholarship has begun to develop along these lines, and continued reflection will be necessary in order to incorporate a hermeneutic of the marginalized, the poor, and underprivileged into a theological aesthetics.[16]

Next, a recovery of beauty will have to take into account the relationship between the body and the mind. Again, the legacy of Kant brings with it a separation of the sensible and the "spiritual" perception of beauty, as explained by Adrienne Dengerink Chaplin:

> A similar separation between the body and the mind can be found in Kant's distinction between a liking for the agreeable, which is rooted in our sensuous bodily nature, and a liking for beauty, which is the result of the contemplative mind's reflection.[17]

This separation is inherited by the discipline of aesthetics via its founder Alexander Baumgarten (1714–1762) and still dominates contemporary aesthetics. Hence, the loss of beauty is linked to the separation of the "pleasing" as sensible and the intellectual contemplation of beauty. Chaplin cites theorists who are moving beyond this separation and attempting to link "truth, beauty, morality, *and* biological viability, a link not normally encountered in traditional modernist aesthetics."[18]

Indeed, the very incarnational feature of Christianity presumes that a theological aesthetics must account for the whole person, body, mind, and spirit. This means that a recovery of beauty will include insights from feminist reflection on embodiment and will also have to establish the philosophical link between the biological-sensitive and the intellectual apprehension of beauty.[19]

Doran's development of Lonergan's generalized empirical method may help provide such a link:

> [W]hat I have called psychic conversion may be the bridge between Balthasar's forgotten transcendental (the beautiful) and the transcendentals that Lonergan has retrieved in interiorly differentiated consciousness (the intelligible, the true, the real, and the good).[20]

While this is not the place for an extensive explanation, recall that psychic conversion involves the changing of what Freud identified as the "psychic" censor from a repressive to a constructive functioning. The fruit of the healing of the censor is the recovery of the creative aesthetic-dramatic dynamism in the psyche. "Psychic conversion is the transformation of that censorship from a repressive to a constructive functioning, thus releasing the aesthetic and dramatic operator into freedom from repression that is required if it is to form its proper function."[21] With psychic conversion we have the possibility of a corrected post-Kantian retrieval of anthropology that provides an explanatory account of the interconnectedness of human experience, understanding, and judgments that strive for ultimate transcendent knowledge.

With respect to the beauty of the body, the doctrine of the Incarnation, the Resurrection, the Ascension (and with this the Assumption of Mary), and the Pauline teaching of the "glorified body" (Phil 3:19) are just a few basic teachings to illustrate the integral relationship between the physical body, the soul, and the heavenly realm. Yet much of Western spirituality and philosophy has for a variety of reasons perpetuated a dualism between the physical and spiritual. The recovery of beauty is an opportunity to reconstrue the intimate relationship between the biological and "spiritual" perception of beauty. On this account, the feminist notion of embodiment may help in recovering a theology of the body whereby it is inextricably connected with the mental and spiritual aspects of the person as a whole, who as created being has the potential to reflect God's glory.[22]

A theological aesthetics will benefit from the fruit of an ecumenical dialogue between Eastern and Western Christianity.[23] Western Christians can look to Eastern Christianity for its rich tradition of "writing" icons. *Writing* as opposed to *painting* an icon signifies the inextricable relationship between the true and the beautiful. Such a rich tradition of religious art gives Eastern Christians a special authority for a theological aesthetics, as exemplified for example by the work of Bulgakov. For him, beauty is bound up with the mission of the Holy Spirit: "All the forms of being, the meanings that clothe the latter, are – as creations in beauty – the artistry of the Holy Spirit, Who is the Artist of the world, the Principle of form and Form of forms ... The beauty of the world is an effect of the Holy Spirit, the Spirit of beauty; and Beauty is Joy, the joy of being."[24]

The Eastern Orthodox theologian David Bentley Hart has sought to respond to the postmodern critical hermeneutics and now seeks to explicate how beauty is a pervasive, inexhaustible feature of the Christian story. He traces that feature in four moments: Trinity, creation, salvation, and eschatology. "In the beautiful God's glory is revealed as something communicable and intrinsically delightful, as including the creature in its ends, and as completely worthy of love."[25] Hart is influenced by various Orthodox thinkers as well as Balthasar in his attempt to articulate a Christian aesthetics, and in this way his work represents the fruits of a theological rapprochement between the East and the West.

Simultaneously, Richard Viladesau is bringing attention to theological aesthetics from the perspective of Western Christianity as he explores the rich relationship between theology and art in Christian history.[26] Art provides the images for a deeper theological understanding, reflection, and communication of the faith.

Finally, something should be said about the role of Mariology in the recovery of beauty. Balthasar states: "The image of Mary is incontestable, and even to nonbelievers it represents a treasure of inviolable beauty ... Mary's image radiates with the evidential power which comes from having been created and shaped by the form of revelation" (*GL*, I, 565). Similarly, Johann Roten writes: "In Mary there is far more than what meets the eye. The overwhelming splendor of her figure reveals the trinitarian groundedness of her being."[27] Mary is the "Christ-bearer" who through the action of the Holy Spirit gives birth to the "Christ-form." The Christ-form is God's ultimate act of artistic beauty to which all creation is ordered, and Mary is inextricably bound up with this work of art in a unique way. Although Balthasar does not explicitly invoke the title, it is nevertheless appropriate to call her "Mother of Beauty." If for Balthasar the Christian task is to conform to the Christ-form, it is through Mary that this can be achieved: "Hence, the image of her interior reality stands before the eyes of Christians and should stand before their eyes whenever the conditions for their becoming conformed to Christ are being considered" (*GL*, I, 563). Just as Mary gives birth to Beauty, Christians (as Christ-bearing or *Christophorus*) also give birth to beauty insofar as the glory (*doxa*) of the Christ-form shines through them, radiating throughout the world.

While this is not the place to develop a Mariology, if we are to recover beauty and enrich a theological aesthetics this will *de facto* imply a recovery of Mary, because she as Mother of Beauty serves an exemplar of how to give birth to beauty in a world too often permeated by the ugliness of sin and violence.

Conclusion

It is time to end this study of beauty. For me it began in the summer of 1994 as I emerged from a traditional Navajo *hooghan* in a remote area in the Southwestern desert. It gained prominence again in my studies in Toronto and my encounter with Balthasar and his penetrating diagnosis of the loss of beauty.

In summer 2005 my query took another turn to the themes of religious iconography and some of its figures, including the ancient image of Sophia. As I close this study, which I hope will contribute to the recovery of beauty in the West, I admit there is a whole other dimension yet to be explored, yet intimately related to beauty. It concerns not only the loss of beauty but also the loss of wisdom. For it is wisdom that informs us of the loss of beauty and its recovery; the recovery of one is inextricable from the recovery of the other.

Notes

Preface

1 Theodor W. Adorno, *Aesthetic Theory*, trans. R. Hullot-Kentor (London: Athlone Press, 1977).
2 Bernard Lonergan, *IN*, xxxviii.
3 Gary Witherspoon, *Language and Art in the Navajo Universe* (Ann Arbor: University of Michigan Press, 1977), 154; emphasis added.

Introduction

1 Armand C. Maurer, *AB*, 14–15.
2 See Arthur Danto, *The Abuse of Beauty: Aesthetics and the Concept of Art* (Peru, IL: Open Court, 2003).
3 David Hume, "Of the Standard of Taste" (1757), http://web.mnstate.edu/gracyk/courses/phil%20of%20art/hume%20on%20taste.htm, §7.
4 See, for example, the first in the proposed trilogy by Grace M. Jantzen, *Death and Displacement of Beauty*, vol. 1: *Foundations of Violence* (London: Routledge, 2004). She examines the inextricable relationship between the loss of beauty and the origins of violence in Western civilization.
5 Hans Urs von Balthasar, *Seeing the Form*, vol. 1 of *GL*, 18–19.
6 Robert M. Doran, *Theology and the Dialectics of History* (Toronto: University of Toronto Press, 1990), 167.
7 Richard Viladesau, *Theological Aesthetics: God in Imagination, Beauty, and Art* (New York: Oxford University Press, 1999), 36.
8 Viladesau, *Theological Aesthetics*, 36.
9 In his book *Theological Aesthetics: God in Imagination, Beauty, and Art*, Richard Viladesau makes use of Lonergan's thought in order to respond

to Balthasar's limitations. While I welcome his attempt, in this work my reliance on Lonergan's thought is more foundational and my attempt to develop Lonergan's thought along these lines more comprehensive.

1. The Eclipse of Beauty and Its Recovery

1   Thomist scholars are still divided on whether or not for Thomas beauty was even a transcendental property of being. I take up this issue in chapter 2. See Jan A. Aertzen, *Medieval Philosophy and the Transcendentals: The Case of Thomas Aquinas* (Leiden: E.J. Brill, 1996), esp. chap. 8.

2   Aiden Nichols, OP, *The Word Has Been Abroad: A Guide through Balthasar's Theological Aesthetics* (Washington, DC: Catholic University of America Press, 1998), 145.

3   Nichols, *The Word*, 146–7.

4   Nichols, *The Word*, 146–7. Negatively, Lonergan names this tendency *general bias*, a bias that resists theoretical knowledge. Such attitudes persist today in the resistance to "abstract" or speculative theology. However, theory and practice go hand in hand, and one must always keep in mind that good theory is always practical. Positively, in Catholicism this emphasis parallels the rise in apostolic religious orders and those seeking to balance contemplation and action. Prior to the medieval period, religious orders were more or less strictly monastic/contemplative.

5   Nichols, *The Word*, 148.

6   Oliver Davies, "The Theological Aesthetics," in *The Cambridge Companion to Hans Urs von Balthasar*, ed. Edward T. Oakes and David Moss (Cambridge: University of Cambridge Press, 2004), 133.

7   Thomas Norris, "The Symphonic Unity of His Theology: An Overview," in *The Beauty of Christ: Introduction to the Theology of Hans Urs von Balthasar*, ed. B. McGregor and Thomas Norris (Edinburgh: T&T Clark, 1994), 229.

8   Nichols, *The Word*, 149.

9   Nichols, *The Word*, 150.

10 I am not sure how comfortable Kierkegaard scholars would be with Balthasar's critique of the former's stages and the result. At least two Kierkegaard scholars have told me in private conversations that they did not agree that Kierkegaard's distinction between aesthetic, ethical, and religious amounts to a "wedge" or bifurcation. As I will argue in chapter 4, I think it is possible to view these spheres as differentiations of consciousness and therefore to respond to Balthasar's critique and satisfy Kierkegaard scholars.

11 On this issue see the important work by John Betz, "Beyond the Sublime: Aesthetics of the Analogy of Being," Parts 1 and 2, *Modern Theology* 21, no. 3 (2005): 367–411, and 22, no. 1 (2006): 1–50.

12 Concerning Aquinas's thought, Francis J. Kovach states: "This system of transcendentals, as can be readily seen, does not contain transcendental beauty, since the derivation is to be found in a relatively early work of Thomas Aquinas, *De veritate* (On Truth). Later on, probably while writing his commentary on Pseudo-Dionysus' *On the Divine Names*, Thomas clearly express his belief in the transcendality of beauty by declaring with Plato that every being is both good and beautiful; also, that the beautiful is convertible with the good; and the beautiful and the good are really identical and only logically distinct ... Is there a place in the above Thomistic system for transcendental beauty? ... the truth is that there definitely is room for transcendental beauty in Thomas's system." *Philosophy of Beauty* (Norman, OK: University of Oklahoma Press, 1974), 241–2.

13 See Étienne Gilson, *Elements of Christian Philosophy* (Garden City, NY: Doubleday, 1960), 159–63.

14 Michael Polanyi, *Personal Knowledge*, (London: Routledge & Kegan Paul, 1962), 269–72.

15 Hans Urs von Balthasar, "On the Tasks of Catholic Philosophy," *Communio* 20 (1993): 177.

16 I will be summarizing the stages of meaning from Bernard Lonergan, *Method in Theology* (Toronto: University of Toronto Press, 1990), 81–99; henceforth cited as *MT*.

17 Frederick Copleston, *History of Philosophy*, vol. 1: *Greece and Rome* (New York: Doubleday, 1993), 257.

18 Mary Mothersill, *Beauty Restored* (Oxford: Oxford University Press, 1984).

19 Paul Guyer, Review of Mary Mothersill's *Beauty Restored*, *The Journal of Aesthetics and Art Criticism* 44, no. 3 (1986): 245.

20 This argument is worked out in chapters 9 to 11 in Bernard Lonergan, *IN*.

21 Strictly speaking, knowing occurs in the act of judgment, but later Lonergan differentiated the fourth-level decision that pertains to constitutive acts based on our knowing.

22 Lonergan, *MT*, 292. The degree of authenticity is the extent to which one is attentive to one's experience, intelligent in one's understanding, reasonable in one's judgments, and responsible in one's decisions. It requires a faithful adherence to one's unrestricted questioning, and asking all the relevant questions in a given inquiry. Equally important is Lonergan's precept to be-in-love: with one's family, neighbour (community), and with God.

23 Giovanni Sala demonstrates that Lonergan is not a Kantian. See his *Lonergan and Kant* (Toronto: University of Toronto Press, 1994).

24 Lonergan's thinking on the good develops further in *Method in Theology* when he treats of the scale of values and the role of affectivity in judgments of value.

25 Robert M. Doran, *Theology and the Dialectics of History* (Toronto: University of Toronto Press, 1990), 168.

26 On the interpenetration, see John D. Dadosky, *The Structure of Religious Knowing* (Albany, NY: SUNY Press, 2004), 113–17.

27 For a more elaborate and concise overview of Lonergan's theory, see chapter 3 of John Dadosky, *The Structure of Religious Knowing: Encountering the Sacred in Eliade and Lonergan* (Albany, NY: SUNY Press, 2004). This section has been adapted, abridged, and rewritten based on the exposition in that chapter.

28 Bernard Lonergan, "The Subject," in *Second Collection* (Philadelphia: Westminster Press, 1974; repr., Toronto: University of Toronto Press, 1996), 80–1.

29 Lonergan, "The Subject," 75.

30 On self-appropriation see Lonergan, *Understanding and Being*, ed. Elizabeth A. Morelli and Mark D. Morelli, vol. 5 of *CW*, 131–2, 271–3.

31 See *IN*, chap. 11, "The Self-Affirmation of the Knower."

32 See also Bernard Lonergan, *TE*, 188.

33 See Lonergan, *TE*, 87. In reality the difference between the patterns of experience and differentiations of consciousness is more complicated, but that is a subject for further study.

34 Robert Doran, *Theology and the Dialectics*, 42.

35 Doran, *Theology and the Dialectics*, 59.

36 Doran, *Theology and the Dialectics*, 61; on internal communication see *MT*, 66–7.

37 Dadosky, *The Structure of Religious Knowing*.

38 Frederick Crowe, "Son of God, Holy Spirit, and World Religions," in *Appropriating the Lonergan Idea*, ed. Michael Vertin (Washington, DC: CUA Press, 1989), 325.

2. Every Being Is Beautiful

1 J. Francis Kovach, *Philosophy of Beauty* (Norman, OK: University of Oklahoma Press, 1974), 236; henceforth cited throughout as *PB*.

2 Umberto Eco, *Art and Beauty in the Middle Ages*, trans. Hugh Bredin (New Haven: Yale University Press, 1986), 19.

3 Umberto Eco, *Art and Beauty*, 20.

4 Cited in Eco, *Art and Beauty*, 22.

5   Quoted in Eco, *Art and Beauty*, 25.

6   Eco, *Art and Beauty*, 26.

7   Eco, *Art and Beauty*, 70.

8   Umberto Eco, *Aesthetics of Thomas Aquinas* (Cambridge, MA: Harvard University Press, 1988), 37.

9   Jacques Maritain, *Art and Scholasticism and the Frontiers of Poetry*, trans. J.W. Evans (New York: Scribner & Sons, 1962), 30.

10   Maritain, *Art and Scholasticism*, 173.

11   Eco, *Aesthetics of Aquinas*, 39.

12   Maritain, *Art and Scholasticism*, 172.

13   Étienne Gilson, *Elements of Christian Philosophy* (Garden City, NY: Doubleday, 1960), 160.

14   Gilson, *Elements* 162.

15   Gilson, *Elements*, 160.

16   Gilson, *Elements*, 162.

17   G.B. Phelan, "The Concept of Beauty in St. Thomas Aquinas," in *Selected Papers*, ed. A.G. Kirn (Toronto: Pontifical Institute of Mediaeval Studies, 1967), 161.

18   Jan Aertsen, *Medieval Philosophy and the Transcendentals: The Case of Thomas Aquinas* (Leiden: E.J. Brill, 1996), 335–59.

19   Piotr Jaroszynski, *Beauty and Being: Thomistic Perspectives,* Étienne Gilson Series 33, trans. Hugh McDonald (Toronto: PIMS, 2011), 205.

20   Aertsen, *Medieval Philosophy*, 354; see P.O. Kristeller, "The Modern System of the Arts," in *Renaissance Thought and the Arts: Collected Essays* (Princeton, NJ, Princeton University Press, 1980), 167.

21   Eco establishes the relationship between light and "bright color" in medieval aesthetics and in Aquinas. See his *Aesthetics of Aquinas*, 103–14.

22   Eco delves further into the various uses of the concept of proportion in Aquinas. See Eco, *Aesthetics of Aquinas*, 83–102.

23   Lonergan makes this argument in chapter 18 of *Insight*.

24   *The Summa Theologica of St. Thomas Aquinas*. 2d rev. ed., 1920; literally translated by Fathers of the English Dominican Province; online edition ©2006 by Kevin Knight.

25   Eco, *Aesthetics of Aquinas*, 66.

26   Mark Jordan, "The Evidence of the Transcendentals and the Place of Beauty in Aquinas," *International Philosophical Quarterly* 29 (1989): 396.

27   Jordan, "Evidence of the Transcendentals," 396.

28   Jordan, "Evidence of the Transcendentals," 396.

29   G.B. Phelan, "The Concept of Beauty in St. Thomas Aquinas," in *Selected Papers*, ed. A.G. Kirn (Toronto: Pontifical Institute of Mediaeval Studies, 1967), 157.

30 Maritain states that this definition of beauty is *per effectum*; we know it by effect. However, when Aquinas assigns the three elements of beauty, he is giving an essential definition of it. Maritain, *Art and Scholasticism*, 161.

31 Eco, *Aesthetics of Aquinas*, 55.

32 Eco, *Aesthetics of Aquinas*, 58

33 Jacques Maritain, *Creative Intuition in Art and Poetry* (New York: Pantheon Books, 1953).

34 Étienne Gilson, *Painting and Reality*, Bolligen Series 35, no. 4 (Princeton, NJ: University Press, 1968), and *The Arts of the Beautiful* (New York: Scribner, 1965).

35 Gilson, *Painting and Reality*, 34.

36 Jordan, "Evidence of the Transcendentals," 395.

37 *Nihil est quod non participat pulchro.*

38 *Unde omnis homo amat pulchrum.*

39 Cited in Eco, *Art and Beauty*, 24.

40 Eco, *Art and Beauty*, 48. In this work we will follow the path in the spirit of Aquinas in the sense that Lonergan appropriated his philosophy for a post-Kantian context.

41 Jaroszynski, *Beauty and Being*, 199–200.

42 See Jaroszynski, *Beauty and Being*, 183.

43 Lonergan, "Method in Theology Lectures," Q&A, Dublin, 1971, unpublished. I am grateful to the Trustees of the Lonergan Estate for permission to cite this passage and specifically to Robert Doran for bringing it to my attention.

44 Lonergan, "Method in Theology Lectures," Q&A, Regis College, 1969, unpublished. I am grateful to the Trustees of the Lonergan Estate for permission to cite this passage and specifically to Robert Doran for bringing it to my attention.

3. Violence and the Loss of Beauty

1 Wendy Steiner documents this especially as part of the post–Kantian legacy. See her *The Trouble with Beauty* (London: William Heinemann, 2001).

2 See Wang Ping, *Aching for Beauty: Footbinding in China* (Minnesota: University of Minnesota Press, 2000), pp. 29–53.

3 Sheila Jeffreys, *Beauty and Misogyny: Harmful Cultural Practices in the West* (Florence, KY: Routledge, 2005), 1.

4 Jantzen, *Death and Displacement of Beauty*, viii.

5 See Bruno Snell, *The Discovery of Mind: The Greek Origins of European Thought* (New York, NY: Harper Torchbook, 1960).

6   Nietzsche, *The Birth of Tragedy*, quoted in Albert Hofstadter and Richard Kuhns, eds., *Philosophies of Art and Beauty: Selected Readings in Aesthetics from Plato to Heidegger* (Chicago: University of Chicago Press, 1976), 498.

7   Nietzsche, *The Birth of Tragedy*, 499.

8   Nietzsche, *The Birth of Tragedy*, 501–2.

9   Nietzsche, *The Birth of Tragedy*, 502.

10 René Girard, *I See Satan Fall Like Lightning* (Maryknoll, NY: Orbis, 2001).

11 Bandura states: "Learning would be exceedingly laborious, not to mention hazardous, if people had to rely solely on the effects of their own actions to inform them what to do. Fortunately, most human behavior is learned observationally through modeling: from observing others one forms an idea of how new behaviors are performed, and on later occasions this coded information serves as a guide for action." *Social Learning Theory* (New York: General Learning Press, 1977), 22; see also his *Aggression: A Social Learning Analysis* (Englewood Cliffs, NJ: Prentice-Hall, 1973).

12 Girard, *I See Satan Fall*, xi.

13 Girard, *I See Satan Fall*, xi.

14 I have argued that more nuance is needed to this discussion. There is a horizontal mimesis (envy) and a vertical mimesis (pride), and Girardians have tended to neglect the latter by focusing exclusively on envy. John D. Dadosky, "'Naming the Demon': The 'Structure' of Evil in Lonergan and Girard," *Irish Theological Quarterly* 75, no. 4 (2010): 358; see also James Alison, *The Joy of Being Wrong: Original Sin through Easter Eyes* (New York: Crossroad, 1998), 246.

15 Girard, *I See Satan Fall*, xi.

16 Girard, *I See Satan Fall*, xii.

17 Girard, *I See Satan Fall*, 173.

18 Girard, *I See Satan Fall*, 174; see Nietsche's *The Will to Power*, trans. Antonio Ludovici, 2010, http://www.digireads.com, 99.

19 Girard, *The Girard Reader*, ed. James Williams (New York: Crossroad Herder, 1996), 246–7.

20 Girard, *I See Satan Fall*, 175.

21 Robert A. Johnson, *Inner Gold: Understanding Psychological Projection* (Kihei, HI: Koa, 2008), 61.

22 Girard, *The Girard Reader*, 249.

23 Nietzsche, *The Will to Power*, #1052.

24 Stijn Latré, "Nietzsche, Heidegger, Girard on 'The Death of God,'" *Revista Portuguesa de Filosofia* 57 (2001): 304–5.

25 René Girard, "Strategies of Madness: Nietzsche, Wagner, Dostoevski," in *"To Double Business Bound": Essays on Literature, Mimesis, and Anthropology* (Baltimore: Johns Hopkins University Press, 1988), 73.

26 Friedrich Nietzsche, *The Gay Science: With a Prelude in German Ryhmes and an Appendix of Songs*, ed. Bernard Williams, trans. Josefine Nauckhoff (Cambridge: Cambridge University Press, 2001), 119–20.
27 Girard, *The Girard Reader*, 256–7.
28 René Girard, "The Founding Murder in the Philosophy of Nietzsche," in *Violence and Truth: On the Work of René Girard*, ed. Paul Dumouchel (Stanford: Stanford University Press, 1988), 237.
29 Girard, "The Founding Murder," 236.
30 This is not Girard's phrase, but I have developed it in my work on Lonergan and Girard on this topic. See John D. Dadosky, "Naming the Demon," 367–70.
31 Girard, Editor's Comments, in *The Girard Reader*, 243.
32 René Girard, "Strategies of Madness," 63–4.
33 Girard, "Strategies of Madness," 82.
34 See the discussion and contribution of Robert Doran on this issue in his *Theology and the Dialectics of History* (Toronto: University of Toronto Press, 1990), 350.
35 Doran, *Theology and the Dialectics of History*, 78.
36 Robert Doran, *What Is Systematic Theology?* (Toronto: University of Toronto Press, 2005), 170.
37 Girard, *I See Satan Fall*, xii; emphasis added.
38 See Max Scheler, *Ressentiment*, trans. William H. Holdheim (New York: Noonday, 1973).
39 This distinction was originally made by Robert Doran in reference to Jung's work when he argued: "The key to a critical appropriation of Jung on the basis of Lonergan's foundations lies in the distinction between two kinds of opposites. There is a dialectic of contraries, exemplified par excellence in the tension of spirit and matter, and there is a dialectic of contradictories manifest in the opposition of good and evil. The integral resolution of the dialectic of contraries is in every instance the path to the good, while the distortion of the dialectic of contraries is at the heart of the mystery of evil." *Theology and the Dialectics of History*, 350.

4. Recovering Beauty in the Subject

1 Hans Urs von Balthasar, *My Work in Retrospect* (San Francisco: Ignatius Press, 1993), 38.
2 Valentine Tomberg, *Meditations on the Tarot: A Journey into Christian Hermeticism*, trans. Robert Powell with an afterword by Hans Urs von Balthasar (New York: Tarcher/Putnam, 2002), 629.

3 James Collins discusses the aptness of the terms "spheres" and "stages." The point is not to think of the three as linear progressions. James Collins, *The Mind of Kierkegaard*, rev. ed. (Princeton, NJ: Princeton University Press, 1983), 45.

4 Søren Kierkegaard, *Either/Or, Part I*, ed. and trans. H.V. Hong and E. Hong (Princeton: Princeton University Press, 1987), 74, 95.

5 Kierkegaard, *Either/Or* I, 94.

6 Kierkegaard, *Either/Or* I, 90.

7 Kierkegaard, *Either/Or* I, 206.

8 Kierkegaard, *Either/Or* I, 206.

9 Kierkegaard, *Either/Or* I, 285.

10 George Price, *The Narrow Pass: A Study of Kierkegaard's Concept of Man* (London: Hutchinson, 1963), 171.

11 For someone who never married, Kierkegaard had a "'high" notion of the sacrament and the institution, although he viewed it as a choice rooted in love.

12 Bernard Lonergan, "The Subject," in A *Second Collection* (Toronto: University of Toronto Press, 1974), 80.

13 Stephen H. Dunning addresses the use of *Aufhebung* ("to perish and to preserve") throughout Kierkegaard's work on the stages. See Stephen Dunning, *Kierkegaard's Dialectic of Inwardness: A Structural Analysis of the Theory of Stages* (Princeton: Princeton University Press, 1985), esp. 10–11.

14 Søren Kierkegaard, *Either/Or, Part II*, ed. & trans. H.V. Hong and E. Hong (Princeton: Princeton University Press, 1987), 64.

15 Price, *The Narrow Pass*, 172.

16 *The Narrow Pass*, 172.

17 *The Narrow Pass*, 172.

18 Price, *The Narrow Pass*, 172–3.

19 Kierkegaard, *Either/Or* II, 321.

20 Kierkegaard, *Either/Or* II, 292.

21 Price, *The Narrow Pass*, 173.

22 Price, *The Narrow Pass*, 174–5.

23 Kierkegaard, *Either/Or* II, 177.

24 Price, *The Narrow Pass*, 179–80.

25 Kierkegaard, *Either/Or* II, 177.

26 Søren Kierkegaard, *Stages on Life's Way*, ed. & trans. H.V. Hong and E. H. Hong (Princeton: Princeton University Press, 1988), 101.

27 Price, *The Narrow Pass*, 186.

28 Søren Kierkegaard, *Fear and Trembling* and *Repetition*, ed. & trans. H.V. Hong and E. Hong (Princeton: Princeton University Press, 1983), 36. It is

worth noting that René Girard has a much different and perhaps better interpretation than Kierkegaard's, one that does not involve human sacrifice. See his *Things Hidden since the Foundation of the World*, ed. S. Bann and M. Metteer (Stanford, CA: Stanford University Press, 1987), 142–3.

29 Kierkegaard, *Stages*, 477.

30 "[W]hen God is pleased to walk here on earth in a strict incognito … impenetrable to the most intimate observation …" Søren Kierkegaard, *Training in Christianity and the Edifying Discourse which "Accompanied" It*, ed. and trans. W. Lowrie (Princeton: Princeton University Press, 1972), 27.

31 Kierkegaard, *Training*, 85.

32 Price, *The Narrow Pass*, 196–8.

33 Kierkegaard, *Training*, 270.

34 Price, *The Narrow Pass*, 201–3.

35 Hans Urs Von Balthasar, "Revelation and the Beautiful," *Theological Explorations*, Vol. 1: *The Word Made Flesh* (San Francisco: Ignatius Press, 1989), 96.

36 Price, *The Narrow Pass*, 159–60.

37 Geza E. Thiessen, ed., *Theological Aesthetics: A Reader* (Grand Rapids, MI: Erdmans, 2004), 169.

38 Balthasar, "Revelation and the Beautiful," 96.

39 In the *Summa* (*ST*, 2-2.145.2. ad 1) the love of beauty is linked with the love of the Good. However, he is more explicit in his commentary on the Psalms: *Super Psalmo* 25 n. 5 at Corpus Thomisticum web site. [87012]. "Unde omnis homo amat pulchrum."

40 See Lonergan, *IN*, 202–12.

41 Lonergan, *IN*, 208. Lonergan's treatment of art is more developed in a later work. See Lonergan, *TE*, chap. 9.

42 Robert M. Doran, *Theology and the Dialectics of History* (Toronto: University of Toronto Press, 1990), 71.

43 There is an implicit suggestion in Lonergan's thought of an additional operator to the unrestricted desire to know. He refers to it in several places: as a *quasi-operator* (see "Mission and the Spirit" in A *Third Collection: Papers by Bernard J.F. Lonergan*, ed. F.E .Crowe [Mahwah, NY: Paulist Press, 1985], 30), a *symbolic operator* (see "Philosophy and the Religious Phenomenon," *Method: Journal of Lonergan Studies* 12, no. 2 [1994], 134), and the *élan vital* (see "Reality, Myth, Symbol" in *Myth, Symbol and Reality*, ed. Alan M. Olson [Notre Dame: University of Notre Dame Press, 1980], 37). Robert Doran attempts to clarify and synthesize these references in terms of a psychic operator; see his *Theology and the Dialectics of History*, esp. 663–4.

44 See chap. 11 of Erik H. Erickson, *Childhood and Society*, 2d ed. (New York: Norton, 1963).

45 Doran, *Theology and the Dialectics*, 42.

46 On dramatic bias see Lonergan, *IN*, 214–15.

47 Doran, *Theology and the Dialectics of History*, 60.

48 Doran, *Theology and the Dialectics of History*, 61; on internal communication see Lonergan, *MT*, 66–7.

49 As Doran states, "It functions by releasing images that integrate underlying biological manifolds but that are also the materials for insight, reflection, and decision in the forging of a work of dramatic art." *Intentionality and Psyche*, vol. 1 of *Theological Foundations* (Milwaukee: Marquette University Press, 1995), 327.

50 "For the spheres [aesthetic and ethical] are existential ... The fact of the matter would seem to be that [humans] live in some blend or mixture of the artistic, dramatic, and practical patterns of experience, that they tend to the positions enouncing their principles and to the counterpositions in living their lives." Lonergan, *IN*, 648.

51 Doran states, "The psychic aspect of interiority lies in the aesthetic dimension that permeates all of our intentional operations. In its integrity, this aesthetic dimension participates in intentionality itself, and constitutes the sensitive orientation to the beautiful." *Theology and the Dialectics of History*, 170.

52 "Hence, since the contemplative life consists in an act of the reason, there is beauty in it by its very nature and essence" (*ST*, 2-2.180.2. ad 3).

53 Doran, *Theological Foundations*, 251.

54 Doran, *Theological Foundations*, 327–8.

55 Bernard Lonergan, *Understanding and Being*, ed. Elizabeth A. Morelli and Mark D. Morelli, vol. 5 of *CW*, 234; emphasis added.

56 Lonergan, A *Third Collection*, 175.

57 On this topic see Robert M. Doran, "Ignatian Themes in the Thought of Bernard Lonergan: Revisiting a Theme that Deserves Further Reflection," *Journal of the Lonergan Workshop* 19 (2006): 83–106.

58 "[B]y deliberate and responsible freedom we move beyond merely self-regarding norms and make ourselves moral beings." Lonergan, A *Third Collection*, 29.

59 Robert Doran, *Theological Foundations*, 327–8.

60 "For beauty includes three conditions, 'integrity' or 'perfection,' since those things which are impaired are by the very fact ugly; due 'proportion' or 'harmony'; and lastly, 'brightness' or 'clarity,' whence things are called beautiful which have a bright color" (*ST*, 1.39.8)

61 "A thing is said to be good in itself (*honestum*) according as it has some quality of excellence worthy of honor because of its spiritual beauty" (*ST,* 2-2.145.3).
62 "The ultimate drama of my life, in fact, is this drama of authenticity and inauthenticity. The authentic person is the person who pursues understanding, who seeks truth, who responds to what is really worth while [value], and who searches for God and God's will. The inauthentic person is the person who flees understanding, who runs from the truth, who resists further questions about his or her decisions, and who tries to escape God. And those feelings never go away. They are present in the entire drama. They are precisely what make it so dramatic." Doran, *Theological Foundations,* 409.
63 Doran, *Theology and the Dialectics of History,* 61.
64 See Fr Egide Van Broeckhoven, S., *Diary of a Worker-Priest: A Friend to All Men* (Rockaway, NJ: Dimension Books, 1977).

5. The End of Aesthetic Experience?

1 Richard Shusterman, "The End of Aesthetic Experience," *Journal of Aesthetics and Art Criticism* 55, no. 1 (1997): 38.
2 Armand A. Mauer, C.S.B., *About Beauty: A Thomistic Interpretation* (Houston: University of Houston, 1983), 25.
3 Hans G. Gadamer, *Truth and Method,* rev. 2d ed., trans. Joel Weinsheimer and Donald G. Marshall (New York: Continuum, 2004), 43.
4 David Hume, "Of the Standard of Taste," (1757), http://web.mnstate. edu/gracyk/courses/phil%20of%20art/hume%20on%20taste.htm, §7.
5 Shusterman, "The End of Aesthetic Experience," 1.
6 Robert Wicks, "Arthur Schopenhauer," in *The Stanford Encyclopedia of Philosophy,* Fall 2009 ed., ed. Edward N. Zalta, http://plato.stanford.edu/archives/fall2009/entries/schopenhauer/.
7 Arthur Schopenhauer, *The World as Will and Idea,* cited in A. Hofstadter and R. Kuhns, *Philosophies of Art and Beauty* (Chicago: University of Chicago Press, 1976), 458.
8 Schopenhauer, *The World as Will and Idea,* 460.
9 Schopenhauer, *The World as Will and Idea,* 488.
10 Schopenhauer, *The World as Will and Idea,* 465.
11 Arthur Danto, "Introduction," in George Santayana, *The Sense of Beauty: Being the Outlines of Æsthetic Theory* (Boston: MIT Press, 1986), xxi.
12 Santayana, *The Sense of Beauty,* 35. Danto elaborates: "'Objectification' is in any case very much a Schopenhauerian term. The world-as-idea (or

as-representation, depending on how we translate Vorstellung) is, in his system, the world-as-will objectified, just as the body, more locally, is the objectification of the will. 'The action of the body,' Schopenhauer writes, 'is nothing but the act of will objectified, i.e., translated into perception.' At one point Santayana portrays an imagined life in which there is only observation and no affect or appreciation – 'in a word, ... a world of idea without a world of will.' It would be attractive to suppose that in his philosophical unconscious he had taken over the structure of Schopenhauer's metaphysics, only substituting feeling for will, and then producing a work – the present one – whose title might as well have been *The World as Feeling and Idea*. This would yield the outline of a fascinating theory in which beauty stands to perception as pleasure stands to will, so that beauty and pleasure would then be the same thing viewed under two perspectives ... Unfortunately for such an elegant reconstruction, objectification, which is a metaphysical relationship in Schopenhauer, appears to be a psychological one in Santayana, who was, after all, too much in the Anglo-American tradition of the 'quaint treatises,' and too much a student of James to be able to take seriously any concept not finally a natural one, and not ultimately matter for science. Objectification is then an act of mind rather than a necessity of being ... So *The Sense of Beauty* is Schopenhauer psychologized and naturalized, and the quaint English treatises yield the method of literary psychology Santayana uses in place of metaphysical speculation. In this respect there is a considerable continuity between the early book and the remaining philosophical system." Danto, "Introduction," 22–3.

13 Santayana, *The Sense of Beauty*, 31.
14 Danto, "Introduction," xv–xvi.
15 John Dewey, *Art as Experience*, cited in A. Hofstadter and R. Kuhns, *Philosophies of Art and Beauty* (Chicago: University of Chicago Press, 1976), 642.
16 Dewey, *Art as Experience*, 584.
17 Roman Ingarden, "The Aesthetic Experience and the Aesthetic Object," in *Readings in Existential Phenomenology*, ed. N. Lawrence and D. O' Connor (Englewood Cliffs, NJ: Prentice Hall, 1967), 303.
18 Ingarden, "The Aesthetic Experience," 313.
19 Ingarden, "The Aesthetic Experience," 313.
20 Mikel Dufrenne, *The Phenomenology of Aesthetic Experience*, trans. E.S. Casey (Evanston, IL: Northwestern University Press, 1973), 228.
21 Monroe C. Beardsley, "Aesthetic Experience Regained," *Journal of Aesthetics and Art Criticism* 28 (1969), 5.

22 Beardsley, "Aesthetic Experience Regained," 5.
23 John Fisher, "Experience and Qualities," in *Aesthetic Quality and Aesthetic Experience*, ed. Michael H. Mitias (Amsterdam: Rodopi, 1988), 4.
24 Monroe Beardsley, "In Defense of Aesthetic Value," *Proceedings and Addresses of the American Philosophical Association* 52 (1979): 741–2.
25 Shusterman, "The End of Aesthetic Experience," 29.
26 Shusterman, "The End of Aesthetic Experience," 30; emphasis added.
27 Shusterman, "The End of Aesthetic Experience," 32.
28 See his chapter entitled "Aesthetic Experience from Analysis to Eros" in Richard Shusterman and Adele Tomlin, eds., *Aesthetic Experience* (New York: Routledge, 2008).
29 Shusterman, *Aesthetic Experience*, 81.
30 Shusterman, *Aesthetic Experience*, 82.
31 Shusterman, *Aesthetic Experience*, 83.
32 Shusterman, "The End of Aesthetic Experience," 85.
33 Shusterman, "The End of Aesthetic Experience," 86.
34 Shusterman, "The End of Aesthetic Experience," 87.
35 For good examples of this aspect of Lonergan's thought see Randall S. Rosenberg, "Lonergan and the Transcendent Orientations of Art," *Renascence* 61, no. 3 (2009): 141–51.
36 Edgar Alan Poe, "The Poetic Principle," http://www.bartleby.com/28/14.html. See also Jacques Maritain, *Art and Scholasticism*, http://www2.nd.edu/Departments/Maritain/etext/artfn.htm#73, note 73.
37 C.E.M. Joad, "A Realist Philosophy of Life," in *Contemporary British Philosophy: Personal Statements*, ed. J.H. Muirhead (New York: Macmillan, 1925), 188.
38 He gleans this definition from his reading of Susanne Langer, *Feeling and Form: A Theory of Art* (New York: Charles Scribner's Sons, 1953), 40.
39 Roger Scruton, *Beauty* (Oxford: Oxford University Press, 2009), 29.
40 "[P]ure will-less knowing, which is presupposed and demanded by all aesthetic contemplation … in every case the object of aesthetical contemplation is not the individual thing, but the Idea in it which is striving to reveal itself." Schopenhaur, *The World as Will and Idea*, cited in Hofstadter and Kuhns, *Philosophies of Art & Beauty*, 467.
41 Gerard Walmsley, *Lonergan on Philosophic Pluralism: The Polymorphism of Consciousness as the Key to Philosophy* (Toronto: University of Toronto Press, 2008), 113–19. "For human consciousness is polymorphic. The pattern in which it flows may be biological, aesthetic, artistic, dramatic, practical, intellectual, or mystical" (IN, 410).
42 Shusterman, "The End of Aesthetic Experience," 30.

43 Hans-Georg Gadamer, *Philosophical Hermeneutics* (Berkeley: University of California Press, 2008), 102.

44 Bernard Lonergan, "Time and Meaning," in *Philosophical and Theological Papers 1958–1964*, ed. R.C. Croken, F.E. Crowe, and R.M. Doran, vol. 6 of *CW*, 119.

45 Joseph Flanagan, SJ, "Lonergan's Philosophy of Art: from *Verbum* to *Topics in Education*," in *Meaning and History in Systematic Theology: Essays in Honor of Robert M. Doran*, ed. John Dadosky (Milwaukee: Marquette University Press, 2009), 144.

46 Paul Ricoeur states: "a sunrise in a poem by Wordsworth signifies more than a simple meteorological phenomenon ... The surplus of meaning is the residue of the literal interpretation." *Interpretation Theory: Discourse and the Surplus of Meaning* (Fort Worth, TX: Texas Christian University Press, 1976), 55.

47 Hans-Georg Gadamer, *Truth and Method*, 70.

48 On withdrawal and return see Arnold Toynbee, A *Study of History*, abridgment of vols. 1–6 by D.C. Somervell (New York: Oxford University Press, 1947), 217–40; Bernard Lonergan, *Early Works on Theological Method 1*, ed. R.M. Doran and R.C. Croken, vol. 22 of *CW*, 42–3.

49 Iain Thomson, "Heidegger's Aesthetics," in *The Stanford Encyclopedia of Philosophy*, Fall 2009 ed., ed. Edward N. Zalta, http://plato.stanford.edu/archives/fall2010/entries/heidegger-aesthetics/.

50 Hans-Georg Gadamer, *The Relevance of the Beautiful* (London: Cambridge University Press, 1986), 133.

51 This should not be confused with Lonergan's notion of the aesthetic pattern – although the same critique would apply if someone tried to remain in the pattern.

52 Shusterman, "The End of Aesthetic Experience," 33.

53 Dewey, *Art as Experience*, 580.

54 Jacques Maritain, *Art and Scholasticism and the Frontiers of Poetry*, trans. J.W. Evans (New York: Scribner's, 1962), 165n56.

55 Juhani Pallasmaa, *The Eyes of the Skin: Architecture and the Senses*, 2d ed. (Hoboken, NJ: John Wiley & Sons, 2005).

56 Philip Shaw, *The Sublime* (Florence, KY: Routledge, 2005), 15.

57 Marjorie Hope Nicholson, *Mountain Gloom and Glory: The Development of the Aesthetics of the Infinite* (New York: Norton, 1963), 295.

58 Rudolf Otto, *The Idea of the Holy: An Inquiry into the Non-rational Factor in the Idea of the Divine and its Relation to the Rational*, trans. J.W. Harvey (London: Oxford University Press, 1924), 31.

59 Cited in Shaw, *The Sublime*, 110.

60 Edmund Burke, *On the Sublime and Beautiful,* Harvard Classics, vol. 24, pt. 2 (New York: P.F. Collier & Son, 1909–14), www.bartleby.com/24/2/313/ (accessed 22 January 2010).

61 Burke, *On the Sublime,* www.bartleby.com/24/2/ (accessed 25 January 2010).

62 Bonnie Mann, *Women's Liberation and the Sublime* (Oxford: Oxford University Press, 2006), 25.

63 See Trudy Griffen-Pierce, *Earth Is My Mother, Sky Is My Father: Space, Time, and Astronomy in Navajo Sandpainting* (Albuquerque, NM: University of New Mexico Press, 1995).

64 Kant, *Critique of Judgment,* trans. J.H. Bernard (New York: Hafner, 1951), §25, 86.

65 Kant, *Critique of Judgment,* §28, 101.

66 Kant, *Critique of Judgment,* §25, 88.

67 Kant, *Critique of Judgment,* §28, 99–100.

68 Kant, *Critique of Judgment,* §28, 101.

69 Kant, *Critique of Judgment,* §28, 104.

70 Kant, *Critique of Judgment,* §25, 89.

71 The following summarizes Arthur Schopenhauer, *The World as Will and Idea*, vol. 1, 7th ed., trans. R.B. Haldane and J. Kemp (London: Kegan, Trench, Trüdner, 1910), §39.

72 Shaw, *The Sublime,* 126.

73 Shaw, *The Sublime,* 133.

74 Jean-Françoise Lyotard, "The Sublime and the Avante Garde," cited in Renée van de Vall, "What Consciousness Forgets: Lyotard's Concept of the Sublime," in A *Companion to Art Theory*, ed. Paul Smith and Carolyn Wilde (London: Blackwell, 2009), 361.

75 Lyotard, "The Sublime and the Avante Garde," cited in van de Vall, "What Consciousness Forgets," 361.

76 Shaw, *The Sublime,* 134–5.

77 Shaw, *The Sublime,* 134–5.

78 It is a manifold experience that I personally experienced, having in summer 1995 slipped into a crevice at the top of the Alps while appreciating their beauty.

6. The Intelligibility of Beauty

1 Mark D. Jordan, "The Evidence of the Transcendentals and the Place of Beauty in Aquinas," *International Philosophical Quarterly* 29 (1989): 395.

2 See Robert Doran, "Reception and Elemental Meaning: An Expansion of the Notion of Psychic Conversion," *Toronto Journal of Theology* 20, no. 2 (2004): 133–57.

3   Christopher Alexander, *The Nature of Order: An Essay on the Art of Building and the Nature of the Universe*, book 1: *The Phenomenon of Life* (Berkeley: Center for Environmental Structure, 2002), 2; henceforth cited as *PL*.

4   See Doran, "Reception and Elemental Meaning."

7. Judgments of Beauty

1   Giovanni Sala, *Lonergan and Kant: Five Essays on Human Knowledge* (Toronto: University of Toronto Press, 1994).

2   Sala, *Lonergan and Kant*, 30.

3   Sala, *Lonergan and Kant*, 32.

4   Immanuel Kant, *Critique of Judgment*, trans. J.H. Bernard (New York: Hafner, 1951), §1; emphasis added. All further quotations attributed to Kant are, unless otherwise indicated, to this work.

5   Hannah Ginsborg, "Kant's Aesthetics and Teleology," in *The Stanford Encyclopedia of Philosophy*, Fall 2008 ed., ed. Edward N. Zalta, http://plato.stanford.edu/archives/fall2008/entries/kant-aesthetics/.

6   Lonergan came to distinguish the fourth level more clearly after completing the manuscript for *Insight* (1953) following his appointment to Rome, and this was probably facilitated by his encounter with existentialist thought after he arrived in Europe to teach at the Gregorian in Rome during the late 1950s.

7   On Lonergan's notion of judgment, see *IN*, chaps. 9, 10.

8   Lonergan, "The Subject," in A *Second Collection* (Toronto: University of Toronto Press, 1996), 76.

9   Bernard Lonergan, *Understanding and Being*, ed. Elizabeth A. Morelli and Mark D. Morelli, vol. 5 of *CW*, 118, 122–3.

10   Lonergan, *Understanding and Being*, 124.

11   Robert M. Doran, *Theology and the Dialectics of History* (Toronto: University of Toronto Press, 1990), 98–9.

12   Bernard Lonergan, "Supplement to *De Verbo Incarnato*: *De Redemptione*," unpublished ms. I am relying on Mike Shields' revised translation (2011). I am grateful to Fr Shields and to the Trustees of the Lonergan Estate for permission to cite this work. All references will be taken from Shields's typed manuscript and cited here as *De Redemptione*.

13   "But one who has been liberated through the technical use of signs is not held back by gnawing worries about material things or drawn this way and that by the notions and decisions of so-called practical people, but follows those deeper yearnings which seek after, contemplate, and desire an understanding of all things, moral rectitude, ideal human happiness, and spiritual immortality. Through literature we come to an explicit

self-consciousness. Through the pure sciences we understand our own nature and that of other things as well. Philosophy and theology raise our mind to contemplate the order of the universe and to know, praise, and serve its creator. History shows us what humankind has been and has done, that we may clearly and distinctly know what has to be corrected, rejected, and implemented.

"This cultural good, since it needs nothing external apart from signs, is easily preserved from very ancient times and transported from one place to another. And since it is rooted very deeply in human nature, it breaks through the particularities of tribe, race, and tradition and tends towards a universal commonwealth of persons. Since it can express all being and all good, it enlarges, enriches, and develops the interior life, so that we exist not merely as a cog or tool in an external biological, technological, economic and political process, but as conscious of our dignity, our freedom, and our responsibility, the arbiters and masters of that same external process." *De Redemptione*, 13–14. On the relationship of literature to aesthetic value, it may be worth consulting Lonergan scholar Hugo Meynell's *The Nature of Aesthetic Value* (Albany, NY: SUNY Press, 1986). He addresses the topic of aesthetic value in literature, music, and the visual arts, with Lonergan's perspective being operative in the background of his thinking.

14 Jacques Maritain, *Art and Scholasticism and the Frontiers of Poetry*, trans. J.W. Evans (New York: Scribner's, 1962), 132n63b. Bonaventure mentions "four conditions of a being, namely that it be one, true, good and beautiful." Umberto Eco explains "the identity and difference of the four conditions as follows: *unum* has to do with efficient cause, *verum* with the formal cause, and *bonum* with the final cause; but *pulchrum* 'encompasses every cause and is common to each … It has to do equally with every cause.'" *Art and Beauty in the Middle Ages*, trans. Hugh Bredin (New Haven: Yale University Press, 1986), 24.

15 "Beauty is something that evokes a response from the whole person – it may be through meanings, as in poetry or drama, but it may be apart from meanings in any ordinary sense. It is a type of meaning of its own kind. *We will have more to say about this kind of meaning in our third chapter* [reference to the chapter on meaning from *Method in Theology*], *which is a rather long one*." Lonergan, "Method in Theology Lectures," Q&A, Dublin, 1971, unpublished, response to question 36; emphasis added. Lonergan probably has elemental meaning in mind here as well, although his indebtedness to Suzanne Langer on art will mean that for him art is inextricably connected with elemental meaning.

16 Joseph de Finance, *Essai su l'agir humain* (Rome: Gregorian University Press, 1962).

17 I have developed Lonergan's thought, especially in terms of religious belief, in what I have called a critical appropriation of one's faith tradition. See John Dadosky, "Is There a Fourth Stage of Meaning?" *Heythrop Journal* 51, no. 5 (2010), 778–9.

18 Roger Scruton, *Beauty* (Oxford: Oxford University Press, 2009), 29.

19 Cynthia Freeman, *But Is It Art?* (Oxford: Oxford University Press, 2001), 11.

20 C.S. Lewis, *The Four Loves* (New York: Harcourt Brace, 1988), 13.

21 This was one of the main emphases of Gadamer's tome *Truth and Method*. He sought to preserve the *Geistewissenschaften* from being dominated and supplanted by the physical sciences. The first third of the work addresses aesthetic value in order to preserve the human sciences from reductionism.

22 In *Insight*, Lonergan refers to this as the twofold liberation of the aesthetic pattern from the biological and theoretical. In *Topics in Education*, he will talk about the freedom from the instrumentalization of consciousness in general, which would include the dramatic-practical patterns and interior differentiations of consciousness. *Topics* provides a further filling out of what he means by the aesthetic pattern. In the aesthetic pattern consciousness is free, spontaneous, and creative by virtue of its not being limited by the other patterns.

23 The liberation is twofold: "As it liberates experience from the drag of biological purposiveness, so it liberates intelligence from the wearying constraints of mathematical proofs, scientific verifications, and common-sense factualness" (*IN*, 208).

24 Merton uses the phrase to describe his famous experience in front of the Buddha statues at Polonnaruwa. See his *The Asian Journal* (New York: New Directions, 1973), 233.

25 Roger Scruton, *Why Beauty Matters*, BBC, 28 November 2009.

26 *Nihil est quod non participat pulchro.*

27 "Ignatian Themes in the Thought of Bernard Lonergan: Revisiting a Theme that Deserves Further Reflection," *Journal of the Lonergan Workshop* 19 (2006): 83–106.

28 I am drawing analogously on Robert Doran's hermeneutics of Lonergan's fourth level of operations; see *Theology and the Dialectics of History*.

29 On Ignatian repetition see George Traub, ed., *An Ignatian Spirituality Reader* (Chicago: Loyola Press, 2008), 67–8. For an overview of the Navajo notion of beauty see John Farella, *Mainstalk: A Synthesis of Navajo Philosophy* (Tuscon: University of Arizona Press, 1990).

30 Étienne Gilson, *Elements of Christian Philosophy* (New York: Doubleday, 1960), 162.
31 Personal communication with author, Boston College, 6 February 2010.
32 Hugo Meynell, *The Nature of Aesthetic Value* (Albany, New York: SUNY Press, 1986), 26.
33 Roger Scruton addresses the differences between art and entertainment. See his *Beauty*, 101–3.
34 See the discussion in Edson José Amâncio, "Dostoevsky and Stendhal's Syndrome," *Arq Neuropsiquiatr* 63, no. 4 (2005): 1099–1103.

8. Creating, Contemplating, and Loving Beauty

 1 He mentions a "quasi-operator" in "Mission and the Spirit" in A *Third Collection*: Papers by Bernard J.F. Lonergan, ed. F.E.Crowe (Mahwah, NY: Paulist Press, 1985), 30; "symbolic operator" in "Philosophy and the Religious Phenomenon," *Method: Journal of Lonergan Studies* 12, no. 2 (1994): 134; and *élan vital* in "Reality, Myth, Symbol" in *Myth, Symbol and Reality*, ed. Alan M. Olson (Notre Dame: University of Notre Dame Press, 1980), 37. Robert Doran attempts to clarify and synthesize these references in terms of a psychic operator; see his *Theology and the Dialectics of History* (Toronto: University of Toronto Press, 1990), esp. 663–4.
 2 Robert M. Doran, *What Is Systematic Theology?* (Toronto: University of Toronto Press, 2005), 122.
 3 For a good overview of the philosophy of art see Richard Eldridge, *An Introduction to the Philosophy of Art* (Cambridge: Cambridge University Press, 2003); chapter 4, "Expression," provides the general influences on Lonergan's thinking of art.
 4 Gerard Walmsley, *Lonergan on Philosophic Pluralism: The Polymorphism of Consciousness as the Key to Philosophy* (Toronto: University of Toronto Press, 2008), 113–19. Lonergan states: "For human consciousness is polymorphic. The pattern in which it flows may be biological, aesthetic, artistic, dramatic, practical, intellectual, or mystical" (*IN*, 410).
 5 It might be better to refer to it as a *liberative pattern of experience* since it pertains to an array of human activity rather than simply the aesthetic.
 6 For a more refined elaboration on Lonergan's treatment of art, see *TE*, chap. 9.
 7 Walmsley, *Lonergan on Philosophic Pluralism*, 117.
 8 Hans George Gadamer, *Philosophical Hermeneutics* (Berkeley: University of California Press, 2008), 102.
 9 Gadamer, *Philosophical Hermeneutics*, 100.

10 Gadamer, *Philosophical Hermeneutics*, 95.
11 See Editor's Note, *IN*, 791: Susanne K. Langer, *Feeling and Form: A Theory of Art Developed from* Philosophy in a New Key (New York: Charles Scribner's Sons, 1953), 120–32 (*IN*, 208).
12 Robert Doran, personal communication, 28 April 2011.
13 Stephen Houlgate, "Hegel's Aesthetics," in *The Stanford Encyclopedia of Philosophy*, Summer 2010 ed., ed. Edward N. Zalta, http://plato.stanford.edu/archives/sum2010/entries/hegel-aesthetics/.
14 "Hegel recognizes that art can portray animals, plants and inorganic nature, but he sees it as art's principal task to present divine and human freedom. In both cases, the focus of attention is on the *human figure* in particular. This is because, in Hegel's view, the most appropriate sensuous incarnation of reason and the clearest visible expression of spirit is the human form. Colors and sounds by themselves can certainly communicate a mood, but only the human form actually embodies spirit and reason. Truly beautiful art thus shows us sculpted, painted or poetic images of Greek gods or of Jesus Christ – that is, the divine in human form – or it shows us images of free human life itself." Houlgate, "Hegel's Aesthetics."
15 Albert Hofstadter and Richard Kuhns, *Philosophies of Art and Beauty: Selected Readings in Aesthetics from Plato to Heidegger* (Chicago: University of Chicago Press, 1976), 555.
16 Collingwood, *Principles of Art* (London: Oxford University Press, 1938), quoted in Stephen David Ross, ed., *Art and Its Significance: An Anthology of Aesthetic Theory*, 3d ed. (Albany, NY: SUNY Press, 1994), 199.
17 Collingwood, *Principles of Art,* quoted in Ross, *Art and Its Significance,* 199.
18 Susanne Langer, *Feeling and Form,* quoted in Ross, *Art and Its Significance,* 223.
19 Martin Heidegger, "Origin of a Work of Art," quoted in Hofstadter and Kuhns, *Philosophies of Art and Beauty,* 665.
20 Iain Thomson, "Heidegger's Aesthetics," in *The Stanford Encyclopedia of Philosophy*, Fall 2010 ed., ed. Edward N. Zalta, http://plato.stanford.edu/archives/fall2010/entries/heidegger-aesthetics/.
21 Thomson, "Heidegger's Aesthetics."
22 Walmsley agrees while also cautioning against the distorting effects of such approaches as Heidegger's and Nietzsche's. See *Lonergan on Philosophic Pluralism*, 118–19.
23 Gadamer, *Philosophical Hermeneutics*, 98.
24 Walmsley, *Lonergan and Philosophic Pluralism*, 118.
25 Gadamer, *Philosophical Hermeneutics*, 95.

26 Susanne Langer, *Feeling and Form*, 40.
27 This is corroborated by the reflections of at least one artist and Lonergan scholar. See Tad Dunne, "What Do I Do When I Paint?" *Method: Journal of Lonergan Studies* 16, no. 2 (1998): 103–32.
28 On iconography see Paul Eudokimov, *The Art of the Icon: A Theology of Beauty*, trans. Steven Bigham (Redondo Beach, CA: Oakwood, 1990). Religious iconography is beyond the scope of our inquiry, since its content pertains more properly to a theological aesthetics.
29 Gadamer, *Philosophical Hermeneutics*, 98.
30 Leonard Koren, *Wabi-Sabi for Artists, Designers, Poets and Philosophers* (Berkeley: Stone Bridge Press, 1994).
31 Doran, *Theological Foundations*, vol. 1: *Intentionality and Psyche* (Milwaukee: Marquette University Press, 1995), 409.
32 Frederick E. Crowe, "Complacency and Concern in the Thought of St. Thomas, in *Three Thomist Studies*, supplement to Boston Workshop, vol. 16 (Boston: Boston College, 2000), 73–187.
33 Crowe, "Complacency and Concern," 83.
34 Crowe, "Complacency and Concern," 90.
35 Portions of the following section, somewhat revised, appeared in John D. Dadosky, "The Proof of Beauty: From Aesthetic Experience to the Beauty of God," *Analecta Hermeneutica* 2 (2010): 1–15.
36 See also Glenn Hughes, *A More Beautiful Question: The Spiritual in Poetry in Art* (Columbia: University of Missouri Press, 2011), esp. chap. 4, "Emily Dickenson and the Unknown God."
37 Edgar Alan Poe, "The Poetic Principle," http://www.bartleby.com/28/14.html. (accessed 21 October 2008). See also Jacques Maritain, *Art and Scholasticism* (New York: Pantheon, 1953), n. 73, http://www2.nd.edu/Departments/Maritain/etext/artfn.htm#73.
38 C.E.M. Joad, "A Realist Philosophy of Life," in *Contemporary British Philosophy: Personal Statements*, 2d ser., ed. J.H. Muirhead (New York: Macmillan, 1925), 188; also quoted by Maritain, *Art and Scholasticism*, n. 73.
39 Sergei Bulgakov, *Sophia: The Wisdom of God* (Hudson, NY: Lindesfarne, 1993), viii–x.
40 Bulgakov, *Sophia*, viii–x.
41 Bulgakov, *Sophia*, x–xi.

9. Philosophy for a Theology of Beauty

1 The majority of the following section, although it has undergone some editorial revisions, appeared in John D. Dadosky, "Philosophy for a Theology of Beauty," *Philosophy & Theology* 19, nos. 1–2 (2007): 7–34.

2   Doran, *What Is Systematic Theology?* (Toronto: University of Toronto Press, 2005), 88.

3   See Robert M. Doran, "Lonergan and Balthasar: Methodological Considerations," *Theological Studies* 58 (1997): 61–84.

4   John Dadosky, "Foundations for a Diné (Navajo) Contribution to a Theology of Beauty," in Cyriac Pullapilly, ed., *Christianity and Native Cultures: Perspectives from Different Regions of the World* (Notre Dame, IN: Cross Cultural Publications, 2004), 43–61.

5   Gary Witherspoon, *Language and Art in the Navajo Universe* (Ann Arbor: University of Michigan Press, 1977), 24.

6   Witherspoon, *Language and Art*, 24.

7   Gary Witherspoon and Glen Peterson, *Dynamic Symmetry and Holistic Asymmetry in Navajo and Western Art and Cosmology* (New York: Peter Lang, 1995), 15.

8   Witherspoon and Peterson, *Dynamic Symmetry*.

9   D.T. Suzuki, *Zen Buddhism: Selected Writings of D.T. Suzuki*, ed. William Barrett (Garden City, NY: Doubleday/Anchor, 1956), 285–7.

10 Crispin Sartwell, *Six Names of Beauty* (New York: Routledge, 2004), 114.

11 Leonard Koren, *Wabi-Sabi for Artists, Designers, Poets and Philosophers* (Berkeley: Stone Bridge, 1994), 51.

12 Stanley J. Grenz, *Theology for the Community of God* (Grand Rapids, MI: Erdmans, 1994), 207.

13 Thomas Berry, *The Great Work* (New York: Bell Tower, 1999), xi.

14 Jürgan Möltmann, *God in Creation: An Ecological Doctrine of Creation* (London: SCM, 1985), 16.

15 Doran, "Lonergan and Balthasar," 84.

16 See Alejandro Garcia-Rivera, *The Community of the Beautiful: A Theological Aesthetics* (Collegeville, MN: Liturgical Press, 1999); Michelle Gonzales, *Sor Juana: Beauty and Justice in the Americas* (Maryknoll, NY: Orbis, 2003); Elaine Scarry, *Beauty and Justice* (Princeton: Princeton University Press, 1999); Susan Ross, *For the Beauty of the Earth: Women, Sacramentality, and Justice* (Mahwah, NJ: Paulist Press, 2006).

17 Adrienne Dengerink Chaplin, "Art and Embodiment," *Contemporary Aesthetics* 3 (2005), www.contempaesthetics.org/newvolume/pages/journal.php, 2.

18 Dengerink, "Art and Embodiment," 2.

19 Michelle Gonzalez, "Hans Urs von Balthasar and Contemporary Feminist Theology," *Theological Studies* 65, no. 3 (2004): 575.

20 Doran, "Lonergan and Balthasar," 78.

21 Doran, *What Is Systematic Theology?*, 170.

22 See Elizabeth Johnson, Susan A. Ross, and Mary Catherine Hilkert, OP, "Current Theology: Feminist Theology: A Review of Literature," *Theological Studies* 56, no. 3 (1995): 327–52.

23   See, for example, Eugene Rogers, *After the Spirit: A Constructive Pneumatology From Resources outside the Modern West (Radical Traditions)* (Grand Rapids, MI: Erdmans, 2005); Jonathan Sutton and W. Van Den Bercken, Ed., *Aesthetics as a Religious Factor in Eastern and Western Christianity* (Leuven: Peeters, 2005).

24   Sergius Bulgakov, *The Comforter*, trans. Boris Jakim (Grand Rapids, MI: Erdmans, 2004), 201.

25   David Bentley Hart, *The Beauty of the Infinite: The Aesthetics of Christian Truth* (Grand Rapids, MI: Erdmans, 2003), 17.

26   See Richard Viladesau, *Theology and the Arts: Encountering God Through Music, Art, and Rhetoric* (New York: Paulist Press, 2000); *The Beauty of the Cross: The Passion of Christ in Theology and the Arts, from the Catacombs to the Eve of the Renaissance* (Oxford: Oxford University Press, 2006); *The Triumph of the Cross: The Passion of Christ in Theology and the Arts, from the Renaissance to the Counter-Reformation* (Oxford: Oxford University Press, 2008).

27   Johann G. Roten, SM, "Mary and the Way of Beauty," *Marian Studies* 49 (1998): 116–17.

Bibliography

Adorno, Theodor W. *Aesthetic Theory*. Trans. R. Hullot-Kentor. London: Athlone Press, 1977.

Aertzen, Jan A. *Medieval Philosophy and the Transcendentals: The Case of Thomas Aquinas*. Leiden: E.J. Brill, 1996.

Alexander, Christopher. *The Nature of Order: An Essay on the Art of Building and the Nature of the Universe, Book 1: The Phenomenon of Life*. Berkeley: Center for Environmental Structure, 2002.

Alison, James. *The Joy of Being Wrong: Original Sin through Easter Eyes*. New York: Crossroad, 1998.

Amâncio, Edson José. "Dostoevsky and Stendhal's Syndrome." *Arquivos de Neuro-Psiquiatria* 63, no. 4 (2005): 1099–103. http://dx.doi.org/10.1590/S0004-282X2005000600034.

Aquinas, Thomas. *Summa Theologica*. http://www.newadvent.org/summa/.

–. *Super Psalmo*. http://www.corpusthomisticum.org/.

Balthasar, Hans Urs Von. *The Glory of the Lord: A Theological Aesthetics*. Edited by Joseph Fessio, SJ, and John Riches. 7 vols. San Francisco: Ignatius Press, 1982–91.

–. *My Work in Retrospect*. San Francisco: Ignatius Press, 1993.

–. "On the Tasks of Catholic Philosophy." *Communio (Spokane, Wash.)* 20 (1993): 147–87.

–. *Theological Explorations*, vol. 1: *The Word Made Flesh*. San Francisco: Ignatius Press, 1989.

Bandura, Albert. *Aggression: A Social Learning Analysis*. Englewood Cliffs, NJ: Prentice-Hall, 1973.

–. *Social Learning Theory*. New York: General Learning Press, 1977.

Beardsley, Monroe C. "Aesthetic Experience Regained." *Journal of Aesthetics and Art Criticism* 28, no. 1 (1969): 3–28. http://dx.doi.org/10.2307/428903.

–. "In Defense of Aesthetic Value." *Proceedings and Addresses of the American Philosophical Association* 52 (1979): 740–52.

Beckley, Bill, and David Shapiro. *Uncontrollable Beauty: Towards a New Aesthetics*. New York: Allworth, 1998.

Berry, Thomas. *The Great Work*. New York: Bell Tower, 1999.

Betz, John R. "Beyond the Sublime: Aesthetics of the Analogy of Being (Part One)." *Modern Theology* 21, no. 3 (2005): 367–411. http://dx.doi.org/10.1111/j.1468-0025.2005.00290.x.

–. "Beyond the Sublime: Aesthetics of the Analogy of Being (Part Two)." *Modern Theology* 22, no. 1 (2006): 1–50. http://dx.doi.org/10.1111/j.1468-0025.2006.00308.x.

Bulgakov, Sergius. *The Comforter*. Trans. Boris Jakim. Grand Rapids, MI: Erdmans, 2004.

–. *Sophia: The Wisdom of God*. Hudson, NY: Lindesfarne, 1993.

Burke, Edmund. *On the Sublime and Beautiful*. Vol. 24, pt. 2. The Harvard Classics. New York: P.F. Collier & Son, 1909–14.

Coleman, F.J. "Can a Smell or a Taste be Beautiful?" *AMPQ* 2 (1965): 319–24.

Collingwood, R.G. *Principles of Art*. London: Oxford University Press, 1938.

Collins, James. *The Mind of Kierkegaard*. Rev. ed. Princeton: Princeton University Press, 1983.

Copleston, Frederick. *History of Philosophy*, vol. 1: *Greece and Rome*. New York: Doubleday, 1993.

Crowe, Frederick E. *Appropriating the Lonergan Idea*. Ed. Michael Vertin. Washington, DC: Catholic University of America Press, 1989.

–. *Three Thomist Studies*. Supplement to Boston Workshop. Vol. 16. Boston: Boston College, 2000.

Dadosky, John. "Foundations for a Diné (Navajo) Contribution to a Theology of Beauty." In *Christianity and Native Cultures*, ed. Cyriac Pullapilly, 43–61. Notre Dame, IN: Cross Cultural Publications, 2004.

–. "Is There a Fourth Stage of Meaning?" *Heythrop Journal*, 51, no. 5 (2010): 768–80.

–. *Meaning and History in Systematic Theology: Essays in Honor of Robert M. Doran*. Milwaukee: Marquette University Press, 2009.

–. "'Naming the Demon': The 'Structure' of Evil in Lonergan and Girard." *Irish Theological Quarterly* 75, no. 4 (2010): 355–72. http://dx.doi.org/10.1177/0021140010377736.

–. "Philosophy for a Theology of Beauty," *Philosophy & Theology* 19, nos. 1–2 (2007): 7–34.

–. "Recovering Beauty in the Subject: Balthasar and Lonergan Confront Kierkegaard." *American Catholic Philosophical Quarterly* 83, no. 4 (2009): 509–32. http://dx.doi.org/10.5840/acpq200983443.

–. *The Structure of Religious Knowing: Encountering the Sacred in Eliade and Lonergan*. NY: Albany: SUNY Press, 2004.

–. "Walking in the Beauty of the Spirit: A Phenomenological Case Study of a Navajo Blessingway Ceremony." *Mission* 6, no. 2 (1999): 210–21.

Danto, Arthur C. *The Abuse of Beauty: Aesthetics and the Concept of Art*. Peru, IL: Open Court, 2003.

Davies, Oliver. "The Theological Aesthetics." In *The Cambridge Companion to Hans Urs von Balthasar*, ed. Edward T. Oakes and David Moss, 131–42. Cambridge: University of Cambridge Press, 2004. http://dx.doi.org/10.1017/CCOL0521814677.010

de Finance, Joseph. *Essai sur l'agir humain*. Rome: Gregorian University Press, 1962.

Dengerink Chaplin, Adrienne. "Art and Embodiment: Biological and Phenomenological Contributions to Understanding Beauty and the Aesthetic." *Contemporary Aesthetics* 3 (2005). www.contempaesthetics.org/newvolume/pages/journal.php

Doran, Robert M. "Ignatian Themes in the Thought of Bernard Lonergan: Revisiting a Theme That Deserves Further Reflection." *Journal of the Lonergan Workshop* 19 (2006): 83–106.

–. "Lonergan and Balthasar: Methodological Considerations." *Theological Studies* 58 (1997): 61–84.

–. "Reception and Elemental Meaning: An Expansion of the Notion of Psychic Conversion." *Toronto Journal of Theology* 20, no. 2 (2004): 133–57.

–. *Theological Foundations*, Vol. 1: *Intentionality and Psyche*. Milwaukee: Marquette University Press, 1995.

–. *Theology and the Dialectics of History*. Toronto: University of Toronto Press, 1990.

–. *What Is Systematic Theology?* Toronto: University of Toronto Press, 2005.

Dufrenne, Mikel. *The Phenomenology of Aesthetic Experience*. Trans. E.S. Casey. Evanston, IL: Northwestern University Press, 1973.

Dumouchel, Paul, ed. *Violence and Truth: On the Work of René Girard*. Stanford: Stanford University Press, 1988.

Dunne, Tad. "What Do I Do When I Paint?" *Method: Journal of Lonergan Studies* 16, no. 2 (1998): 103–32.

Eco, Umberto. *Aesthetics of Thomas Aquinas*. Cambridge, MA: Harvard University Press, 1988.

–. *Art and Beauty in the Middle Ages*. New Haven: Yale University Press, 1986.

Eldridge, Richard. *An Introduction to the Philosophy of Art*. Cambridge: Cambridge University Press, 2003. http://dx.doi.org/10.1017/CBO9781139164740.

Erickson, H. Erik. *Childhood and Society*. 2nd ed. New York: Norton, 1963.

Eudokimov, Paul. *The Art of the Icon: A Theology of Beauty*. Trans. Steven Bigham. Redondo Beach, CA: Oakwood, 1990.

Farella, John R. *The Main Stalk: A Synthesis of Navajo Philosophy*. Tucson: University of Arizona Press, 1993.

Fields, Stephen. "Balthasar and Rahner on the Spiritual Senses." *Theological Studies* 57, no. 2 (1996): 224–41.

Freeman, Cynthia. *But Is It Art?* Oxford: Oxford University Press, 2001.

Gadamer, Hans George. *Philosophical Hermeneutics*. Berkeley: University of California Press, 2008.

–. *The Relevance of the Beautiful*. London: Cambridge University Press, 1986.

–. *Truth and Method*. Rev. 2d ed. Trans. Joel Weinsheimer and Donald G. Marshall. New York: Continuum, 2004.

Garcia-Rivera, Alejandro. *The Community of the Beautiful: A Theological Aesthetics*. Collegeville, MN: Liturgical Press, 1999.

Gilson, Étienne. *Elements of Christian Philosophy*. Garden City, NY: Doubleday, 1960.

–. *Painting and Reality*. Rev. 2d ed. Princeton: Princeton University Press, 1969.

Girard, René. I *See Satan Fall Like Lightning*. Maryknoll, NY: Orbis, 2001.

–. *The Girard Reader*. Ed. James Williams. New York: Crossroad Herder, 1996.

–. "Strategies of Madness: Nietzsche, Wagner, Dostoevski." In *"To Double Business Bound": Essays on Literature, Mimesis, and Anthropology* (61–83). Baltimore: Johns Hopkins University Press, 1988.

–. *Things Hidden since the Foundation of the World*. Ed. S. Bann and M. Metteer. Stanford: Stanford University Press, 1987.

Gonzalez, Michelle A. "Hans Urs Von Balthasar and Contemporary Feminist Theology." *Theological Studies* 65, no. 3 (2004): 566–96.

–. *Sor Juana: Beauty and Justice in the Americas*. Maryknoll, NY: Orbis, 2003.

Grenz, Stanley J. *Theology for the Community of God*. Grand Rapids, MI: Erdmans, 1994.

Griffen-Pierce, Trudy. *Earth Is My Mother, Sky Is My Father: Space, Time, and Astronomy in Navajo Sandpainting*. Albuquerque: University of New Mexico Press, 1995.

Guyer, Paul. "Review of Mary Mothersill's *Beauty Restored*." *Journal of Aesthetics and Art Criticism* 44, no. 3 (1986): 245–55. http://dx.doi.org/10.2307/429734.

Hart, David Bently. *The Beauty of the Infinite: The Aesthetics of Christian Truth*. Grand Rapids, MI: Erdmans, 2003.

Hofstadter, Albert, and Richard Kuhns. *Philosophies of Art and Beauty: Selected Readings in Aesthetics from Plato to Heidegger*. Chicago: University of Chicago Press, 1976. http://dx.doi.org/10.7208/chicago/9780226348117.001.0001

Hughes, Glenn. A *More Beautiful Question: The Spiritual in Poetry in Art*. Columbia, MO: University of Missouri Press, 2011.

Hume, David. "Of the Standard of Taste," (1757). http://web.mnstate.edu/gracyk/courses/phil%20of%20art/hume%20on%20taste.htm, §7.

Jantzen, Grace M. *Foundations of Violence: Death and the Displacement of Beauty*. Vol. 1. London: Routledge, 2004.

Jaroszynski, Piotr. *Beauty and Being: Thomistic Perspectives*. Trans. Hugh McDonald. Etienne Gilson Series no. 33. Toronto: PIMS, 2011.

Jeffreys, Sheila. *Beauty and Misogyny: Harmful Cultural Practices in the West*. Florence, KY: Routledge, 2005.

Joad, C.E.M. "A Realist Philosophy of Life." In *Contemporary British Philosophy: Personal Statements. Second Series*, ed. J.H. Muirhead, 185–96. New York: Macmillan, 1925.

Johnson, Elizabeth, Susan A. Ross, and Mary Catherine Hilkert, OP. "Current Theology: Feminist Theology: A Review of Literature." *Theological Studies* 56, no. 3 (1995): 327–52.

Jordan, Mark D. "The Evidence of the Transcendentals and the Place of Beauty in Aquinas." *International Philosophical Quarterly* 29 (1989): 393–407. http://dx.doi.org/10.5840/ipq198929426.

–. "The Grammar of *Esse*: Re-reading Thomas on the Transcendentals." *Thomist* 44 (1980): 1–26.

Kant, Immanuel. *Critique of Judgment*. Trans. J.H. Bernard. New York: Hafner, 1951.

Kierkegaard, Søren. *Either/Or, Part I*. Trans. and ed. H.V. Hong and E. Hong. Princeton: Princeton University Press, 1987.

–. *Stages on Life's Way*. Trans. and ed. H.V. Hong and E. Hong. Princeton: Princeton University Press, 1988.

–. *Training in Christianity and the Edifying Discourse which "Accompanied" It*. Trans. and ed. W. Lowrie. Princeton: Princeton University Press, 1972.

Koren, Leonard. *Wabi-Sabi for Artists, Designers, Poets & Philosophers*. Berkeley: Stone Bridge, 1994.

Kovach, Francis, J. *Philosophy of Beauty*. Norman: University of Oklahoma Press, 1974.

Langer, Susanne. *Feeling and Form: A Theory of Art*. New York: Charles Scribner's Sons, 1953.

Latré, Stijn. "Nietzsche, Heidegger, Girard on 'The Death of God.'" *Revista Portuguesa de Filosofia* 57 (2001): 299–305.

Lawrence, N., and D. O' Connor, eds. *Readings in Existential Phenomenology*. Englewood Cliffs, NJ: Prentice Hall, 1967.

Lewis, C.S. *The Four Loves*. New York: Harcourt Brace, 1988.

Lonergan, Bernard. *Early Works on Theological Method 1*. Ed. R.M. Doran and R.C. Croken. Vol. 22 of *Collected Works of Bernard Lonergan*. Toronto: University of Toronto Press, 2010.

–. *Insight: A Study in Human Understanding*. Ed. F.E.Crowe and R.M. Doran. Vol. 3 of *Collected Works of Bernard Lonergan*. Toronto: University of Toronto Press, 1992.

–. *Method in Theology*. Toronto: University of Toronto Press, 1990.

–. "Method in Theology Lectures" (1971). Dublin Ireland. Unpublished Q&A portion.

–. "On the Redemption." Unpublished translation by Michael Shields. Supplement to *De Verbo Incarnato: De Redemptione*. Lonergan Research Institute, Toronto, 2011.

–. "Philosophy and the Religious Phenomenon." *Method: Journal of Lonergan Studies* 12, no. 2 (1994): 125–46.

–. *A Second Collection*. Toronto: University of Toronto Press, 1996.

–. *A Third Collection: Papers by Bernard J.F. Lonergan*. Ed. FE.Crowe. Mahwah, NY: Paulist Press, 1985.

–. *Topics in Education*. Ed. F.E.Crowe and R.M. Doran. Vol. 10 of *Collected Works of Bernard Lonergan*. Toronto: University of Toronto Press, 1993.

–. *Understanding and Being*. Ed. Elizabeth A. Morelli and Mark D. Morelli. Vol. 5 of *Collected Works of Bernard Lonergan*. Toronto: University of Toronto Press, 1990.

Mann, Bonnie. *Women's Liberation and the Sublime*. Oxford: Oxford University Press, 2006. http://dx.doi.org/10.1093/0195187458.001.0001.

Maritain, Jacques. *Art and Scholasticism*. New York: Pantheon, 1953.

–. *Creative Intuition in Art and Poetry*. New York: Scribner, 1930.

Maurer, Armand A., C.S.B. *About Beauty: A Thomistic Interpretation*. Houston: University of Houston, 1983.

Merton, Thomas. *The Asian Journal*. New York: New Directions, 1973.

Meynell, Hugo. *The Nature of Aesthetic Value*. Albany, NY: SUNY Press, 1986.

Mitias, Michael, H., ed. *Aesthetic Quality and Aesthetic Experience*. Amsterdam: Rodopi, 1988.

Moltmann, Jürgan. *God in Creation: An Ecological Doctrine of Creation*. London: SCM Press, 1985.

Mothersill, Mary. *Beauty Restored*. Oxford: Oxford University Press, 1984.

Muirhead, J.H., ed. *Contemporary British Philosophy: Personal Statements, Second Series*. New York: Macmillan, 1925.

Nichols, Aiden, OP. *The Word Has Been Abroad: A Guide through Balthasar's Theological Aesthetics*. Washington, DC: Catholic University of America Press, 1998.

Nicholson, Marjorie Hope. *Mountain Gloom and Glory: The Development of the Aesthetics of the Infinite*. New York: Norton, 1963.

Nietzsche, Friedrich. *The Gay Science: With a Prelude in German Ryhmes and an Appendix of Songs*. Ed. Bernard Williams. Trans. Josefine Nauckhoff. Cambridge: Cambridge University Press, 2001.

–. *The Will to Power*. Trans. Antonio Ludovici. 2010. http://www.digireads.com.

Norris, Thomas. "The Symphonic Unity of His Theology: An Overview." In *The Beauty of Christ: Introduction to the Theology of Hans Urs von Balthasar*, ed. B. McGregor and Thomas Norris, 1–9. Edinburgh: T&T Clark, 1994.

Olson, Alan M., ed. *Myth, Symbol and Reality*. Notre Dame: University of Notre Dame Press, 1980.

Otto, Rudolf. *The Idea of the Holy: An Inquiry into the Non-rational Factor in the Idea of the Divine and Its Relation to the Rational*. Trans. J.W. Harvey. London: Oxford University Press, 1924.

Pallasmaa, Juhani. *The Eyes of the Skin: Architecture and the Senses*. 2d ed. Hoboken, NJ: John Wiley & Sons, 2005.

Phelan, G.B. *Selected Papers*. Ed. A.G. Kirn. Toronto: Pontifical Institute of Medieval Studies, 1967.

Ping, Wang. *Aching for Beauty: Footbinding in China*. Minnesota: University of Minnesota Press, 2000.

Poe, Edgar Allan. "The Poetic Principle." http://www.bartleby.com/28/14.html.

Polanyi, Michael. *Personal Knowledge*. London: Routledge & Kegan Paul, 1962.

Price, George. *The Narrow Pass: A Study of Kierkegaard's Concept of Man*. London: Hutchinson, 1963.

Ricoeur, Paul. *Interpretation Theory: Discourse and the Surplus of Meaning*. Fort Worth: Texas Christian University Press, 1976.

Rogers, Eugene. *After the Spirit: A Constructive Pneumatology from Resources outside the Modern West (Radical Traditions)*. Grand Rapids, MI: Erdmans, 2005.

Rosenberg, Randall S. "Lonergan and the Transcendent Orientations of Art." *Renascence* 61, no. 3 (2009): 141–51.

Ross, Stephen David, ed. *Art and Its Significance: An Anthology of Aesthetic Theory*. 3d ed. Albany, NY: SUNY Press, 1994.

Ross, Susan. *For the Beauty of the Earth: Women, Sacramentality, and Justice*. Mahwah, NJ: Paulist Press, 2006.

Roten, Johann G.S.M. "Mary and the Way of Beauty." *Marian Studies* (annual publication of the Mariological Society of America, Marian Library, University of Dayton) 69 (1998): 109–27.

Sala, Giovanni. *Lonergan and Kant*. Toronto: University of Toronto Press, 1994.

Santayana, George. *The Sense of Beauty: Being the Outlines of Æsthetic Theory*. Introduction by Arthur Danto. Boston: MIT Press, 1986.

Sartwell, Crispin. *Six Names of Beauty*. New York: Routledge, 2004.

Scarry, Elaine. *Beauty and Justice*. Princeton: Princeton University Press, 1999.

Schopenhauer, Arthur. *World as Will and Idea*, Volume I. Trans. R.B. Haldane and J. Kemp. 7th ed. London: Kegan, Trench, Trüdner, 1910.

Scruton, Roger. *Beauty*. Oxford: Oxford University Press, 2009.

Shaw, Philip. *The Sublime*. Florence: Routledge, 2005.

Shusterman, Richard. "An End to Aesthetic Experience." *Journal of Aesthetics and Art Criticism* 55, no. 1 (1997): 29–41. http://dx.doi.org/10.2307/431602.

Shusterman, Richard, and Adele Tomlin, eds. *Aesthetic Experience*. New York: Routledge, 2008.

Smith, Paul, and Carolyn Wilde, eds. A *Companion to Art Theory*. London: Blackwell, 2009.

Snell, Bruno. *The Discovery of Mind: The Greek Origins of European Thought*. New York: Harper Torchbook, 1960.

Steiner, Wendy. *The Trouble with Beauty*. London: William Heinemann, 2001.

Sutton, Jonathan, and W. Van Den Bercken, eds. *Aesthetics as a Religious Factor in Eastern and Western Christianity*. Leuven: Peeters, 2005.

Suzuki, D.T. *Zen Buddhism: Selected Writings of D.T. Suzuki*. Ed. William Barrett. Garden City, NY: Doubleday/Anchor, 1956.

Thiessen, Geza E., ed. *Theological Aesthetics: A Reader*. Grand Rapids, MI: Erdmans, 2004.

Thomson, Ian. "Heidegger's Aesthetics." In *The Stanford Encyclopedia of Philosophy*, Fall 2010 ed. Ed. Edward N. Zalta. http://plato.stanford.edu/archives/fall2010/entries/heidegger-aesthetics/.

Tomberg, Valentine. *Meditations on the Tarot: A Journey into Christian Hermeticism*. Afterword by Hans Urs von Balthasar. Trans. Robert Powell. New York: Tarcher/Putnam, 2002.

Toynbee, Arnold. A *Study of History*, Abridgment of vols. 1–6 by D.C. Somervell. New York: Oxford University Press, 1947.

Traub, George, ed. *An Ignatian Spirituality Reader*. Chicago: Loyola Press, 2008.

Van Broeckhoven, Egide, SJ. A *Friend to All Men: The Diary of a Worker-Priest*. Rockaway, NJ: Dimension, 1977.

Viladesau, Richard. *The Beauty of the Cross: The Passion of Christ in Theology and the Arts, from the Catacombs to the Eve of the Renaissance*. Oxford: Oxford University Press, 2006.

–. *Theological Aesthetics: God in Imagination, Beauty, and Art*. New York: Oxford University Press, 1999.

–. *Theology and the Arts: Encountering God through Music, Art, and Rhetoric*. New York: Paulist Press, 2000.

The Triumph of the Cross: The Passion of Christ in Theology and the Arts, from the Renaissance to the Counter-Reformation. Oxford: Oxford University Press, 2008.

Walmsley, Gerard. *Lonergan on Philosophic Pluralism: The Polymorphism of Consciousness as the Key to Philosophy.* Toronto: University of Toronto Press, 2008.

Wicks, Robert. "Arthur Schopenhauer." In *The Stanford Encyclopedia of Philosophy,* Fall 2009 ed. Ed. Edward N. Zalta. http://plato.stanford.edu/archives/fall2009/entries/schopenhauer/>.

Wilhelmsen, F. "The Aesthetic Object and the Act of Being." *Modern Schoolman* 29 (1950): 277–91.

Witherspoon, Gary. *Language and Art in the Navajo Universe.* Ann Arbor, MI: University of Michigan Press, 1977.

Witherspoon, Gary, and Glen Peterson. *Dynamic Symmetry and Holistic Asymmetry in Navajo and Western Art and Cosmology.* New York: Peter Lang, 1995.

Wyman, Leland C. *Blessingway.* Tucson: University of Arizona Press, 1970.

Zalta, Edward N., ed. *The Stanford Encyclopedia of Philosophy,* Fall 2008 ed. http://plato.stanford.edu/archives/fall2008/entries/kant-aesthetics/.

Zolbrod, Paul G. *Diné bahane': The Navajo Creation Story.* Albuquerque: University of New Mexico Press, 1984.

Index

Fully erased Sept 30, 2014   MUR

? : 175, 210, 120, 122, 125,
one : 11, 14, see Eye cw on beauty,
Interpenetration : 218,
": 100,

Dogearing noted Jan 11/17 } #
OK otherwise